DEDICATION PAGE

<u>Soli Deo Gloria</u>

This book is dedicated to the
Baptist Churches
whom I was privileged to serve as
Secretary of the Baptist Union of Ireland
from 1976 to 1995
and
especially to
nine of the above Churches
whom I was privileged to serve as
Pastor between 1962 and 2006

Thank You, Heavenly Father

'As The Spirit Enabled Them'

INTRODUCTION

The Holy Bible is a wonderful book. It has a way of throwing light on things that have become familiar so that they shine with new light. Having completed the **Devotional Readings in the Gospel of Luke**, I found myself restless until I continued reading and making notes on Luke's second book.

If Luke's Gospel introduced us to Jesus, then his second book introduces us to the person we know as The Holy Spirit.

I am using the **Anglicised New International Version text of the Book of Acts** for these studies. I still use the (by now) familiar method of study in Acts. First comes a reading, (one of seventy in this case), followed by a meditation. You will see right away that the notes are a little fuller than before: this is because some of the Scripture sections are lengthy, and deserve attention. For example, we cannot easily gloss over the events of the Day of Pentecost or Peter's sermon on that occasion, or Stephen's defence before the Sanhedrin, or the conversion of Saul of Tarsus, or Peter's visit to the house of Cornelius in Caesarea, or the account of the Council in Jerusalem, or Paul's trials and journey to Rome. Luke gave these plenty of time and space.

The meditations take us in all kinds of directions but I assure you that they arise naturally from the readings. To conclude the meditations each section closes with a **'THANK YOU, HEAVENLY FATHER'** item. It is so framed that the adoration and thanksgiving suggested lead immediately and naturally to further prayers, both supplications and intercessions.

The title for this book was found in Acts 2:4.

'All of them were filled with the Holy Spirit and began to speak in other tongues as the Spirit enabled them.'

The point being made is a very simple one. Anyone who ever did worthwhile service for Jesus Christ within the Book of Acts did so ***as the Spirit enabled them***. The same is true in today's Church and world. If every Christian is a missionary, then every Christian needs and can be assured of the Spirit's enabling. Never fear, this will not send us into the Lord's service feeling like super-humans. We are more likely than ever to be cast on Him, the Spirit, for the supply of all we need.

I came across a wonderful illustration of the Spirit's enabling at a Sunday school teachers' conference at Alloa in Scotland when I was a young pastor. One of the visiting speakers quoted a little rhyme. I don't know where she got it, so I cannot quote the source.

'The Spirit clothed Himself with Gideon,
He makes the record say:
So he became the working-clothes
The Spirit wore that day.'

My wife and I are continuing to prove the Lord's ability to supply all our need, and that was during an autumn (or fall if you prefer) when I had a spell of broken health. As a salute to her I include one of our Golden Anniversary photographs on the back cover.

I wonder if any of my readers embarked on their own exploration of a selected part of the Bible. I would like to hear from them if they did. Remember I won't be your chief critic, more of a sympathetic listener.

An Outline of Acts

For the purposes of this book it is not necessary to provide an exhaustive outline of the contents. There are editions of the NIV which provide an Introduction and an Outline of Contents for every book of the Bible. Readers may also have access to a *Bible Dictionary* or *An Introduction to the Books of the Bible*. I always keep my copy of ***The Zondervan Pictorial Bible Dictionary by Merrill C. Tenney*** at hand. My copy is the 1963 edition. I bought it in Northern Ireland, and fifty-one years later simply cannot remember the price in £ sterling.

However, we may simply want to read the book of ACTS. If that is the case then Jesus' words in Acts 1:8 offer a convenient outline of the book.

> *But you will receive power when the Holy Spirit comes on you; and you will be my witnesses in Jerusalem, and in all Judea and Samaria, and to the ends of the earth.*

In Jerusalem:	Acts 1:1–8:3
In Judea and Samaria:	Acts 8:4–12:25
To the ends of the earth:	Acts 13:1–28:31

The Coming of the Holy Spirit on the day of Pentecost empowered the infant Church of Jesus Christ to be his witnesses. Jesus promised that the Holy Spirit would come in answer to his prayers. Pray that God will reveal all that he has for us to learn about this wonderful Third Person of the Holy Trinity.

When you have read this book you might wish to pass on your comments and/or criticisms to me at *jamesgrant754@btinternet.com*. Perhaps you have thoughts about Acts to share with me. If so, I will be pleased to receive them.

Before I sign off I would like to record sincere thanks to my colleague James Greenwood, a friend of many years, who from start to finish of this writing project supported me fully. We made a happy discovery: the definition of the word 'fellowship' now includes 'proofreading'!

Your friend in Christ,
REA GRANT
January 2014

CONTENTS

Acts 1:1 – 26

Introduction

I. Acts 2:1 – 8:3

You shall be My witnesses in Jerusalem and Judea

II. Acts 8: 4 – 12: 25

You shall be My witnesses in Samaria

III. Acts 13:1 – 28:31
You shall be My witnesses to the ends of the earth

Acts 13:1 – 15:35
Paul's First Missionary Journey

Acts 15:36–18:22
Paul' Second Missionary Journey

ACTS 18:23 – 21:26
PAUL'S THIRD MISSIONARY JOURNEY

ACTS 21:17-26:32
PAUL'S ARREST & TRIALS

Acts 27:1 – 28:31
ROME AT LAST

1. Acts 1:1–11

JESUS TAKEN UP INTO HEAVEN

[1]In my former book, Theophilus, I wrote about all that Jesus began to do and to teach [2]until the day he was taken up to heaven, after giving instructions through the Holy Spirit to the apostles he had chosen.

[3]After his suffering, he showed himself to these men and gave many convincing proofs that he was alive. He appeared to them over a period of forty days and spoke about the kingdom of God.

[4]On one occasion, while he was eating with them, he gave them this command: "Do not leave Jerusalem, but wait for the gift my Father promised, which you have heard me speak about. [5]For John baptised with water, but in a few days you will be baptised with the Holy Spirit."

[6]So when they met together, they asked him, "Lord, are you at this time going to restore the kingdom to Israel?" Acts 1:1-6.

Luke began his second book with a neat summary of his gospel: **'*In my former book, Theophilus, I wrote about all that Jesus began to do and to teach [2]until the day he was taken up to heaven.*'** He is now embarking on telling the story of Jesus (Part Two) following his ascension to heaven.

We wonder how deeply the disciples had assimilated the possibility that Jesus would be taken from them one day. It was not that Jesus hadn't spoken with them about his ascension. For example see John 12:23; 13:1; 14:1-4 & 28f; 16:5f & 28f. It is certain that he thought about it more frequently than they did.

In the interim period from his resurrection until his ascension Jesus concentrated on ministering to his apostles. Note their preparation.

> **(1)** [2]***After giving instructions through the Holy Spirit to the apostles he had chosen.***

Jesus had chosen these men for a very special ministry to his church in its infancy. He did not withhold from them any information they would need to be leaders of his church. All that he said to them at this stage isn't on record anywhere so we do not know the entire content of it. His main instruction was that they should remain in Jerusalem until the promised Holy Spirit would come upon them (vv. 5 & 8).

> **(2)** [3]***After his suffering, he showed himself to these men and gave many convincing proofs that he was alive.***

The necessity for this was that an apostle's knowledge of Jesus had to include being a witness of his resurrection. Of all people the apostles of Jesus were the chief witnesses to the truth of Jesus' bodily resurrection.

> **(3)** [3]***He appeared to them over a period of forty days and spoke about the kingdom of God.***

How we wish we had been allowed to hear all that he shared with the apostles about this great subject. I imagine that it would have stretched our minds and saved us from parochialism.

> ***(4)*** [4]***On one occasion, while he was eating with them, he gave them this command:***

We learn here that sessions Jesus had with the apostles were frequently informal. He shared with them what was on his mind during a meal. The informality didn't take away from the importance of what he had to say. His command was:

> *[4]Do not leave Jerusalem, but wait for the gift my Father promised, which you have heard me speak about. [5]For John baptised with water, but in a few days you will be baptised with the Holy Spirit.* Acts 1:4-5

'The gift my Father promised' was the gift of the Holy Spirit. In time past the Holy Spirit came to certain individuals to equip them for special purposes: so with the apostles. The Holy Spirit would empower them for the various ministries they would discharge following Jesus' ascension to his Father until the Spirit would be poured out on all the believers at Pentecost.

The word *'baptism'* was used with reference to John's baptism, and also with the advent of the Spirit. It is not too much to say that the Spirit would *'immerse them'* in himself.

> **(5)** ***[6]So when they met together, they asked him, Lord, are you at this time going to restore the kingdom to Israel?***

This matter was on the minds of the apostles because they believed that the earthly kingdom of the Messiah was soon to be established. They also knew some OT scriptures in Ezekiel 36 and Joel 2 that connected the kingdom and the outpouring of the Holy Spirit. The subject was an important one, but time was short and Jesus had to get their minds to focus on what lay ahead. To this day the exact time of the Second Coming of Jesus remains unrevealed. They had to be content with that. He was not giving them a *'put-down'* by answering as he did.

> **(6)** ***[7]He said to them: It is not for you to know the times or dates the Father has set by his own authority. [8]But you will receive power when the Holy Spirit comes on you; and you will be my witnesses in Jerusalem, and in all Judea and Samaria, and to the ends of the earth.***
>
> ***[9]After he said this, he was taken up before their very eyes, and a cloud hid him from their sight.*** **Acts 1:7-9**

Those were Jesus' last words to the apostles. The physical Jesus was received up into heaven in the body of his resurrection and so he returned to the glory that he had with the Father since before the world began (John 17:5) and took his seat at the Father's right hand (Hebrews 1:3). In heaven he represents his people before the throne of God.

Did the apostles think of the cloud of God's presence that led Israel through the wilderness, that filled the tabernacle Moses built and the temple that Solomon built? Did they remember the cloud of God's presence on the Mount of Transfiguration? The cloud of God's presence had descended to receive the King of Glory returning in triumph to his Father's side. Read Psalm 24:7-10 for his welcome in heaven.

> **(7)** ***[10]They were looking intently up into the sky as he was going, when suddenly two men dressed in white stood beside them. [11]Men of Galilee, they said, why do you stand here looking into the sky? This same Jesus, who has been taken from you into heaven, will come back in the same way you have seen him go into heaven.*** **Acts 1:10-11**

Two matters they needed to comprehend were (1) the promise they had been given and (2) the programme they were charged to fulfil.

The Spirit's power was not given to the apostles so that they would be super-charged super-men sitting around all day with nothing to do. No, it was in the power of the Holy Spirit they would embark on Jesus' programme of world evangelisation until such time as *'this same Jesus will come back.'*

THANK YOU, HEAVENLY FATHER:

For Jesus' mentoring of the apostles at a time of great change in their lives, so that they would be enabled by the power of the Holy Spirit to lead the infant Church;

For the well-attested fact of Jesus' bodily resurrection: it was not a myth but a miracle of the power of God. Like Job we are able to say 'I know that my Redeemer lives!'

For the well-grounded hope of believers that Jesus will come again in power and great glory to receive his people home and to judge the world of ungodly men;

For the privilege of being witnesses for Jesus in today's world – in the power of the Holy Spirit.

IN JESUS' NAME, AMEN

2. Acts 1: 12 - 26

MATTHIAS CHOSEN TO REPLACE JUDAS.

[12]Then they returned to Jerusalem from the hill called the Mount of Olives, a Sabbath day's walk from the city. [13]When they arrived, they went upstairs to the room where they were staying. Those present were Peter, John, James and Andrew; Philip and Thomas, Bartholomew and Matthew; James son of Alphaeus and Simon the Zealot, and Judas son of James. [14]They all joined together constantly in prayer, along with the women and Mary the mother of Jesus, and with his brothers. Acts 1:12-14

It was from the Mount of Olives, a hill about 200ft. higher than the City of Jerusalem that Jesus ascended into heaven. Luke says it was a Sabbath day's walk into the city or about half a mile. When the Tabernacle was in the centre of the Israelite encampment in the wilderness half a mile was the furthest anyone had to walk to reach the Tabernacle on the Sabbath.

The Upper Room in Jerusalem held memories for the apostles and the others who were with them. Luke says that *'it was where they were staying.'* Here the last Passover of Jesus' life was celebrated and the first Lord's Supper was instituted. Luke even includes a roll-call and names all eleven apostles (v. 13).

Luke also shows that everyone was mindful of Jesus' farewell words and so the Upper Room became the prayer room for the group of believers. He reports that there were women present, among them Mary the mother of Jesus. The brothers of Jesus were there (v. 14). He also notes that when all the believers were gathered in there were about 120 of them (v. 15).

We wonder why Peter was the apostle who took the lead in what happened next in v. 15. Perhaps the Holy Spirit had put the matter of a successor to Judas in his mind as a matter of priority. It really was a matter of importance.

But how would he proceed? Peter gained the attention of the group by speaking about the need to appoint a twelfth apostle, to take the place of Judas.

> [15]*In those days Peter stood up among the believers (a group numbering about a hundred and twenty) and said* [16]*Brothers, the Scripture had to be fulfilled which the Holy Spirit spoke long ago through the mouth of David concerning Judas, who served as guide for those who arrested Jesus —* [17]*he was one of our number and shared in this ministry.* [18]*(With the reward he got for his wickedness, Judas bought a field; there he fell headlong, his body burst open and all his intestines spilled out.* [19]*Everyone in Jerusalem heard about this so they called that field in their language Akeldama that is, Field of Blood.)* Acts 1:15-19

Notice what Peter believed about the Old Testament scriptures: '*the Holy Spirit spoke long ago through the mouth of David*.' He reveals that the scripture he has in mind was spoken specifically about Judas. He reminds the group of the sin of Judas – '*he served as guide to those who arrested Jesus*'. He speaks of Judas with mixed feelings: [17]"*he was one of our number and shared in this ministry*". He went on to speak of Judas' death by suicide (vv. 18-20). Peter told the group about the scriptures he had in mind (v. 20).

> [20] *'For,' said Peter, 'it is written in the Book of Psalms, 'May his place be deserted; let there be no-one to dwell in it,' (Psalm 69:25) and, 'May another take his place of leadership' (Psalm 109:8).* Acts 1:20

Peter stated the qualifications of an apostle.

> [21] *Therefore it is necessary to choose one of the men who have been with us the whole time the Lord Jesus went in and out among us,* [22]*beginning from John's baptism to the time when Jesus was taken up from us. For one of these must become a witness with us of his resurrection.* Acts 1:21-22

The successor to Judas must be a disciple who had been with Jesus from the beginning of his ministry right through to his ascension. There were no dissenting voices and so the meeting was open for proposals *from the floor* (as we say).

Two proposals were forthcoming: the two names were Joseph Barsabbas and Matthias. I don't think we heard either name previously in the Gospels. Then they prayed. What sanctified common sense marked their prayer!

> [24]*"Lord, you know everyone's heart. Show us which of these two you have chosen* [25]*to take over this apostolic ministry, which Judas left to go where he belongs."* [26]*Then they cast lots and the lot fell to Matthias; so he was added to the eleven apostles.* Acts 1:24-26.

This is the last mention of the casting of lots in the New Testament.

In Christian bookshops nowadays there is a section labelled 'CHRISTIAN FICTION.' I know what the classification means–but what a horrid title. There is nothing whatever fictitious about Christianity. But if we had a 'C.F.N.I.V.' there might be an extra verse in Acts 1 somewhat as follows:

> [27]And because he hadn't been appointed, Joseph Barsabbas rose up and leaving the room in a rage, he banged the door so hard that it was nearly lifted off its hinges. He went down the road and started a church of his own.

I am sure that didn't happen. More likely Joseph crossed the room threw his arm around Matthias' shoulder and said, *'The Lord bless you Matthias. You have my support'.*

THANK YOU, HEAVENLY FATHER:

For the fellowship of believers when gathered in Jesus' name;

For the guidance of the Holy Spirit when church leaders encounter fresh and baffling situations;

For answers to prayer when a church needs guidance and seeks it in humble, believing prayer;

For the spirit of unanimity when believers humbly follow the Holy Spirit's guidance in any matter;

For gifting the members of a church so that when the right time comes their fellow-members have confidence to call them to leadership positions, and the individual(s) concerned recognise God's call to them and accept appointment as from the Lord.

IN JESUS' NAME, AMEN

I. Acts 2:1 – 8:3

You shall be My witnesses in Jerusalem and Judea

3. Acts 2:1-13

THE HOLY SPIRIT COMES AT PENTECOST (1)

[1]When the day of Pentecost came, they were all together in one place. [2]Suddenly a sound like the blowing of a violent wind came from heaven and filled the whole house where they were sitting.

[3]They saw what seemed to be tongues of fire that separated and came to rest on each of them. [4]All of them were filled with the Holy Spirit and began to speak in other tongues as the Spirit enabled them.

[5]Now there were staying in Jerusalem God-fearing Jews from every nation under heaven. [6]When they heard this sound, a crowd came together in bewilderment, because each one heard them speaking in his own language.

[7]Utterly amazed, they asked: "Are not all these men who are speaking Galileans? [8]Then how is it that each of us hears them in his own native language? [9]Parthians, Medes and Elamites; residents of Mesopotamia, Judea and Cappadocia, Pontus and Asia, [10]Phrygia and Pamphylia, Egypt and the parts of Libya near Cyrene; visitors from Rome. [11](both Jews and converts to Judaism); Cretans and Arabs—we hear them declaring the wonders of God in our own tongues!"

[12]Amazed and perplexed, they asked one another, "What does this mean?" [13]Some, however, made fun of them and said, "They have had too much wine." Acts 2:1-13

The Events of Pentecost

The word 'Pentecost' means 'fiftieth' and is a reference to the Feast of Weeks (Exod. 34:22, 23) or Feast of Harvest (Lev. 23:16) which was celebrated fifty days after Passover in May/June (Lev.

23:15-22). It was one of three annual feasts of the Jews for which the nation was to come to Jerusalem.

That year Pentecost would be different because in God's economy the hour had come for the Holy Spirit to be poured out on the infant Church. The believers '*were all together in one place*', which most likely refers back to 1:13, where they gathered for prayer in anticipation of the coming of the Holy Spirit.

THE COMING OF THE HOLY SPIRIT HAD FOUR IMPORTANT FEATURES.

[2]Suddenly a sound like the blowing of a violent wind came from heaven and filled the whole house where they were sitting. This experience was audible.

[3]They saw what seemed to be tongues of fire that separated and came to rest on each of them. This experience was visible. What looked like tongues or flames of fire, sat on each believer without harm or heat or burning.

[4]All of them were filled with the Holy Spirit. This experience was personal. The Holy Spirit filled each person present, identifying them as believers in Jesus their Lord and Saviour and equipping them to be his witnesses (Acts 1:8).

[4]And began to speak in other tongues as the Spirit enabled them. This experience was oral and possibly involuntary. This was a miraculous manifestation of the Holy Spirit's presence and activity. He used the voices of the apostles but the language and the words they spoke were supplied by the Spirit. This had to be the case because the apostles could not speak other languages, much less think in them. The tongues of the believers were loosed and they began to speak in known languages of earth's people.

How do we know this? The following verses provide hard evidence of this phenomenon. The whole paragraph from vv. 5 to 12 is thrilling reading. Jews from all over the known world were present and witnessed this event. What caught their attention?

> [5]*Now there were staying in Jerusalem God-fearing Jews from every nation under heaven.* [6]*When they heard this sound, a crowd came together in bewilderment, because each one heard them speaking in his own language.* [7]*Utterly amazed, they asked: "Are not all these men who are speaking Galileans?* [8]*Then how is it that each of us hears them in his own native language?* Acts 2:5-8

They knew that the speakers were native Galileans yet Jews from other countries heard them speaking recognisable languages belonging to other nations.

> [9]*Parthians, Medes and Elamites; residents of Mesopotamia, Judea and Cappadocia, Pontus and Asia,* [10]*Phrygia and Pamphylia, Egypt and the parts of Libya near Cyrene; visitors from Rome.* [11]*(both Jews and converts to Judaism); Cretans and Arabs—we hear them declaring the wonders of God in our own tongues!"* [12]*Amazed and perplexed, they asked one another,*
>
> *What does this mean?* Acts 2:9-12

The nations listed here more or less define the vast area of the Roman Empire. It is hardly possible for us to imagine how quickly the gospel would spread as the Pentecost pilgrims returned home. We will let Luke tell the story.

The Pentecost event stands in complete contrast to Genesis 11, when in a different era and circumstances God confused the languages of earth so that people did not understand each other.

However, for reasons known only to God it is necessary for prospective missionaries to foreign countries and language groups within them to undergo language training before they ever leave home to commence their gospel work.

A good evangelist is always looking for a point of contact with those he is trying to reach. In the question of the crowd, *"What does this mean?"* Peter found his point of contact (v. 12).

A few 'smart-alecs' made fun of the speakers by saying that they were drunk! Peter immediately stood up, refuted the wisecrack and began to answer the question that was on everyone's mind.

THANK YOU, HEAVENLY FATHER:

For the advent of the Holy Spirit when the believers were 'filled with the Spirit;'

For the person of the Holy Spirit; He is a distinct member of the Godhead;

For the sovereignty of the Holy Spirit; He moves as He wills;

For the primary task of the Holy Spirit; He makes Jesus known;

For the indwelling of the Holy Spirit, through whom Jesus lives in his people;

For the indispensability of the Holy Spirit in the life and ministry of the Church of Jesus Christ;

For that beautiful phrase in Acts 2:4 ***'as the Spirit enabled them'.*** We will always need His enabling until our lifework is done.

IN JESUS' NAME, AMEN

4. Acts 2: 14-41

THE HOLY SPIRIT COMES AT PENTECOST (2)

[14]Then Peter stood up with the Eleven, raised his voice and addressed the crowd: "Fellow Jews and all of you who live in Jerusalem, let me explain this to you; listen carefully to what I say. [15]These men are not drunk, as you suppose. It's only nine in the morning!

[16]No, this is what was spoken by the prophet Joel: [17]"In the last days, God says, I will pour out my Spirit on all people. Your sons and daughters will prophesy, your young men will see visions, your old men will dream dreams. [18]Even on my servants, both men and women, I will pour out my Spirit in those days, and they will prophesy. [19]I will show wonders in the heaven above and signs on the earth below, blood and fire and billows of smoke. [20]The sun will be turned to darkness and the moon to blood before the coming of the great and glorious day of the Lord. [21]And everyone who calls on the name of the Lord will be saved."

[22]"Men of Israel, listen to this: Jesus of Nazareth was a man accredited by God to you by miracles, wonders and signs, which God did among you through him, as you yourselves know. [23]This man was handed over to you by God's set purpose and foreknowledge; and you, with the help of wicked men, put him to death by nailing him to the cross. [24]But God raised him from the dead, freeing him from the agony of death, because it was impossible for death to keep its hold on him. [25]David said about him: "I saw the Lord always before me. Because he is at my right hand, I will not be shaken. [26]Therefore my heart is glad and my tongue rejoices; my body also will live in hope, [27]because you will not abandon me to the grave, nor will you let your Holy One see decay. [28]You have made known to me the paths of life; you will fill me with joy in your presence."

[29]"Brothers, I can tell you confidently that the patriarch David died and was buried and his tomb is here to this day. [30]But he was a prophet and knew that God had promised him on oath that he would place one of his descendants on his throne. [31]Seeing what was ahead, he spoke of the resurrection of the Christ, that he was not abandoned to the grave, nor did his body see decay. [32]God has raised this Jesus to life, and we are all witnesses of the fact.

[33]Exalted to the right hand of God, he has received from the Father the promised Holy Spirit and has poured out what you now see and hear.

[34]For David did not ascend to heaven, and yet he said, "The Lord said to my Lord: "Sit at my right hand [35]until I make your enemies a footstool for your feet."

[36]"Therefore let all Israel be assured of this: God has made this Jesus, whom you crucified, both Lord and Christ."

[37]When the people heard this, they were cut to the heart and said to Peter and the other apostles, "Brothers, what shall we do?"

[38]Peter replied, "Repent and be baptised, every one of you, in the name of Jesus Christ for the forgiveness of your sins. And you will receive the gift of the Holy Spirit. [39]The promise is for you and your children and for all who are far off—for all whom the Lord our God will call."

[40]With many other words he warned them; and he pleaded with them, "Save yourselves from this corrupt generation." [41]Those who accepted his message were baptised, and about three thousand were added to their number that day. Acts 2: 14-41

The Explanation of Pentecost

Once the Holy Spirit had come, the next major event in Church History was Peter's sermon on the day of Pentecost, which resulted in 3,000 conversions and greatly increased the size of the young church of Jesus Christ.

How do we explain Peter's power in preaching and the effect of his sermon? The answer to the question is in v. 4, where in relation to the apostles speaking in other known languages, it is said that they '*began to speak in other tongues* ***as the Spirit enabled them.***' Peter preached as the Spirit enabled him.

Peter found his point of contact with the crowd in their question '*What does this mean?*' (vv. 12-13). He was also aware that the crowd he was addressing was entirely Jewish. This is why his preaching was based on the Old Testament prophecies of Joel (vv. 17-21) and David (vv. 25-28). In preaching like this he was drawing on the crowd's knowledge of the Hebrew Scriptures.

> [14]*"Fellow Jews and all of you who live in Jerusalem, let me explain this to you; listen carefully to what I say* [16] *this is what was spoken by the prophet Joel."* Acts 2:14 & 16

He quoted the prophecy of Joel (Joel 2:28-32) in full. Joel had prophesied the outpouring of the Holy Spirit in the way it had happened (vv. 17-18). Another part of the prophecy would be fulfilled before '*the coming of the great and glorious day of the Lord*' (vv. 19-20). That day would come with the return of Jesus Christ. He was careful to add the gospel call that concluded Joel's prophecy:

> [21]*'And everyone who calls on the name of the Lord will be saved'*
> [22]*"Men of Israel, listen to this: Jesus of Nazareth was a man accredited by God to you by miracles, wonders and signs, which God did among you through him, as you yourselves know."*
> Acts 1:21-22

With the mention of Jesus of Nazareth Peter had renewed the crowd's attention. Local Jews in the crowd possibly had firsthand knowledge of Jesus' crucifixion and death, his burial and resurrection and possibly his ascension to heaven. Few could have known their significance.

Peter's first point was a neat summary of Jesus' ministry (v. 22). He followed this with an indictment of the *'men of Israel'* who had wilfully put Jesus to death *'by nailing him to a cross.'*

> [23]*This man was handed over to you by God's set purpose and foreknowledge; and you, with the help of wicked men, put him to death by nailing him to the cross.* [24]*But God raised him from the dead, freeing him from the agony of death, because it was impossible for death to keep its hold on him.* Acts 2: 23-24

The crucifixion of Jesus was a crime committed by men but permitted by God (v. 23). The resurrection of Jesus was an act of God. Death's sting was neutralised and the grave was robbed of its victory. Death could not keep its prey.

In support of this declaration Peter turned again to the Hebrew Scriptures, this time to Psalm 16:8-11, which was part of a Messianic Psalm by King David. The subject of the passage was resurrection. Was David referring to his own resurrection, or that of someone else? Peter's preface to the quotation, *'David said about him'* clarified the matter (v. 25). David was prophesying the resurrection of Jesus.

Everyone present knew that David's body had never been raised, in fact it was still in his tomb nearby (v. 29. Enabled by the Holy Spirit David had prophesied centuries before that a descendant of his would succeed him on his throne (v. 30). His descendant would be the Messiah, the Christ. The Psalm predicted '*that he was not abandoned to the grave, nor did his body see decay' (v.31).*

> [32]God *has raised this Jesus to life, and we are all witnesses of the fact.* [33]*Exalted to the right hand of God, he has received from the Father the promised Holy Spirit and has poured out what you now see and hear.* Acts 2:32-33

The events of the Day of Pentecost were acts of God who, in faithfulness to his promise to send the Holy Spirit, had poured out what everyone had seen and heard. This was the dawn of a new age of the Holy Spirit that would stretch between the first and second advents of Christ.

Another reference to the Scriptures (Ps. 110:1) reinforced the fact of Christ's exaltation.

> [34] *For David did not ascend to heaven, and yet he said, " 'The Lord said to my Lord: "Sit at my right hand* [35] *until I make your enemies a footstool for your feet." '* [36] *"Therefore let all Israel be assured of this: God has made this Jesus, whom you crucified, both Lord and Christ."* Acts 2:34-36

It is little wonder that the mood of the crowd had changed somewhat: Peter's preaching had taken a turn that was unexpected. His final statement declared that Jesus, whom they had crucified, was both God and the anointed Messiah.

The Holy Spirit moved freely in convicting and converting power in the crowd, bringing some 3,000 individuals face to face with the risen Lord, whom they had crucified.

> [37] *When the people heard this, they were cut to the heart and said to Peter and the other apostles, "Brothers, what shall we do?"* Acts 2:37

Their conviction of sin was deep, literally they were *'stabbed to the quick'*; Peter's words *'pierced their hearts'*. They were *'conscience-stricken'*. An urgent cry went up from the crowd, *"Brothers, what shall we do?"* The crowd looked to Peter and the other apostles for an answer.

> [38] *Peter replied, "Repent and be baptised, every one of you, in the name of Jesus Christ for the forgiveness of your sins. And you will receive the gift of the Holy Spirit.* Acts 2:38

Peter's instructions had to be crystal clear. He called on those who had been awakened to the enormity of their sin to repent (turn from it to God) and be baptised (as Jesus had commanded the apostles in the Great Commission) for the forgiveness of sins.

Peter promised the new believers two gifts from God: forgiveness of sins, and the gift of the Holy Spirit. With these in mind he continued:

> [39] *The promise is for you and your children and for all who are far off—for all whom the Lord our God will call."* Acts 2:39

What promise was Peter referring to? The answer is in 1:4: *'the gift my Father promised.'* People must not think that the gift of the Holy Spirit was confined to the apostles alone, or to the 120 other disciples who were with them, or limited to Jews only, or to that generation alone. So he clarified who the recipients of the promise of the Holy Spirit were, namely: '*you and your children and all who are far off—for all whom the Lord our God will call*." The term *'all who are far off'* is a reference to Gentiles who would believe in Jesus Christ.

> [40] *With many other words he warned them; and he pleaded with them, "Save yourselves from this corrupt generation."* [41] *Those who accepted his message were baptised, and about three thousand were added to their number that day.* Acts 2:41-42

Peter gave the crowd a clear answer to their question. He warned them. He pleaded with them. Thereafter the consequences were in the capable hands of the Holy Spirit.

Somewhere in the region of 3,000 souls accepted the message, repented of their sins, called on the name of the Lord and were baptised and added to the number of the believers that day. No-one was baptised without being added; no-one was added without being baptised. Modern practice has departed somewhat from apostolic precedent.

Let no one stumble over the logistics of baptising 3,000 new believers in one day, or wonder where enough water was found. Archaeologists have confirmed that on the south side of the Temple Mount numerous Jewish baptistery-like facilities have been found where worshippers immersed themselves before entering the temple. We are assured there were more than enough of these stone water-tanks to facilitate a large number of baptisms in a short space of time.

THANK YOU, HEAVENLY FATHER:

For the power of the Holy Spirit that energised the witness of the believers and the preaching of Peter;

For the convicting and converting power of the Holy Spirit, a factor that marked the events of Pentecost and the growth of the Church as the work of God and not of men;

For the historic Pentecost in Jerusalem following Jesus' ascension to heaven; and for the promised Holy Spirit which he received from the Father and shed forth on his church.

IN JESUS' NAME, AMEN

5. Acts 2:42-47

THE FELLOWSHIP OF THE BELIEVERS

[42]And they continued steadfastly in the apostles' doctrine and fellowship, in the breaking of bread, and in prayers. [43]Then fear came upon every soul, and many wonders and signs were done through the apostles.

[44]Now all who believed were together, and had all things in common, [45]and sold their possessions and goods, and divided them among all, as anyone had need.

[46]So continuing daily with one accord in the temple, and breaking bread from house to house, they ate their food with gladness and simplicity of heart, [47]praising God and having favour with all the people. And the Lord added to the church daily those who were being saved. Acts 2:42–47

How we long for such days in which the Holy Spirit takes matters into his own power and accomplishes his will, so that when people view a true work of God they will instantly acknowledge that the Holy Spirit did it.

The 120 believers now numbered 3,120 which was 26 times their original number. A group of that size would keep the apostles busy. It wasn't a matter of getting people into line or keeping order, or even writing a constitution! No, a spiritual bonding was taking place, and a pattern of church life began to emerge. Luke records:

[42]And they continued steadfastly in the apostles' doctrine and fellowship, in the breaking of bread, and in prayers. Acts 2:42

A Spirit-filled Church

The believers had a keen appetite for instruction. The apostles were the leaders in teaching the truth about Jesus and the facts of the gospel. *'The apostles' doctrine'* simply means *'the apostles' teaching'*. The new believers devoted themselves to this teaching. If we refer to some things that Jesus had taught them about the Holy Spirit we can see that he had a major role in this: John 14:26; 15:26 – 27; 16:13.

'Fellowship' was another feature of the entire group. This is the spiritual sharing that takes place when believers meet in the Lord's presence. The Holy Spirit makes this sharing a reality in believers' lives.

'The breaking of bread' was a third factor in the life of the group. The apostles would explain the meaning of the elements of bread and wine. These were symbols of the Lord's body. The observance of 'the Lord's supper' was a command of Jesus before his death on the cross.

'Prayers' were a fourth factor. The 120 had experience of this spiritual discipline while waiting for the Spirit to come, the 3,000 had not. However, we may presume that the elements of thanksgiving and worship were among the priorities in their meetings for prayer.

> [43]*Then fear came upon every soul, and many wonders and signs were done through the apostles.* Acts 2:43

There was *'a sense of God'* among them, and the Spirit continued to further the work of God through the apostles.

> [44]*Now all who believed were together, and had all things in common,* [45]*and sold their possessions and goods, and divided them among all, as anyone had need.* [46]*So continuing daily with one accord in the temple, and breaking bread from house to house, they ate their food with gladness and simplicity of heart,* [47]*praising God and having favour with all the people.* Acts 2:44-47

There was *'a strong sense of belonging'* among them and an extraordinary amount of mutual care and help could be seen.

Every day was *'a day of worship and fellowship'* when they went to the temple to praise God and to witness to the gospel. Their testimonies were transparently genuine. Meanwhile, their numbers kept increasing as '*the Lord added to the church daily those who were being saved.*'

If, before moving on, we take a parting glance back into the chapter we see a group of recently born-again believers who are the body of Christ in Jerusalem. They are not an organisation held together by human arrangement. They are a living organism, their hearts beating with the life of the risen Lord. They are also a community of the Holy Spirit. This is a very heart-warming concept. Many local churches have lost this identity and this awareness.

The Watching World

It is easy to overlook the fact that the believers' whole way of life was being observed by the watching world.

Worship had a large place in their lives which underscores the fact that this spirit-filled church was Christ-centered. People could see this, even if they could not put a name on it; it was a visual aid to the watching world.

If we are joining them in one of their meetings for the first time, what is it that impresses us? I suggest that it is the caring attitude of these people for one another. **Christian love** is a big factor with them. Every member matters. I leave you to imagine the needs that might have arisen at any time of the week, and what measures the whole body of believers might have taken to meet it.

Remembering the Lord's Death was a central feature of their worship. Try to forget any resemblance to golden chalices or trays of individual cups or candles or incense or any other things with which we surround the Lord's Table. You can be sure of this: there was no organ music in the background to help the congregation cope with long silences (something modern believers cannot do) when they were partaking of bread and wine in remembrance of the Lord's death, burial and resurrection. Let nothing get in the way of a meaningful and grateful remembrance of the Lord. That was the reason for being there.

Another factor was important: their open air **Witness** in the Temple Courts kept them in touch with the world of lost people (v. 46). The Lord added to their number daily those who were being saved (v. 47).

You may have noticed in the above paragraphs that I have resisted the temptation to squeeze the Jerusalem church into our mould. It is not a case of them being like us – God forbid! The burning question is: When are we going to be like them?

A final contrast. What held everyone together? We could say 'the Holy Spirit'. That would be a good answer. Think a little more about this. I suggest that it was **their mutual commitment to Jesus Christ as God and Saviour** that bound them together. From that centre, the life of the church expressed itself in ever increasing circles until most people in Jerusalem knew about the Christians, whom they worshipped, how they worshipped, and how they lived together.

The Believers' Love for Jesus Christ

What is it that gets you out of bed on a Sunday morning and takes you to Church? Oh, I understand. When you joined that church you signed a covenant of membership that obliges you to be present unless hindered by a conscientious reason. That is a sentence from the church constitution. I know it well. The real 'down-deep' issue still needs to be faced. Is it loyalty to your church's constitution or sheer love for Jesus your Lord and Saviour that takes you to church?

The believers at Jerusalem were not only a community of believers; they were a unity of believers, their hearts beating as one, in devotion to their Lord and Saviour Jesus Christ.

THANK YOU, HEAVENLY FATHER:

For the birth of the Christian church on the day of Pentecost; we almost wish that the church could be young again;

For Your promise, 'the promise of the Father', faithfully kept and generously fulfilled in the out-pouring of the Holy Spirit on the infant Church;

For visitations of the Holy Spirit at various points in history with reviving and saving power;

IN JESUS' NAME, AMEN

6. Acts 3: 1-10

PETER HEALS THE CRIPPLED BEGGAR

One day Peter and John were going up to the temple at the time of prayer—at three in the afternoon.

[2]Now a man crippled from birth was being carried to the temple gate called Beautiful, where he was put every day to beg from those going into the temple courts. [3]When he saw Peter and John about to enter, he asked them for money. [4]Peter looked straight at him, as did John. Then Peter said, "Look at us!"

[5]So the man gave them his attention, expecting to get something from them. [6]Then Peter said, "Silver or gold I do not have, but what I have I give you. In the name of Jesus Christ of Nazareth, walk." [7]Taking him by the right hand, he helped him up, and instantly the man's feet and ankles became strong. [8]He jumped to his feet and began to walk. Then he went with them into the temple courts, walking and jumping, and praising God.

[9]When all the people saw him walking and praising God, [10]they recognised him as the same man who used to sit begging at the temple gate called Beautiful, and they were filled with wonder and amazement at what had happened to him. Acts 3: 1-10

Perhaps it was a good place to meet people and talk to them about Jesus, but there is a strong hint in the opening sentence that Peter and John were developing a habit of going up to the temple at one of the daily times of prayer. They were going to the 3 o'clock prayer meeting. It may also have been a good place to be if you were a beggar, and one such man was there. There was the possibility that folks who came to worship were more disposed to give charity to a beggar than the generality of the citizens of Jerusalem. This man had a congenital condition; for forty years he had never been able to walk properly (4:22).

Probably worshippers got used to him sitting there day after day. Peter later made a point about this in v. 16 when he spoke of *this man whom you see and know.* Today was different because two men who were apostles of Jesus came along, Peter and John by name, and they were genuinely interested in him. The beggar was in the act of asking for money (v. 3) when Peter and John looked him straight in the eye and said, 'Look at us!' He gave them his full attention, because his hopes had been raised that he might receive a generous donation.

> [6]*Then Peter said, "Silver or gold I do not have, but what I have I give you. In the name of Jesus Christ of Nazareth, walk."* [7]*Taking him by the right hand, he helped him up, and instantly the man's feet and ankles became strong. Then he went with them into the temple courts, walking and jumping, and praising God.* Acts 3:6-7

Peter and John were speaking truthfully when they said they were without means of their own, but they were able to minister to the man in a way that no amount of money could buy. Peter took the man by his right hand and commanded him *'in the name of Jesus Christ of Nazareth to rise and walk'*. For the first time in his life the man could feel strength coming into *his feet and ankles*. Within seconds he had jumped to his feet and begun to walk. He became euphoric and there was no holding him as he walked and jumped and praised God. His place by the temple gate was left vacant and the three men entered the temple courts. This thing had not been done in a corner, but in full view of the people who were passing by.

> [9]*When all the people saw him walking and praising God,* [10]*they recognised him as the same man who used to sit begging at the temple gate called Beautiful, and they were filled with wonder and amazement at what had happened to him.* Acts 1:9-10

The onlookers were utterly astonished. There may have been a smaller prayer meeting than usual in the temple that afternoon because many people had followed the trio into Solomon's Colonnade.

We would like to know what had motivated the two apostles to go to the Temple for prayer. Whatever it was, they were not wrapped up in their own thoughts. They were alert to this man and his condition. We are very impressed with their readiness to act. In fact, they behaved toward the cripple as Jesus would have done. There was no hesitation on their part, *'will we?'* or *'won't we?'*, but rather they were ready to minister to a man in need in the name of Jesus of Nazareth. There was no wavering about the possibility of failure, but a straightforward command was issued in Jesus' name and a crippled man walked.

I can recall a number of times in the course of pastoral work, when God answered definite prayer and some who were sick recovered very quickly and were soon restored to their families and to their everyday occupations. I didn't rush around telling everybody I met because I believed that the patient was the best judge of that. Anyhow, pastoral etiquette didn't permit me to talk about the people I visited.

Now, in retirement, I look back and wish I had acted with a firm faith much more often. Christ's touch has still its ancient power. To Him be the glory.

THANK YOU, HEAVENLY FATHER:

For this example of the many wonders and miraculous signs that were done by the apostles (2:43);

For this simple narrative of the power of Jesus to make a crippled man walk;

For the working relationship that Peter and John were developing;

For the alertness of Peter and John to recognise a man in need and their readiness to minister to him in the name of Jesus;

For the Christ-like way in which Peter and John ministered to the crippled man;

For the witness of this miracle to the power of the risen Jesus, and for the praise of God on the lips of the healed man.

IN JESUS' NAME, AMEN

7. Acts 3:11 - 26

PETER SPEAKS TO THE ONLOOKERS

While the beggar held on to Peter and John, all the people were astonished and came running to them in the place called Solomon's Colonnade.

[12]When Peter saw this, he said to them: "Men of Israel, why does this surprise you? Why do you stare at us as if by our own power or godliness we had made this man walk? [13]The God of Abraham, Isaac and Jacob, the God of our fathers, has glorified his servant Jesus. You handed him over to be killed, and you disowned him before Pilate, though he had decided to let him go. [14]You disowned the Holy and Righteous One and asked that a murderer be released to you. [15]You killed the author of life, but God raised him from the dead. We are witnesses of this.

[16]By faith in the name of Jesus, this man whom you see and know was made strong. It is Jesus' name and the faith that comes through him that has given this complete healing to him, as you can all see.

[17]Now, brothers, I know that you acted in ignorance, as did your leaders. [18]But this is how God fulfilled what he had foretold through all the prophets, saying that his Christ would suffer. [19]Repent, then, and turn to God, so that your sins may be wiped out, that times of refreshing may come from the Lord, [20]and that he may send the Christ, who has been appointed for you even Jesus. [21]He must remain in heaven until the time comes for God to restore everything, as he promised long ago through his holy prophets.

[22]For Moses said, 'The Lord your God will raise up for you a prophet like me from among your own people; you must listen to everything he tells you. [23]Anyone who does not listen to him will be completely cut off from among his people.'

[24]"Indeed, all the prophets from Samuel on, as many as have spoken, have foretold these days. [25]And you are heirs of the prophets and of the covenant God made with your fathers. He said to Abraham, 'Through your offspring all peoples on earth will be blessed.' [26]When God raised up his servant, he sent him first to you to bless you by turning each of you from your wicked ways." Acts 3:11-26

The more we get to know Peter the more we are surprised at his resourcefulness. For instance he was a born evangelist. Just as he found a point of contact with the crowd on the day of Pentecost (2:14), so here he is quick to begin preaching. He began with the question that he could read on every face:

Men of Israel, why does this surprise you? Why do you stare at us as if by our own power or godliness we had made this man walk? Acts 3:12

It can be a difficult task to maintain the interest of a crowd, so Peter pressed on with the answer to his questions.

[13] The God of Abraham, Isaac and Jacob, the God of our fathers, has glorified his servant Jesus. Acts 3:13

He got them thinking about the God of their fathers, the God of the patriarchs. He told them Israel's God had performed the miracle and in doing so had glorified his servant Jesus.

Mention of the name of Jesus should have touched consciences in the crowd. Peter rehearsed the actions of the people (and others like them) with regard to Jesus' crucifixion.

'You handed him over to be killed, and you disowned him before Pilate, though he had decided to let him go. [14]You disowned the Holy and Righteous One and asked that a murderer be released to you. [15]You killed the author of life, but God raised him from the dead. We are witnesses of this.' Acts 3:13-15

There was no mincing of words in that indictment. They ought to be ashamed of how the Jewish people and their leaders had behaved towards Jesus.

> [16]'*By faith in the name of Jesus, this man whom you see and know was made strong. It is Jesus' name and the faith that comes through him that has given this complete healing to him, as you can all see.'* Acts 3:16

The healing of the cripple was ascribed to Jesus Christ. The Jesus who had been crucified was no longer dead because God had raised him from the dead. It was the power of Jesus' name and faith in that name that explained the complete healing they had witnessed.

Peter knew that it wasn't only what men had done to Jesus that was important; what God had done in the death of Jesus was of overriding importance.

> [17]*"Now, brothers, I know that you acted in ignorance, as did your leaders.* [18]*But this is how God fulfilled what he had foretold through all the prophets, saying that his Christ would suffer."* Acts 3: 17-18

So how can Jewish men and women, full of guilt for their sin in murdering Jesus, find peace with God?

Here was the good news. This was the gospel of the day of Pentecost in slightly different words, simply because of different circumstances. The gospel demanded that guilty sinners repent (turn from their sin to God). The gospel promised that their sins would be wiped out (like cleaning a blackboard in a classroom), and times of further blessing would come from the Lord. This would be their experience when they would welcome the Christ, God's anointed Son,

> [19]*"Repent, then, and turn to God, so that your sins may be wiped out, that times of refreshing may come from the Lord,* [20]*and that he may send the Christ, who has been appointed for you—even Jesus."* Acts 3:19-20

This would be their experience when they would welcome the Christ, God's anointed Son, into their lives. They should now know God's purpose in the suffering of Christ (v. 18).

Where is the resurrected Jesus now?

> [21]*"He must remain in heaven until the time comes for God to restore everything, as he promised long ago through his holy prophets.*
>
> [22]*For Moses said, 'The Lord your God will raise up for you a prophet like me from among your own people; you must listen to everything he tells you.* [23]*Anyone who does not listen to him will be completely cut off from among his people.'* [24]*"Indeed, all the prophets from Samuel on, as many as have spoken, have foretold these days."* Acts 3: 21-24

Peter was preaching to Jews within Solomon's Colonnade, This is why he majored on Jewish terminology and the Hebrew Scriptures and prophets. When the right time comes in God's programme of the ages Jesus Christ will return (v. 21). Moses spoke about that event (v. 22). All the prophets from Samuel have spoken of these gospel days.

> [25] *"And you are heirs of the prophets and of the covenant God made with your fathers. He said to Abraham, 'Through your offspring all peoples on earth will be blessed."*
>
> [26]*"When God raised up his servant, he sent him first to you to bless you by turning each of you from your wicked ways."* Acts 3:25-26

What an inheritance of spiritual blessing was theirs because of the covenant that God made with their fathers. God promised to bless the world through the seed of Abraham. He was still keeping that promise. When God raised Jesus from the dead he sent him to bless them (the Jews) by turning them from their sins to himself.

THANK YOU, HEAVENLY FATHER:

For the preaching of the gospel of Christ; it is truly the power of God for salvation of everyone who believes: first for the Jew, then for the Gentile;

For our appeal to the God of the patriarchs both in prayer and preaching; he is the everlasting God;

For the glory that the preaching of Christ's life and death, resurrection and ascension brings to him;

For the silent, unseen ministry of the Holy Spirit wherever the gospel is preached;

IN JESUS' NAME, AMEN

8. Acts 4: 1-22

PETER AND JOHN BEFORE THE SANHEDRIN

The priests and the captain of the temple guard and the Sadducees came up to Peter and John while they were speaking to the people.

[2]They were greatly disturbed because the apostles were teaching the people and proclaiming in Jesus the resurrection of the dead. [3]They seized Peter and John, and because it was evening, they put them in jail until the next day. [4]But many who heard the message believed and the number of men grew to about five thousand.

[5]The next day the rulers, elders and teachers of the law met in Jerusalem. [6]Annas the high priest was there, and so were Caiaphas, John, Alexander and the other men of the high priest's family. [7]They had Peter and John brought before them and began to question them: "By what power or what name did you do this?"

[8]Then Peter, filled with the Holy Spirit, said to them: "Rulers and elders of the people! [9]If we are being called to account today for an act of kindness shown to a cripple and are asked how he was healed, [10]then know this, you and all the people of Israel: It is by the name of Jesus Christ of Nazareth, whom you crucified but whom God raised from the dead, that this man stands before you healed. [11]He is "the stone you builders rejected, which has become the capstone." [12]Salvation is found in no-one else, for there is no other name under heaven given to men by which we must be saved."

[13]When they saw the courage of Peter and John and realised that they were unschooled, ordinary men, they were astonished and they took note that these men had been with Jesus. [14]But since they could see the man who had been healed standing there with

them, there was nothing they could say. [15]So they ordered them to withdraw from the Sanhedrin and then conferred together.

[16]"What are we going to do with these men?" they asked. "Everybody living in Jerusalem knows they have done an outstanding miracle, and we cannot deny it.

[17]But to stop this thing from spreading any further among the people, we must warn these men to speak no longer to anyone in this name." [18]Then they called them in again and commanded them not to speak or teach at all in the name of Jesus.

[19]But Peter and John replied, "Judge for yourselves whether it is right in God's sight to obey you rather than God. [20]For we cannot help speaking about what we have seen and heard."

[21]After further threats they let them go. They could not decide how to punish them, because all the people were praising God for what had happened. [22]For the man who was miraculously healed was over forty years old. Acts 4:1-22

'The Israeli Religious Police' were on the trail of the apostles and interrupted them while they were speaking to the people; in the same way as they had dogged the footsteps of Jesus during his ministry. They were exasperated with Peter and John and arrested them because they were teaching the people and declaring in Jesus the resurrection of the dead. Meanwhile Peter and John spent the night in jail because it was too late in the day for a session of the Sanhedrin to be convened.

However, the Jewish authorities were helpless to prevent the silent work of the Holy Spirit who was drawing people to faith in Jesus (v. 4) to the extent that the number of men in the Christian community increased to about 5,000.

Next day a full complement of the Sanhedrin met in Jerusalem. All the 'top brass' were there (vv. 6-7). Peter and John were brought into the court to answer for their actions and their message: *"By what power or what name did you do this?"*

Peter, formerly a fisherman, but now a Spirit-filled apostle, stood up and answered the Council's question forthrightly and without a hint of fear:

> *"Rulers and elders of the people! [9]If we are being called to account today for an act of kindness shown to a cripple and are asked how he was healed, [10]then know this, you and all the people of Israel: it is by the name of Jesus Christ of Nazareth, whom you crucified but whom God raised from the dead, that this man stands before you healed."* Acts 4:9-10

Peter had no hesitation in telling the Council of their crime in putting Jesus to death; neither did he hesitate in declaring that God had since raised him from the dead. He exposed the folly of what the Council had done by quoting Psalm 118:22:

> *[11]"He is "the stone you builders rejected, which has become the capstone." [12]Salvation is found in no-one else, for there is no other name under heaven given to men by which we must be saved."* Acts 4:11-12

Peter declared that the apostles had acted with the authority of Jesus Christ, as proof of which they could see the man who had been healed standing there. Peter also made it clear that it was the belief of the apostles that Jesus Christ was the only Saviour of sinners. The Council had cast Jesus aside, like builders on a building site discarding the most important stone of all. The apostles believed that Jesus was the capstone, the key-stone that sat where two walls met thus giving shape to the building, in this case the Christian Church.

It was at this point that something dawned on the Council members. They thought to themselves: 'How was it that these men who were artisans, non-university types, who had never been to a rabbinical school, spoke and acted as they did?' Then the answer became obvious. The last time they had met someone who spoke and acted as these men did was when Jesus of Nazareth had stood before them! That was it! These men had been with Jesus. The Council was embarrassed.

> [14] *But since they could see the man who had been healed standing there with them, there was nothing they could say.* [15] *So they ordered them to withdraw from the Sanhedrin and then conferred together.* Acts 4:14-15

If they were to punish the apostles they would face the wrath of the crowd.

> [16]*"What are we going to do with these men?" they asked. "Everybody living in Jerusalem knows they have done an outstanding miracle, and we cannot deny it."*

> [17]*But to stop this thing from spreading any further among the people, we must warn these men to speak no longer to anyone in this name."* [18] *Then they called them in again and commanded them not to speak or teach at all in the name of Jesus.* Acts 4:16-18

The Council resolved to forbid the apostles to preach in the name of Jesus, in spite of the fact that '*they have done an outstanding miracle, and we cannot deny it*'. Accordingly they had them brought back into the court and *commanded them not to speak or teach at all in the name of Jesus*. Did they expect that the apostles would submit meekly to the Council's decision? If they did, they were mistaken.

> [19]*But Peter and John replied, "Judge for yourselves whether it is right in God's sight to obey you rather than God.* [20]*For we cannot help speaking about what we have seen and heard."* Acts 4:19-20

Can't we see the pomp and dignity of the Jewish Council on one hand, and the two coarse-looking, former fishermen, apostles of Christ, on the other? So far as the apostles were concerned their consciences were captive to the command of Christ. So far as the council was concerned preaching and teaching in the name of Jesus must stop! Neither side was giving way in this matter.

> [21]*After further threats they let them go. They could not decide how to punish them, because all the people were praising God for what had happened.* [22]*For the man who was miraculously healed was over forty years old.* Acts 4:21-22

Had the crowd known the hymn we love so well, they might have sung it: 'To God be the glory, great things He has done.'

The subject of the persecution of God's people has a long history. It didn't begin with Jesus and the apostles, but in the Book of Genesis when Cain killed his brother Abel because his own actions were evil and his brother's were righteous. It is probable that the majority of people who read these lines have never been in a life-threatening situation because of persecution for Christ's sake. This is all the more reason why we should remember the Suffering Church in our prayers and intercessions on a daily basis.

THANK YOU, HEAVENLY FATHER:

For ordering all things according to the counsel of Your own will;

For the Holy Spirit's ministry to Peter and John, who without formal training or high-level education, were enabled to face the Jewish Council, and courageously witness for Jesus;

For the fact that genuine miracles stand up to scrutiny; the reality of this man's healing was beyond dispute; the enemies of the gospel could not deny it; the Council acknowledged that the apostles *'have done an outstanding miracle, and we cannot deny it'*.

For the way in which prohibitions against gospel preaching frequently become opportunities for Christ's name to be made known where it had not been heard before;

For the abiding truth that *'there is no other name under heaven given to men by which we are saved.'*

IN JESUS' NAME, AMEN

9. Acts 4: 23 to 31

THE BELIEVERS' PRAYER

It is easy to read these familiar lines and miss the seriousness of the threat made by the Jewish Sanhedrin against the apostles Peter and John.

> *They called them in again and commanded them not to speak or teach at all in the name of Jesus.* Acts 4:18

However shambolic the Council meeting had been, the Statute Book would record the prohibition as being entered into law. Peter's spirited and emphatic refusal to comply with the law in this instance did not lessen the prohibition in the least degree (v. 19 – 20). The apostles reported back to their own people.

> *On their release, Peter and John went back to their own people and reported all that the chief priests and elders had said to them.* Acts 4:23

Notice the working-relationship between the apostles and the members of the Jerusalem church. This is good. Such were the pressures of the times that urgent news was shared at the next prayer meeting. We may assume that there were no long silences in this prayer meeting. It seems that prayer started immediately and with urgency.

> [24]*When they heard this, they raised their voices together in prayer to God. "Sovereign Lord," they said, "you made the heaven and the earth and the sea, and everything in them.* [25]*You spoke by the Holy Spirit through the mouth of your servant, our father David:"*
>
> *'Why do the nations rage and the peoples plot in vain?* [26] *The kings of the earth take their stand and the rulers gather together against the Lord and against his Anointed One.'* Acts 4:24-26

Urgency didn't prevent a thoughtful and reverent approach to God. They didn't dash into his presence without being aware of where they had come.

Notice their approach to God: *"Sovereign Lord," they said, "you made the heaven and the earth and the sea, and everything in them."* They gratefully acknowledged God's sovereignty – and cast themselves on it. They recalled the opening verses of Psalm 2. Following in the spirit of the Psalm they quoted recent instances of human rebellion against God.

> [27]*Indeed Herod and Pontius Pilate met together with the Gentiles and the people of Israel in this city to conspire against your holy servant Jesus, whom you anointed.* [28]*They did what your power and will had decided beforehand should happen.* Acts 4:27-28

Democracy is a much used and abused word in our world. Has any country direct democracy? Democracy means 'the rule of the people'. At best we live in a parliamentary democracy, that is to say we are governed by elected representatives. Anyhow, we are proud of our democracy. Alas, for many people democracy simply means they can protest against the current government and cause any amount of public disruption. Sometimes the result is chaos.

It is correct to say that the believers in Jerusalem had no intention of protesting against the ruling of the Sanhedrin. What did they do? They met to pray and laid the matter before God. What was the burden of their prayer? They prayed specifically:

> [29]*"Now, Lord, consider their threats and enable your servants to speak your word with great boldness.* [30]*Stretch out your hand to heal and perform miraculous signs and wonders through the name of your holy servant Jesus."* Acts 4:29-30

Not only did heaven hear their prayer, a physical phenomenon signalled the presence and power of the Holy Spirit.

> [31] *After they prayed, the place where they were meeting was shaken. And they were all filled with the Holy Spirit and spoke the word of God boldly.* Acts 4:31

THANK YOU, HEAVENLY FATHER,

For the place and power of prayer in the life of a local church;

For the courage of Peter and John in the public place, and the confidence of the church when praying in the secret place;

For the encouragement of the Scriptures when we come to pray about any matter;

For your sovereignty in all the affairs of men and nations;

For the helplessness of the Jewish Council in the face of a praying church;

For equipping your people so that the Word of God was spoken boldly;

IN JESUS' NAME, AMEN

10. Acts 4:32-37

THE BELIEVERS SHARE THEIR POSSESSIONS

[32]All the believers were one in heart and mind. No-one claimed that any of his possessions was his own, but they shared everything they had. [33]With great power the apostles continued to testify to the resurrection of the Lord Jesus and much grace was upon them all. [34]There were no needy persons among them. Acts 4:32-34

The members of the early Church were an economically mixed group. Some of them had considerable means and others lived on the breadline. Almost from day one (2:44) they learned to share their resources.

This was a spontaneous development which met the needs of many people. However, it never became a rule of the church. Here in Acts 4 there is a second instance of this generosity to one another. Their sharing of material things was an expression of their spiritual unity (v. 32).

Meanwhile the work of the apostles continued unabated. Never mind the prohibition placed on them by the Sanhedrin they went on preaching the resurrection of Jesus, and much grace was on them all.

That is to say that people outside the church were impressed by what they saw of Christian people, and God continued to bless the witness. Within the church the needs of all were met. An instance of the generosity of the believers concludes this chapter.

[34]For from time to time those who owned lands or houses sold them, brought the money from the sales [35]and put it at the apostles' feet, and it was distributed to anyone as he had need.

[36]Joseph, a Levite from Cyprus, whom the apostles called Barnabas (which means Son of Encouragement), [37]sold a field

he owned and brought the money and put it at the apostles' feet.
Acts 4:34-37

Joseph (also called Barnabas by the apostles), a member of the Old Testament priestly tribe of Levi, was a Cypriot. He had a reputation for encouraging people, hence the derivation of his 'nickname'. His gift to the apostles was very generous. *He sold a field he owned and brought the money and put it at the apostles' feet.*

This is a good point at which to pause and think about possessions, ownership, stewardship and giving.

The Scriptures teach that we came into the world with nothing and we can take nothing out of it (1 Tim. 6:7). Therefore, largely dependent on the family into which we were born, we either grew up wanting for nothing or we lived very plainly and frugally while others were somewhere between high and low on the economic scale.

Then as we grew into adulthood and found employment we earned either a low or modest or a high salary. The way we used the money we had inherited or earned, determined whether we became people of some means or even independent means. By that time there were possessions that we regarded as **'ours', 'belonging to us'.**

It is perfectly legitimate to have personal possessions, either in money or in kind. However, when we become Christians it is not long until we learn that everything we have **'belongs to the Lord'.** What is **'ours'** at that point is **the stewardship of the money or property.** In other words the Lord will hold us accountable for how we use our possessions.

Suppose, like Joseph Barnabas, the Lord lays it on our hearts to give either some or a lot of our possessions to his work, to whom do they belong then?

We need to understand that while the money or property is in our possession it is **'ours'**. When we give the money to the Lord's work by placing it in the hands of the apostles (as Joseph did), or handing it to the Treasurer of a Christian charity, or our local church, to whom does the money belong then? One thing should be clear: **it is no longer 'ours'**. So far as we are concerned **'it now belongs to the Lord'**. We relinquished all claims to it when we handed it over. So far as the Charity or Church Treasurer is concerned it doesn't belong to him personally, **it belongs to the charity or to the church to be used specifically for its purposes.**

A failure to understand this was the reason for a serious disruption in the life of the Jerusalem Church in the following chapter.

THANK YOU, HEAVENLY FATHER:

For meeting all our needs according to your glorious riches in Christ Jesus (Phil 4:19);

For the ability to work and to earn a living, and for the health and strength that you gave us to do so;

For the discipline of work and the discipline of thrift, both of which went a long way in helping us to develop a sense of value;

For the generosity of your people in financing your work at home and abroad; they too will have a share in the spiritual harvest that will follow;

For demonstrating to us that we are never poorer 'for lending to the Lord;'

For the superintendence of the Holy Spirit in every part of your work, including the provision of the necessary finance;

For the assurance that you love a cheerful giver (2 Cor. 9:7);

For Jesus Christ, who though he was rich, yet for our sakes he became poor, so that we through his poverty might become rich (2 Cor. 8:9);

IN JESUS' NAME, AMEN

11. Acts 5:1-11

ANANIAS AND SAPPHIRA

[1]Now a man named Ananias, together with his wife Sapphira, also sold a piece of property.

[2]With his wife's full knowledge he kept back part of the money for himself, but brought the rest and put it at the apostles' feet.

[3]Then Peter said, "Ananias, how is it that Satan has so filled your heart that you have lied to the Holy Spirit and have kept for yourself some of the money you received for the land? [4]Didn't it belong to you before it was sold? And after it was sold, wasn't the money at your disposal? What made you think of doing such a thing? You have not lied to men but to God."

[5]When Ananias heard this, he fell down and died. And great fear seized all who heard what had happened. [6]Then the young men came forward, wrapped up his body, and carried him out and buried him.

[7]About three hours later his wife came in, not knowing what had happened. [8]Peter asked her, "Tell me, is this the price you and Ananias got for the land?" "Yes," she said, "that is the price."

*[9]Peter said to her, "How could you agree to test the Spirit of the Lord? **Look!** The feet of the men who buried your husband are at the door, and they will carry you out also."*

[10]At that moment she fell down at his feet and died. Then the young men came in and, finding her dead, carried her out and buried her beside her husband. Great fear seized the whole church and all who heard about these events. Acts 5:1-10

Unless we know the background to this section we might be among the first to thank Ananias and Sapphira for their generosity to the Jerusalem Church. The sad truth is that they became entangled in a snare of the devil and faked their spirituality to impress their fellow members. Until this happened we may safely assume that they were two godly church members. What actually happened?

Before anything came to light about their motives, Luke relates that Ananias, with his wife's full knowledge kept back part of the price they had received for a piece of property that they owned. In other words, they entered into a conspiracy to deceive their fellow-members. Why did one of them not see the wrongfulness of their thoughts and step back from doing evil? No, that didn't happen. They then brought the balance of the sale money and presented it to the apostles: *put it at the apostles' feet* is Luke's expression.

However, something wasn't quite right. Did Peter sense it independently of the Holy Spirit, or did the Spirit reveal the matter to him? Much to the surprise of Ananias his wrong-doing was exposed by Peter.

> *"Ananias, how is it that Satan has so filled your heart that you have lied to the Holy Spirit and have kept for yourself some of the money you received for the land?* ***Didn't it belong to you before it was sold? And after it was sold, wasn't the money at your disposal?*** *What made you think of doing such a thing? You have not lied to men but to God."* Acts 5:3-4:

Do you recognise some points made in the previous study? Joseph Barnabas made his gift openly and honestly. It has been said somewhere 'To make a gift is a divine act; to make it perfectly is a divine art.' How true.

Read Peter's words again: [4] *"Didn't it belong to you before it was sold? And after it was sold, wasn't the money at your disposal?"*

Keeping back part of the price was not a sin in itself. Their wrong-doing lay in professing that they were giving the whole price received for the property, and then keeping back part of the price. They were guilty of hypocrisy and lying. The seriousness of it was that they were not only lying to men but to God!

> *"What made you think of doing such a thing? You have not lied to men but to God."*

When Ananias heard this, he fell down and died. And great fear seized all who heard what had happened. Somehow or other Satan had filled Ananias and Sapphira with this Christ-dishonouring idea. They had entertained the idea, which led to a sinful action.

> *[7]About three hours later his wife came in, not knowing what had happened. [8]Peter asked her, "Tell me, is this the price you and Ananias got for the land?" "Yes," she said, "that is the price." [9]Peter said to her, "How could you agree to test the Spirit of the Lord?"* Acts 5: 7-9

Perhaps Sapphira wondered how Peter had obtained his information. There was no avoiding Peter's question. If we are to put a name on their sin, the word is embezzlement!

> *[9]"Look! The feet of the men who buried your husband are at the door, and they will carry you out also." [10]At that moment she fell down at his feet and died. Then the young men came in and, finding her dead, carried her out and buried her beside her husband.* Acts 5:9-10

What effect did these two sudden deaths have on the rest of the membership? *Great fear seized the whole church and all who heard about these events.*

The believers' great fear arose from discovering the seriousness of hypocrisy and sin in the church, and learning that death can follow as the consequence of sin.

There is no escaping the fact that they were removed from the church by sudden death: in other words, by an act of God.

THANK YOU, HEAVENLY FATHER,

For the unvarnished truth that marks this section of Acts; and for Luke's honesty in reporting this sad affair;

For the Spirit of holiness who was present and active in the church's life; illuminating Peter and giving him wisdom to handle this new and sorry situation;

For the limiting the potential damage to the church's testimony, by causing a spirit of awe (great fear) to come on the whole church and also on all who heard of these events;

IN JESUS' NAME, AMEN

12. Acts 5:12-16

THE APOSTLES HEAL MANY

> [12]*The apostles performed many miraculous signs and wonders among the people. And all the believers used to meet together in Solomon's Colonnade.*
>
> [13]*No-one else dared join them, even though they were highly regarded by the people.* [14]*Nevertheless, more and more men and women believed in the Lord and were added to their number.*
>
> [15]*As a result, people brought the sick into the streets and laid them on beds and mats so that at least Peter's shadow might fall on some of them as he passed by.*
>
> [16]*Crowds gathered also from the towns around Jerusalem, bringing their sick and those tormented by evil spirits, and all of them were healed.* Acts 5:12-16

It is important for us to know the aftermath of the sorry episode in vv. 1 – 11. We probably expected things to go downhill, with every part of the church's life being hindered. Not so! The church's prayer of chapter 4:30 was being abundantly answered: *The apostles performed many miraculous signs and wonders among the people.*

The whole body of believers continued to meet in Solomon's Colonnade for worship and witness, but there was a mixed response to them by the people. Think about these two opposite statements:

> *No-one else dared join them, even though they were highly regarded by the people v. 13.*
>
> *Nevertheless, more and more men and women believed in the Lord and were added to their number v. 14.*

There was hesitation on the part of the public to be associated with the church, despite having a high regard for it (v. 13). At the same time the church was seeing great missionary success (v 14).

Clearly the church's welfare was in the hand of the Lord. There are people who are 'put off' by the church, while others are 'drawn to it' by the Holy Spirit.

> [15] *As a result, people brought the sick into the streets and laid them on beds and mats so that at least Peter's shadow might fall on some of them as he passed by.* Acts 5:15

Luke's readers are left to conclude that some sick folk were healed by this means; somewhat after the style of the woman in the crowd around Jesus, who touched the hem of his garment and was made whole (Luke 8:43 – 47).

> [16]*Crowds gathered also from the towns around Jerusalem, bringing their sick and those tormented by evil spirits, and all of them were healed.* Acts 5:16

We recall that not everyone who was sick, disabled or demon-possessed was healed in the course of Jesus' ministry. No explanation was ever given, except that at times those who needed to be healed were so numerous that Jesus had to keep moving on. Here crowds gathered from the towns around Jerusalem (v. 16). Many sick and those tormented by evil spirits were brought to the apostles – *and all of them were healed.* These healings were signs of a divine presence and power in Jerusalem.

THANK YOU, HEAVENLY FATHER:

For using the apostles as You did, thus continuing 'all that Jesus began to do and to teach' during his earthly ministry;

For the awesome sense of Your presence in the church, so that people had reverent regard for Your presence and power;

For adding to the church, and in this way minimising the Satanic setback to the church's witness due to the sins of Ananias and Sapphira;

For the fact that the welfare of the church was in the hands of the Holy Spirit;

For the increased opportunities to glorify the name of Jesus through the ministry of the apostles in the healing of so many people;

IN JESUS' NAME, AMEN

13. Acts 5:17-42
THE APOSTLES PERSECUTED

[17]Then the high priest and all his associates, who were members of the party of the Sadducees, were filled with jealousy.

[18]They arrested the apostles and put them in the public jail. [19]But during the night an angel of the Lord opened the doors of the jail and brought them out. [20]"Go, stand in the temple courts," he said, "and tell the people the full message of this new life."

[21]At daybreak they entered the temple courts, as they had been told, and began to teach the people.

When the high priest and his associates arrived, they called together the Sanhedrin—the full assembly of the elders of Israel—and sent to the jail for the apostles. [22]But on arriving at the jail, the officers did not find them there. So they went back and reported, [23]"We found the jail securely locked, with the guards standing at the doors; but when we opened them, we found no-one inside."

[24]On hearing this report, the captain of the temple guard and the chief priests were puzzled, wondering what would come of this.
Acts 5:17-24

Nothing but sheer jealousy motivated the Sanhedrin to move against the apostles this time. They couldn't bear to see the apostles having such success and acceptance among the people.

The apostles were arrested and put in jail. But heaven had other plans for them. The Lord sent an angel during the night to open the prison doors and free the apostles.

Meanwhile the members of the Sanhedrin were assembling in their chambers preparatory to trying the apostles for some offence, as yet to be defined. They sent to the jail for the apostles.

[22] But on arriving at the jail, the officers did not find them there. So they went back and reported, [23]"We found the jail securely locked, with the guards standing at the doors; but when we opened them, we found no-one inside." Acts 5:22-23

But the officers did not find the apostles where they had secured them the night before and reported to the Sanhedrin accordingly: There was consternation in the court:

[24]On hearing this report, the captain of the temple guard and the chief priests were puzzled, wondering what would come of this.

There was an interruption:

[25]Then someone came and said, "Look! The men you put in jail are standing in the temple courts teaching the people."

[26]At that, the captain went with his officers and brought the apostles. They did not use force, because they feared that the people would stone them.

[27]Having brought the apostles, they made them appear before the Sanhedrin to be questioned by the high priest. [28]"We gave you strict orders not to teach in this name," he said. "Yet you have filled Jerusalem with your teaching and are determined to make us guilty of this man's blood." Acts 5:24-27

The high priest didn't have to search the Statute Book. He had clear remembrance of the last time the apostles had been in his court. He had put them under a prohibition to stop them teaching or preaching at all in the name of Jesus (4:18). The high priest was beginning to pick up on another point when he said: '*You are determined to make us guilty of this man's blood."* How right he was! What would the apostles have to say for themselves this time?

[29]Peter and the other apostles replied: "We must obey God rather than men! [30]The God of our fathers raised Jesus from the dead—whom you had killed by hanging him on a tree. [31]God exalted him to his own right hand as Prince and Saviour that he might give repentance and forgiveness of sins to Israel.

> *[32]We are witnesses of these things, and so is the Holy Spirit, whom God has given to those who obey him." [33]When they heard this, they were furious and wanted to put them to death.* Acts 5:29-33

The apostles were adamant that they had a duty to obey God rather than the Sanhedrin. For what reason?

In his defence Peter stated that the apostles were witnesses of the crucifixion of Jesus – a crime for which the Sanhedrin was responsible – but God had raised him from death and exalted him to his own right hand as Prince and Saviour so that Israel (the Jews) could repent and be forgiven for their sins. The Holy Spirit also was a witness to these events, and God had given the Spirit to those who obey him. The Council wanted to have Peter and John killed.

Then a GOM (grand old man) of the Sanhedrin stood up. He was a teacher of the law and a respected figure in Jerusalem. He ordered the apostles to be taken out of the court for a time.

> *[33]When they heard this, they were furious and wanted to put them to death. [34]But a Pharisee named Gamaliel, a teacher of the law, who was honoured by all the people, stood up in the Sanhedrin and ordered that the men be put outside for a little while.*
>
> *[35]Then he addressed them: "Men of Israel, consider carefully what you intend to do to these men. [36]Some time ago Theudas appeared, claiming to be somebody, and about four hundred men rallied to him. He was killed, all his followers were dispersed, and it all came to nothing.*
>
> *[37]After him, Judas the Galilean appeared in the days of the census and led a band of people in revolt. He too was killed, and all his followers were scattered. [38]Therefore, in the present case I advise you: Leave these men alone! Let them go! For if their purpose or activity is of human origin, it will fail. [39]But if it is from God, you will not be able to stop these men; you will only find yourselves fighting against God."* Acts 5:33-39

Gamaliel sounded like a Daniel come to judgment! There was a great deal of sense in what he said, but please note that Gamaliel didn't order an investigation into the truth of what the apostles were preaching and teaching; his closing argument sounds profound, but he himself had not made up his mind about Jesus. Gamaliel himself side-stepped the main issue. He was neutral towards Jesus. *His speech persuaded them*, says v. 40. It did not prevent the apostles being brutally flogged.

> [40]*They called the apostles in and had them flogged. Then they ordered them not to speak in the name of Jesus, and let them go*. Acts 5:40

The ban imposed by the Sanhedrin was still in place (4:28). The apostles left the Council, beaten and bruised, but not cast down.

> [41]*The apostles left the Sanhedrin, rejoicing because they had been counted worthy of suffering disgrace for the Name.*
>
> [42]*Day after day, in the temple courts and from house to house, they never stopped teaching and proclaiming the good news that Jesus is the Christ*. Acts 5:41-42

When human rules and regulations countermand the expressed will of God then Christians, in every culture of the world, are conscience bound to obey God. This has always been the case, and while an unbelieving world continues to persecute them, Christians will still obey God.

THANK YOU, HEAVENLY FATHER,

For Your intervention in the circumstances in which Peter and John found themselves; You opened prison doors and set the apostles free to continue preaching the gospel;

For the focus of the apostles when they knew themselves to be in danger; their concern was not for their own safety but to uplift Christ;

For demonstrating to the apostles that You can deliver your servants
from the world's oppression any time You see fit;
For the assurance that Your people are blessed when they are persecuted for righteousness' sake;

IN JESUS' NAME, AMEN

14. Acts 6:1 - 7

THE CHOOSING OF THE SEVEN

[1]In those days when the number of disciples was increasing, the Grecian Jews among them complained against the Hebraic Jews because their widows were being overlooked in the daily distribution of food.

[2]So the Twelve gathered all the disciples together and said, "It would not be right for us to neglect the ministry of the word of God in order to wait on tables.

[3]Brothers, choose seven men from among you who are known to be full of the Spirit and wisdom. We will turn this responsibility over to them [4]and will give our attention to prayer and the ministry of the word."

[5]This proposal pleased the whole group. They chose Stephen, a man full of faith and of the Holy Spirit; also Philip, Procorus, Nicanor, Timon, Parmenas, and Nicolas from Antioch, a convert to Judaism. [6]They presented these men to the apostles, who prayed and laid their hands on them.

[7]So the word of God spread. The number of disciples in Jerusalem increased rapidly, and a large number of priests became obedient to the faith. Acts 6:1-7

Whatever adjectives or collective nouns we may use to describe a local church, one obvious characteristic remains. It is a very human body. When people become believers they don't immediately become angels so it should not surprise us if their behaviour as people often baffles us. Pastors and deacons will know what I mean. This is my way in to explaining an administrative problem that arose in the Jerusalem church.

> [1]*In those days when the number of disciples was increasing, the Grecian Jews among them complained against the Hebraic Jews because their widows were being overlooked in the daily distribution of food.* Acts 6:1

We have just discovered one of the fault lines in the Jerusalem church. There were Grecian Jews and Hebraic Jews. Some of these were elderly people. The Hebraic Jews had probably come to settle in Jerusalem and the surrounding area so that their family circles could provide for them in their old age. The Grecian Jews were far from home and therefore most likely did not have their extended families to rely on. There may have been a language problem between the two groups. Anyhow the church leaders had introduced what we might call 'The Widows' Benevolent Fund' which enabled food to be distributed on a daily basis. This was either an early version of 'Meals on Wheels' or 'A Meal in a Basket.' Whether the meals were cooked centrally and then served centrally, or delivered to widows in their homes is not our concern.

Doesn't it astonish you how the best laid schemes of men *'gang aft a-gley'* as Robert Burns the Scottish bard once wrote? People could easily forget how the widows fared when there was no benevolent fund. Then the fund (or ministry) was introduced and in no time at all differences arose about how it was being administered. The bottom line in all this is that it was occupying too much of the apostles' time.

'The Twelve' became aware of this problem, gathered all the disciples (the church members) together, and suggested a solution to the problem.

> [2]*So the Twelve gathered all the disciples together and said, "It would not be right for us to neglect the ministry of the word of God in order to wait on tables.* [3]*Brothers, choose seven men from among you who are known to be full of the Spirit and wisdom. We will turn this responsibility over to them* [4]*and will give our attention to prayer and the ministry of the word."* Acts 6:2-3

Well, what do you know? [5]*This proposal pleased the whole group.* I imagine the apostles heaved a collective sigh of relief.

> *They chose Stephen, a man full of faith and of the Holy Spirit; also Philip, Procorus, Nicanor, Timon, Parmenas, and Nicolas from Antioch, a convert to Judaism.* [6]*They presented these men to the apostles, who prayed and laid their hands on them.* Acts 6:5-6

Here is a question: 'Is looking after a Widows' Benevolent Fund spiritual service?'

Answer: Of course it is. This was one of the reasons why the seven men were set apart to the work with prayer and laying on of hands.

Go back to v. 2 where the apostles said 'It would not be right for us to neglect the ministry of the word of God in order to *'deacon'* (which being translated means: '*wait on tables*') and you will find the reason why this section of Acts is viewed as the origin of the office of Deacon. There is a difference of opinion about this, because the men appointed were not called 'deacons' at the time.

We need to notice also that the men appointed to this administrative task were required to be men of godly character and reputation. This is why in the Pastoral Epistles the standards for Elders and Deacons are equally high. They must be respected in their families, in their churches and in the communities in which they live and work.

Some of the men appointed in v. 5 were men of considerable spiritual gifts and godly character. Stephen, a man full of faith and the Holy Spirit, and six others were appointed. All seven men had Greek names. Perhaps they were deliberately chosen to satisfy the group who were complaining.

> [7]*So the word of God spread. The number of disciples in Jerusalem increased rapidly, and a large number of priests became obedient to the faith.* Acts 6:7

The administrative problem seemed to evaporate and the apostles were released to get on with their ministry of teaching and preaching with the result that the number of disciples increased rapidly and a large number of priests also became believers.

THANK YOU, HEAVENLY FATHER:

For Your astonishing providence so that the solution to an administrative problem became the opportunity for an influx of new believers into the church;

For the availability of men of godliness and good character who could be appointed to the new work, and for their willingness to serve in their new role;

For the ongoing life and testimony of the church of Jesus Christ down the centuries since then: one of the evidences of God is the existence of the Christian church;

IN JESUS' NAME, AMEN

15. Acts 6: 8-15

STEPHEN SEIZED

In the introduction to this book I gave a three-part outline of the contents based on the geographical spread of the gospel: in Jerusalem, in Judea and Samaria, and to the ends of the earth. If you were a student at a theological seminary you would need to know the book in a much more thorough way, if you expect to pass examinations. It is very unlikely that the majority of those who read this book are students who are currently at seminary. Therefore I want to suggest another outline which the reader can fill out without my help.

Make a list of the succession of characters around which the narratives in Acts take place. So far, from chapters 1 to 6, Peter and John have been leading figures. We met Stephen for the first time in chapter 6 where he was appointed with six others to administer the Widows' Relief Fund. We shall stay with him for a number of chapters. Then we shall meet Saul of Tarsus, and Philip the Evangelist, Simon the sorcerer, the Ethiopian eunuch, and so the list goes on. To have this list of people in mind is to have a useful 'handle' on the book of Acts.

> [8]*Now Stephen, a man full of God's grace and power, did great wonders and miraculous signs among the people.*
>
> [9]*Opposition arose, however, from members of the Synagogue of the Freedmen (as it was called)—Jews of Cyrene and Alexandria as well as the provinces of Cilicia and Asia. These men began to argue with Stephen,* [10]*but they could not stand up against his wisdom or the Spirit by whom he spoke.* Acts 6:8-10

Opposition arose against the apostles from a particular synagogue in Jerusalem, known as the 'Synagogue of the Freedmen'.

Its membership was drawn from various parts of the world: Egypt and North Africa, Cilicia and Asia (the area between Syria and the Aegean Sea). The concensus seems to be that these were Jews who had been freed from slavery, hence the name 'Freedmen'. Mention of Cilicia may be a hint that Saul of Tarsus belonged to that synagogue. If this is true, then perhaps the young Saul was flexing his muscles against Christians.

> [11]*Then they secretly persuaded some men to say, "We have heard Stephen speak words of blasphemy against Moses and against God."*
>
> [12]*So they stirred up the people and the elders and the teachers of the law. They seized Stephen and brought him before the Sanhedrin.*
>
> [13]*They produced false witnesses, who testified, "This fellow never stops speaking against this holy place and against the law.* [14]*For we have heard him say that this Jesus of Nazareth will destroy this place and change the customs Moses handed down to us."* Acts 6:11-14

The Freedmen thought nothing of stooping to lies, deceit and character assassination. They got some shady characters to spread the rumour: *"We have heard Stephen speak words of blasphemy against Moses and against God."* Soon this reached the ears of the Sanhedrin who immediately had Stephen arrested and brought before them. More false witnesses were found who were prepared to state that *"This fellow never stops speaking against this holy place and against the law.* [14] *For we have heard him say that this Jesus of Nazareth will destroy this place and change the customs Moses handed down to us."*

The witnesses had used two phrases that ignited the fury of the Sanhedrin: *'the holy place'* (i.e. the temple) *'and the law'*. The temple was Judaism's *'holy place'*, the sanctuary of God's presence.

'The law' was *'holy scripture'* given to them by God. Therefore to speak against one or both of these sacred things was to be guilty of blasphemy. Stephen was facing a most serious accusation.

What would Stephen have said about the temple other than what he knew Jesus had said? More than once in his ministry Jesus had spoken of the destruction of the man-made temple, and in three days he would build another one. To which people had responded in surprise: 'It took forty-six years to build this place, and you are going to raise it in three days' (John 2:20-21). Jesus was speaking about his own body. In future the way of approach to God would be through him.

Regarding *'the law'*, Jesus said that he had come to fulfil the law, not destroy it. What Jesus did in his ministry was to redefine the law as *'a greater than Moses'*. So to summarise the issues we can say that Stephen was teaching what Jesus taught.

We may imagine that the atmosphere in the courtroom was tense, to put it mildly, when a strange thing happened.

> [15]*All who were sitting in the Sanhedrin looked intently at Stephen, and they saw that his face was like the face of an angel.* Acts 6:15

We recall that when Moses had received the law from God at Mount Sinai, and came down the mountain to speak to the people he was not aware that his face was radiant because he had spoken with the Lord. When Aaron and all the Israelites saw Moses, his face was radiant, and they were afraid to come near him.

When Moses finished speaking to them, he put a veil over his face (Exod. 34:29–35). Moses' radiant face was the result of his being in the Lord's presence and speaking to him face to face. In the courtroom in Jerusalem Stephen's face *'was like the face of an angel'*.

God was in that courtroom, *'unseen, yet forever at hand'*, and was showing that his servant's witness had his approval. Judges are known to study the face of the accused person who is before them because they are looking for signs of either guilt or innocence. Stephen had never looked better in his life than he did at that moment! Luke records that *'all who were sitting in the Sanhedrin looked intently at Stephen'*. What were they thinking?

THANK YOU, HEAVENLY FATHER:

For Your work of grace in the lives of believers, changing us into the likeness of Jesus;

For Your presence with your servant Stephen, when in addition to his natural gifts, the Holy Spirit gave him wisdom and courage (v. 10);

For the unconscious shining of Stephen's face, which enhanced his witness and brought glory to Jesus, his Lord and Saviour;

IN JESUS' NAME, AMEN

16. Acts 7:1-60

STEPHEN'S SPEECH TO THE SANHEDRIN

[1] *Then the high priest asked him, "Are these charges true?"*

[2] *To this he replied: "Brothers and fathers, listen to me!"*

Stephen's speech has had a very mixed reception down the centuries, with many people saying they just can't understand it. The latest comment I came across was that Stephen's speech doesn't seem to answer the high priest's question!

We shall lose ourselves completely in Stephen's speech if we fail to keep in mind that he is replying to the two accusations that were made against him: *'he never stops speaking against* ***this holy place*** *and against* ***the law'*** (v. 13). These were very serious charges, because these were two of Judaism's most sacred things.

Although Stephen may appear to be taking the longest distance between two points, he is doing a masterly job of defending himself against the charges that were made in court. He never deviates. He is also getting a very pointed message across to the Sanhedrin.

He decides to speak first against the charge that was made about ***his alleged disrespect for the temple*** – taking some 52 verses to do this.

He had only begun to speak against the second charge about ***his alleged disrespect for the law*** (v. 53), when pandemonium broke out in the court, overflowed into the street and he was taken outside the city and stoned to death.

There are actually five sections in Stephen's defence – they combine to give us a précis of Old Testament history from Abraham to Kings David and Solomon, who built a house for the Lord in Jerusalem.

The basis of Stephens' defence is that
GOD DOES NOT LIVE IN A TEMPLE MADE BY MEN.
God is not nor can he be confined to any locality on earth.
(vv. 2-52)

1. vv. 2 – 8 GOD DID NOT HAVE A TEMPLE IN ABRAHAM'S TIME

[2]To this he replied: "Brothers and fathers, listen to me! The God of glory appeared to our father Abraham while he was still in Mesopotamia, before he lived in Haran. [3]'Leave your country and your people,' God said, 'and go to the land I will show you.'

[4]"So he left the land of the Chaldeans and settled in Haran. After the death of his father, God sent him to this land where you are now living. [5]He gave him no inheritance here, not even a foot of ground. But God promised him that he and his descendants after him would possess the land, even though at that time Abraham had no child.

[6]God spoke to him in this way: 'Your descendants will be strangers in a country not their own, and they will be enslaved and ill-treated for four hundred years. [7]But I will punish the nation they serve as slaves,' God said, 'and afterwards they will come out of that country and worship me in this place.'

[8]Then he gave Abraham the covenant of circumcision. And Abraham became the father of Isaac and circumcised him eight days after his birth. Later Isaac became the father of Jacob, and Jacob became the father of the twelve patriarchs." Acts 7:2-8

Abraham lived in Mesopotamia, where he was originally a moon-worshipper! Distance was no object when God wanted to reveal himself to Abraham. He called Abram, who was an idolater, and gave him promises of a land and innumerable descendants, even though at the time he was childless and didn't own a square inch of Canaan, the promised land.

God revealed to Abraham that his descendants would spend four hundred years as slaves in another land, after which they would come out and worship God in Canaan. In due time Abraham became the father of Isaac, the grandfather of Jacob and Esau, and great-grandfather of the twelve patriarchs.

God had all these communications with Abraham and achieved his purposes without a temple. For centuries since then the Hebrew/ Jewish people have been proud to think of themselves as children of Abraham.

2. vv. 9 – 18 GOD DID NOT HAVE A TEMPLE IN JOSEPH'S TIME.

> *"Because the patriarchs were jealous of Joseph, they sold him as a slave into Egypt. But God was with him [10]and rescued him from all his troubles. He gave Joseph wisdom and enabled him to gain the goodwill of Pharaoh king of Egypt; so he made him ruler over Egypt and all his palace.*
>
> *[11]"Then a famine struck all Egypt and Canaan, bringing great suffering, and our fathers could not find food. [12]When Jacob heard that there was grain in Egypt, he sent our fathers on their first visit. [13]On their second visit, Joseph told his brothers who he was and Pharaoh learned about Joseph's family.*
>
> *[14]After this, Joseph sent for his father Jacob and his whole family, seventy-five in all. [15]Then Jacob went down to Egypt, where he and our fathers died. [16]Their bodies were brought back to Shechem and placed in the tomb that Abraham had bought from the sons of Hamor at Shechem for a certain sum of money.*
>
> *[17]"As the time drew near for God to fulfil his promise to Abraham, the number of our people in Egypt greatly increased. [18]Then another king, who knew nothing about Joseph, became ruler of Egypt."* Acts 7:9-18

The narrative moves from Mesopotamia to Egypt, and God continued his work there–without a temple. Joseph's brothers sold him into Egypt, but God was with him there. Divine providence did more for Joseph than he could ever have asked or thought. Ultimately Joseph became ruler over Egypt and the palace of Pharaoh.

Then a famine struck Canaan and many of the surrounding countries, but Jacob heard that there was grain to be had in Egypt. In time the whole family moved down to Egypt and Joseph became their saviour and also the saviour of the Egyptians through his wise administration of plentiful harvests against the possibility of famine. In time Jacob and the twelve patriarchs died and their bodies were brought back to Shechem where Abraham was buried.

Meanwhile, God's clock was moving on; it was time for God to fulfil his promise to Abraham. Within Egypt another king had come to the throne, who knew nothing about Joseph and dealt treacherously with the Israelites, even using infanticide to repress their numbers.

3. vv. 19–43 GOD DID NOT HAVE A TEMPLE IN MOSES' TIME.

[[18]Then another king, who knew nothing about Joseph, became ruler of Egypt.]

[19]He dealt treacherously with our people and oppressed our forefathers by forcing them to throw out their newborn babies so that they would die. [20]At that time Moses was born, and he was no ordinary child. For three months he was cared for in his father's house. [21]When he was placed outside, Pharaoh's daughter took him and brought him up as her own son. [22]Moses was educated in all the wisdom of the Egyptians and was powerful in speech and action.

[23]"When Moses was forty years old, he decided to visit his fellow Israelites. [24]He saw one of them being ill-treated by an Egyptian, so he went to his defence and avenged him by killing

the Egyptian. [25]Moses thought that his own people would realise that God was using him to rescue them, but they did not. [26]The next day Moses came upon two Israelites who were fighting. He tried to reconcile them by saying, 'Men, you are brothers; why do you want to hurt each other?' [27]"But the man who was ill-treating the other pushed Moses aside and said, 'Who made you ruler and judge over us? [28]Do you want to kill me as you killed the Egyptian yesterday?' [29]When Moses heard this, he fled to Midian, where he settled as a foreigner and had two sons.

[30]"After forty years had passed, an angel appeared to Moses in the flames of a burning bush in the desert near Mount Sinai. [31]When he saw this, he was amazed at the sight. As he went over to look more closely, he heard the Lord's voice: [32]'I am the God of your fathers, the God of Abraham, Isaac and Jacob.' Moses trembled with fear and did not dare to look.

[33]"Then the Lord said to him, 'Take off your sandals; the place where you are standing is holy ground. [34]I have indeed seen the oppression of my people in Egypt. I have heard their groaning and have come down to set them free. Now come, I will send you back to Egypt.' [35]This is the same Moses whom they had rejected with the words, 'Who made you ruler and judge?' He was sent to be their ruler and deliverer by God himself, through the angel who appeared to him in the bush.

[36]He led them out of Egypt and did wonders and miraculous signs in Egypt, at the Red Sea and for forty years in the desert. [37]"This is that Moses who told the Israelites, 'God will send you a prophet like me from your own people.' [38]He was in the assembly in the desert, with the angel who spoke to him on Mount Sinai, and with our fathers; and he received living words to pass on to us. [39]But our fathers refused to obey him. Instead, they rejected him and in their hearts turned back to Egypt.

[40]They told Aaron, 'Make us gods who will go before us. As for this fellow Moses who led us out of Egypt—we don't know what has happened to him!' [41]That was the time they made an idol in the form of a calf. They brought sacrifices to it and held a celebration in honour of what their hands had made.

> [42]*But God turned away and gave them over to the worship of the heavenly bodies. This agrees with what is written in the book of the prophets: 'Did you bring me sacrifices and offerings for forty years in the desert, O house of Israel?* [43]*You have lifted up the shrine of Molech and the star of your god Rephan, the idols you made to worship. Therefore I will send you into exile beyond Babylon.'* Acts 7:19-43

Moses' story is a long one, however we approach it. Stephen referred to Moses' birth and deliverance from the Nile by an Egyptian princess, his Egyptian upbringing and education, his exceptional learning ability, his visit to the Hebrews within Egypt where he murdered an Egyptian who was mistreating a Hebrew. Next day he found two Hebrews fighting, and when he intervened one of them challenged him about his murder of the Egyptian on the previous day.

Moses then fled to Midian. Forty years later God appeared to him in the flames of a burning bush in the desert of Mount Sinai. There God revealed himself as 'I AM' and as the God of Abraham, Isaac and Jacob. Moses was told to remove his sandals because he was standing on holy ground.

In the following exchanges God told Moses that he was sending him to Egypt as the deliverer of the Hebrew/Israelite people. He was rejected by his people at first but eventually led them out of Egypt on Passover night via the Red Sea and for the next forty years he and the Israelites wandered in the desert. God spoke to Moses on Mount Sinai and gave him 'living words to pass on' to his people.

The Israelites refused to obey Moses, they rejected him and wanted to turn back to Egypt, and they made other gods and worshipped them. God turned away from them and gave them over to the worship of the heavenly bodies. The prophets strongly denounced the people in the years that followed (Amos 5:25-27). Meanwhile the Israelites went into exile in Babylon.

4. vv. 44–46 GOD DID NOT HAVE A TEMPLE IN JOSHUA'S TIME

but he provided a Tabernacle of Testimony for Israel.

> [44]"*Our forefathers had the tabernacle of the Testimony with them in the desert. It had been made as God directed Moses, according to the pattern he had seen.* [45]*Having received the tabernacle, our fathers under Joshua brought it with them when they took the land from the nations God drove out before them. It remained in the land until the time of David,* [46]*who enjoyed God's favour and asked that he might provide a dwelling-place for the God of Jacob.* Acts 7:44-46

The Tabernacle was a portable building constructed to a pattern that God had given Moses. Its construction was a means of teaching the Israelites how God ought to be worshipped. It was at this point that the Aaronic priesthood and sacrificial system were instituted in Israel. When the *'fiery, cloudy pillar'* of God's presence moved on, the Tabernacle had to be taken down and then reconstructed on a new site.

Right up until the Israelites entered Canaan under Joshua the tabernacle was at the centre of national life. It remained in use until the time of David, who enjoyed God's favour and asked that he might be permitted to provide a dwelling-place for the God of Jacob.

5. vv. 47 – 50 GOD DID NOT HAVE A TEMPLE ON EARTH UNTIL HE PERMITTED SOLOMON TO BUILD ONE.

> *[David,* [46]*enjoyed God's favour and asked that he might provide a dwelling-place for the God of Jacob.]*

> [47]*But it was Solomon who built the house for him.*[48]"*However, the Most High does not live in houses made by men. As the prophet says:* [49]*'Heaven is my throne, and the earth is my foot-stool. What kind of house will you build for me? says the Lord.*

Or where will my resting place be? [50]Has not my hand made all these things?' " Acts 7:47-50

At this point Stephen spoke to the Sanhedrin as no one had ever spoken to them before. The Jewish leaders placed great store by the temple where God dwelt among his people. But Stephen, on the authority of the prophet Isaiah, had news for the Sanhedrin:

> ***The Most High does not live in houses made by men. As the prophet says: [49]'Heaven is my throne, and the earth is my foot-stool. What kind of house will you build for me?'*** **Acts 7:48-49**

God didn't live in the temple for the simple reason that he had never lived there. It was the place where God was pleased to meet with his people. Ever since Jesus had died on the cross the Holy of Holies in the temple had been lying wide open to the world and completely empty There had been an earthquake and the veil of the temple was ripped from top to bottom on the day that Jesus died. It had been an act of God. Here Stephen closes part one of his defence by emphasising that:

GOD DOES NOT LIVE IN A TEMPLE MADE BY MEN.

'The Most High does not live in houses made by men' (v. 48) God is not nor can he be confined to any locality on earth. God is always on the move, and is not restricted to any one place.

Stephen was also saying:

GOD HAS ANOTHER TEMPLE IN WHOM HE LIVES AND THROUGH WHOM MEN MAY MEET GOD.

> **Jesus the Messiah had come to replace the temple and fulfil the law. Jesus said: *'I am the way, the truth and the life; no one comes to the Father except through me.'***

When the Sanhedrin condemned Jesus to death they were destroying God's temple.

'You have betrayed and murdered Him, the Righteous One (v. 52)

God would destroy them. That is the point of Stephen's blazing condemnation of them in vv. 51-53. Just like their fathers, the present generation of Jews was guilty of unfaithfulness to the law and the prophets.

> [51]*"You stiff-necked people, with uncircumcised hearts and ears! You are just like your fathers: You always resist the Holy Spirit!*
>
> [52]*Was there ever a prophet your fathers did not persecute? They even killed those who predicted the coming of the Righteous One. And now you have betrayed and murdered him —* [53] *you who have received the law that was put into effect through angels but have not obeyed it."* Acts 7: 51-53

Stephen only got speaking one sentence about the law (v. 53), therefore his defence was incomplete. At this point pandemonium broke out, as the Sanhedrin unleashed their undisguised hatred of Stephen. He knew his life was in danger. Once the Sanhedrin got their hands on him, there was no one among his friends who could save him.

> [54]*When they heard this, they were furious and gnashed their teeth at him.* [55]*But Stephen, full of the Holy Spirit, looked up to heaven and saw the glory of God, and Jesus standing at the right hand of God*
>
> [56]*"Look," he said, "I see heaven open and the Son of Man standing at the right hand of God."* [57]*At this they covered their ears and, yelling at the top of their voices, they all rushed at him,* [58]*dragged him out of the city and began to stone him.*
>
> *Meanwhile, the witnesses laid their clothes at the feet of a young man named Saul.* [59]*While they were stoning him, Stephen prayed, "Lord Jesus, receive my spirit."* [60]*Then he fell on his knees and cried out, "Lord, do not hold this sin against them." When he had said this, he fell asleep.* Acts 7:54-60

And Saul was there, giving approval to his death. Acts 8:1

The Holy Spirit was enabling Stephen to speak despite being mishandled and abused. He was granted a vision of Jesus. *"Look," he said, "I see heaven open and the Son of Man standing at the right hand of God"* (v. 56).

Stephen had stood up for Jesus and courageously confessed him on earth. Jesus was standing to receive his martyr into heaven.

By this time stones were raining down on him, but he managed to pray *"Lord Jesus, receive my spirit"* (v. 59). Then he fell on his knees and cried out *"Lord, do not hold this sin against them"* (v. 60). When he had said this, he fell asleep. It must have been a merciful release from suffering.

Someone has said that Stephen's death was *'full of Christ'*. Whoever they were, they were absolutely right.

THANK YOU, HEAVENLY FATHER:

For the witness of Your servant Stephen, a believer who was filled with the Holy Spirit;

For the Old Testament Scriptures inspired by the Holy Spirit as holy men of God wrote and spoke down the years;

For the Holy Spirit's inspiration of Stephen, so that he could have clear recall of the Scriptures and expound them with power;

For the fact that changing times do not silence the voice of the Scriptures; the Holy Spirit enables your servants to preach and expound them in every generation and to every culture;

IN JESUS' NAME, AMEN

17. Acts 8:1-3

THE CHURCH PERSECUTED AND SCATTERED

> [1]*And Saul was there, giving approval to his death. On that day a great persecution broke out against the church at Jerusalem, and all except the apostles were scattered throughout Judea and Samaria.*
>
> [2]*Godly men buried Stephen and mourned deeply for him.* [3]*But Saul began to destroy the church. Going from house to house, he dragged off men and women and put them in prison.* Acts 8:1-2

Saul of Tarsus had been unmasked. He had been a willing guarantor for the clothing that Stephen's murderers laid at his feet for safe-keeping. He had approved of Stephen's death. It was an experience he would never forget. Saul never had peace of conscience until he met the risen Christ on the Damascus Road. He refers to this period of his life in his first letter to Timothy. These verses are a great testimony from a great sinner.

> [12]*I thank Christ Jesus our Lord, who has given me strength, that he considered me faithful, appointing me to his service.*
>
> [13]*Even though I was once a blasphemer and a persecutor and a violent man, I was shown mercy because I acted in ignorance and unbelief.*
>
> [14]*The grace of our Lord was poured out on me abundantly, along with the faith and love that are in Christ Jesus.*
>
> [15]*Here is a trustworthy saying that deserves full acceptance: Christ Jesus came into the world to save sinners—of whom I am the worst.* 1 Tim. 1:12-15

The Jerusalem Church had been severely wounded by the martyrdom of Stephen. Simultaneously a great persecution broke out against the church there, beginning on the day of Stephen's death. It had the effect of dispersing the members throughout Judea and Samaria.

Who would be responsible for Stephen's burial? Luke says godly men buried him and mourned deeply for him.

> [3]*But Saul began to destroy the church. Going from house to house, he dragged off men and women and put them in prison.* Acts 8:3

The KJV renders the word *'destroy'* as *'made havoc'* of the church, a term that could be used of a wild animal killing its prey. We might say *'worrying it to death'*. That paints a harrowing picture of the church's suffering. Saul showed no consideration for age or sex, he hauled off both men and women and put them in prison. No mention is made of their children. No doubt other families did their best to help them.

We are looking at the Suffering Church in Jerusalem in the First Century AD. The mother-church was scattered throughout Judea and Samaria. It was a Christian diaspora.

THANK YOU, HEAVENLY FATHER:

For the memory of your servant Stephen and the remarkable gifts You gave him as a believer and as a church member;

For the demonstration of the Holy Spirit's enabling as Stephen defended himself before the Sanhedrin;

For the great truth to which he witnessed: that You are not confined anywhere within the created world and because You are a God who is on the move;

For the men who, possibly at some personal risk, were not ashamed of Stephen, but buried him with dignity and respect;

For Stephen's translation to heaven; absent from the body and immediately present with the Lord;

IN JESUS' NAME, AMEN

II. Acts 8:4-12:25
You shall be My witnesses in Samaria

18. Acts 8:4-8
PHILIP IN SAMARIA

[4]Those who had been scattered preached the word wherever they went. [5]Philip went down to a city in Samaria and proclaimed the Christ there.

[6]When the crowds heard Philip and saw the miraculous signs he did, they all paid close attention to what he said. [7]With shrieks, evil spirits came out of many, and many paralytics and cripples were healed. [8]So there was great joy in that city. Acts 8:4-8

I have heard preachers say that the phrase *'proclaimed the word'* (v. 4) could be better expressed by the words *'they gossiped the gospel'*. To put that another way is to say that '*the Christians became missionaries'* wherever they went.

These insights really challenge us about the effectiveness of our witness for Christ in the 21st century of the Christian era.

Philip, who had been appointed as one the seven 'deacons' in chapter 6:1-7, was a very gifted servant of God. When the Christians were scattered he left Jerusalem and went down to a (or perhaps 'the') city of Samaria and preached Christ there. He *'heralded'* the Messiah.

The Samaritans were descendants of the ten tribes of Northern Kingdom of Israel who had parted from the two southern tribes and had made Samaria their capital. Samaria was captured by Assyria in 722BC and thousands of the people were deported. In the sixth century BC, when the Jews returned to their land, they refused the help of the Samaritans in building the temple. Two centuries later the Samaritans had built a rival temple at Mount Gerizim.

They believed that was where God ought to be worshipped, as the woman of Samaria had told Jesus (John 4:19). The Samaritans rejected all of the Hebrew Scriptures with the exception of the Pentateuch (the five books of Moses).

However the Samaritans, like the Jews, were also looking for the Messiah to come. Philip's message was a declaration that the Messiah had come in Jesus Christ. The Holy Spirit gave him a fruitful ministry there.

> [6]*When the crowds heard Philip and saw the miraculous signs he did, they all paid close attention to what he said.* [7]*With shrieks, evil spirits came out of many, and many paralytics and cripples were healed.* Acts 8:6-7

Up to this point in Acts only the apostles Peter and John had performed miracles of healing, but the Holy Spirit is sovereign and he saw fit to use Philip in Samaria as he had used Peter and John in Jerusalem and Judea. Evil spirits were cast out of demon-possessed people, and many others were healed. We wonder if those who had believed on Jesus in John 4, following the witness of the Samaritan woman, were among those who heard Philip gladly.

> *So there was great joy in that city.* Acts 8:8

Our hearts rejoice also when we read this concluding sentence. Before we move on we ask 'Why was Philips' ministry so fruitful in Samaria?' Part of the answer is in v. 6:

> [6]*When the crowds heard Philip and saw the miraculous signs he did, they all paid close attention to what he said.* Acts 8:6

Here is assurance, if we need it, that faith comes by hearing, and hearing by the word of God. I think that modern congregations need this reminder.

> *Faith comes from hearing the message, and the message comes through the word of Christ* (Romans 10:17).

Luke records that the Samaritans '*all paid close attention to what Philip said*'. Their believing response to the gospel message brought salvation and healing and great joy to the city.

THANK YOU, HEAVENLY FATHER:

For the blessings that the gospel brings to those who sit in darkness: life and light and the joy of salvation;

For the work of divine providence that moved Philip to Samaria following the dispersion of the Jerusalem Church, and for his courage in going there despite the centuries-old conflict between the Jews and Samaritans;

For the sovereignty of the Holy Spirit in evangelism, enabling the hearers to believe the message preached;

For the work of the Holy Spirit in our world where so many nations are in conflict or are divided by civil war; and for the witness of your church in these situations;

IN JESUS' NAME, AMEN

19. Acts 8: 9 - 25

SIMON THE SORCERER

[9]Now for some time a man named Simon had practised sorcery in the city and amazed all the people of Samaria. He boasted that he was someone great, [10]and all the people, both high and low, gave him their attention and exclaimed, "This man is the divine power known as the Great Power."

[11]They followed him because he had amazed them for a long time with his magic.

[12]But when they believed Philip as he preached the good news of the kingdom of God and the name of Jesus Christ, they were baptised, both men and women. Acts 8:9-12

Philip could hardly have known in advance the nature of some of the influences that were at work in Samaria. One of these was the brand of magic practised by Simon the Sorcerer.

[13]Simon himself believed and was baptised. And he followed Philip everywhere, astonished by the great signs and miracles he saw. [14]When the apostles in Jerusalem heard that Samaria had accepted the word of God, they sent Peter and John to them. Acts 8:13-14

There were no telecommunications or mobile phones in those days but somehow news reached the church in Jerusalem very quickly (v. 14). Consequently the apostles sent Peter and John to Samaria.

[15]When they arrived, they prayed for them that they might receive the Holy Spirit, [16]because the Holy Spirit had not yet come upon any of them; they had simply been baptised into the name of the Lord Jesus. [17]Then Peter and John placed their hands on them, and they received the Holy Spirit. Acts 8:15-17

How shall we understand this? The most straightforward way to understand it is to recall *'the Jewish Pentecost'* (Chapter 2), and then think of this as *'the Samaritan Pentecost'* (Chapter 8). It didn't happen on the calendar date of Pentecost, but the word *'Pentecost'* is a convenient (and helpful) label to identify this event in Samaria. Later in Acts we shall come across *'the Gentile Pentecost'* (Chapter 10).

The great effect of this outpouring of the Holy Spirit was that Jews and Samaritans, previously irreconcilable due to a mixture of religion and politics, were now united in the body of Christ through the indwelling Holy Spirit.

However, Philip had a problem with the Sorcerer. Thankfully Peter and John were with him at the time.

> [18]*When Simon saw that the Spirit was given at the laying on of the apostles' hands, he offered them money* [19]*and said, "Give me also this ability so that everyone on whom I lay my hands may receive the Holy Spirit."* Acts 8:18-19

Probably Simon believed that his *'faith'* was the same kind as the others who had been converted. He asked for baptism and was baptised on profession of *'faith'*. He was mesmerised by the ministry of Philip,

One thought led to another and Simon was soon thinking *'I could do with a new act for my repertoire. Perhaps I could purchase this act the preachers have'*. This explains his request to the apostles.

Peter took the initiative in dealing with Simon, and he didn't mince his words.

> [20]*Peter answered: "May your money perish with you, because you thought you could buy the gift of God with money!* [21]*You have no part or share in this ministry, because your heart is not right before God.*

> [22]*Repent of this wickedness and pray to the Lord. Perhaps he will forgive you for having such a thought in your heart.*
>
> [23]*For I see that you are full of bitterness and captive to sin."* Acts 8:20-23

This is why, ever since Acts 8, the purchase of ecclesiastical preferment, and such-like privileges, is known as 'simony'.

> [24]*Then Simon answered, "Pray to the Lord for me so that nothing you have said may happen to me."* Acts 8:24

Simon didn't repent, nor did he show remorse for his error. Instead of praying for himself he asked Peter to pray for him that he might escape the judgement of God.

> [25]*When they had testified and proclaimed the word of the Lord, Peter and John returned to Jerusalem, preaching the gospel in many Samaritan villages.* Acts 8:25

Peter and John made good use of their homeward journey. It became an evangelistic tour of many Samaritan villages. Philip remained in Samaria. His work was not yet done, or to put it another way, God hadn't given him new marching orders.

THANK YOU, HEAVENLY FATHER:

For placing your servants in strategic locations to 'catch the wind of the Spirit' and bring glory to the name of Jesus in their various ministries;

For the spiritual gift of discernment, here exercised by Peter when dealing with Simon the sorcerer;

For purging the young church in Samaria from the negative influence of Simon's false profession of 'faith';

For the evangelistic opportunities that opened up for Peter and John so that many Samaritan villages heard the Gospel message;

IN JESUS' NAME, AMEN

20. Acts 8:26-40

PHILIP AND THE ETHIOPIAN

[26]Now an angel of the Lord said to Philip, "Go south to the road—the desert road—that goes down from Jerusalem to Gaza."

[27]So he started out, and on his way he met an Ethiopian eunuch, an important official in charge of all the treasury of Candace, queen of the Ethiopians. This man had gone to Jerusalem to worship, [28]and on his way home was sitting in his chariot reading the book of Isaiah the prophet. Acts 9:26-28

Many adjectives could be used to describe Philip. Among them I would include the word 'moveable'. He had been busy in what might be described as 'revival conditions' in Samaria, when an angel sent by the Lord directed him to the desert road from Jerusalem to Gaza. He started out immediately to go to that lonely place, not knowing why he had been directed to go there, not knowing what new experience lay ahead. I admire Philip very much.

> Somewhere in the wilderness Philip's path crossed the path of another traveller. Luke simply writes '*on his way he met an Ethiopian eunuch, an important official in charge of all the treasury of Candace, queen of the Ethiopians*' (v. 27).

In those days Ethiopia generally covered the Nile delta – in other words a significant part of the country could be described as African. There is a strong possibility that the man whom Philip met was black-skinned. He was employed in the service of Candace, queen of the Ethiopians. It is now thought that Candace was the Queen Mother in the Ethiopian royal family. This man was Chancellor of the Exchequer in charge of all her treasury. His employment required him to be frequently in the palace, perhaps even based there. In various cultures men who served in royal courts in the presence of so many women were required to be castrated. This is why he is described as a eunuch.

The Ethiopian becomes even more interesting because he had been to Jerusalem to worship and, on his homeward journey was reading from the scroll of the prophet Isaiah. So was this man a Jew? Was he a proselyte? We don't know the answers to these questions. We know that he was completely absorbed as he read this portion of the Hebrew Scriptures.

> [29]*The Spirit told Philip, "Go to that chariot and stay near it."* [30]*Then Philip ran up to the chariot and heard the man reading Isaiah the prophet. "Do you understand what you are reading?" Philip asked.*
>
> [31]*"How can I," he said, "unless someone explains it to me?" So he invited Philip to come up and sit with him.* [32]*The eunuch was reading this passage of Scripture:*
>
> *"He was led like a sheep to the slaughter and as a lamb before the shearer is silent, so he did not open his mouth.* [33]*In his humiliation he was deprived of justice. Who can speak of his descendants? For his life was taken from the earth."*
>
> [34]*The eunuch asked Philip, "Tell me, please, who is the prophet talking about, himself or someone else?"* [35]*Then Philip began with that very passage of Scripture and told him the good news about Jesus.* Acts 8:29-35

So he invited Philip to come up and sit with him. Luke explains that the Ethiopian was reading from Isaiah chapter 53, in particular from verses 7 and 8.

The eunuch asked Philip, *"Tell me, please, who is the prophet talking about, himself or someone else?"* [35] Then Philip began with that very passage of Scripture and told him the good news about Jesus.

We imagine that the conversation may have lasted for quite a few miles. Someone had taught Philip that Isaiah 53 was about the Messiah's sufferings. Philip was able to tell the Ethiopian the story of Jesus and his atoning death for the salvation of sinners. There came a point in the conversation when the Ethiopian became a believer in Jesus Christ.

One thing is clear: the Holy Spirit introduced these two men, who otherwise might never have met. The Spirit directed Philip: *"Go to that chariot and stay near it"* and he obeyed. As Philip ran beside the chariot he could hear the Ethiopian reading aloud from a passage of the prophecy of Isaiah that was familiar to Philip. So Philip, with the alertness of an evangelist asked *"Do you understand what you are reading?"* Immediately a conversation began between the two men.

> [36] *As they travelled along the road, they came to some water and the eunuch said, "Look, here is water. Why shouldn't I be baptised?"*

[Verse 37 is not found in all MSS,
and is omitted in the NIV translation.]

> [38] *And he gave orders to stop the chariot. Then both Philip and the eunuch went down into the water and Philip baptised him.* Acts 8:36-38

This reflects the fact that Philip had explained the meaning of Jesus' death, burial and resurrection, and that those who believed on him confessed their new faith in Jesus and their new relationship with him in baptism. The Ethiopian requested that the chariot be stopped and in a nearby wadi (we may presume) Philip baptised him.

> [39] *When they came up out of the water, the Spirit of the Lord suddenly took Philip away, and the eunuch did not see him again, but went on his way rejoicing.* Acts 8:39

Please notice the joy of this new believer in Jesus. Oh, to be young again, and a new believer again (as I was, aged 11 – almost 12) and experience the peace and joy of believing for the first time.

We were told in v. 26 that an angel of the Lord spoke to Philip. Here in v. 29 and again in v. 39 the record says that it was the Spirit, that is the Holy Spirit, who directed him so that he met the Ethiopian, and also when it was time to move to another place. We cannot be emphatic about whether his being transported from Samaria to the desert had a miraculous element in it.

> [40] *Philip, however, appeared at Azotus and travelled about, preaching the gospel in all the towns until he reached Caesarea.* Acts 8:40

The Lord's agenda for Philip required him to be at Azotus (Ashdod). On his journey from the wilderness he preached the gospel in all the towns between there and Caesarea. Herod the Great had built this city to serve as the sea-port for Jerusalem.

In Acts 21:8 we learn that Philip had made his home there, had four unmarried daughters 'who prophesied' (preached). By that time he was known as Philip the Evangelist.

THANK YOU, HEAVENLY FATHER:

For this beautiful narrative of the Holy Spirit superintending the meeting of Philip and the Ethiopian at the precise moment when he needed help in understanding the Scripture passage he was reading;

For Philip's sensitivity and obedience to the Holy Spirit, and for the blessing that followed both for him and those to whom he was sent;

For the Holy Scriptures, inspired by the Holy Spirit, involving many writers over some 1500 years; for their 'speaking' power (when the voice of man is silent) and their ability to make us wise for salvation;

IN JESUS' NAME, AMEN

21. Acts 9:1 - 19

SAUL'S CONVERSION

[1]Meanwhile, Saul was still breathing out murderous threats against the Lord's disciples. He went to the high priest [2]and asked him for letters to the synagogues in Damascus, so that if he found any there who belonged to the Way, whether men or women, he might take them as prisoners to Jerusalem. Acts 9:1-2

Saul of Tarsus had gone far in pursuing the life of a Pharisee. He would go further and earn himself the reputation of being a persecutor of Christians, '*the people of the Way*'. This description of Christians was derived from the name that Jesus had given himself in John 14:6. It is a most appropriate name, because Jesus is the way to the Father, and the new and living way into the Holy Place (Heb. 10:19-20).

So Saul obtained letters of authority from the High Priest in Jerusalem to the synagogues in Damascus so that if he found any there '*who belonged to the Way*' he would arrest them and take them as prisoners to Jerusalem. His intention was that the Christians had yet to see how cruel this Pharisee could be.

Unknown to Saul, God was on his track. He would go so far in his campaign of persecution, and no further. This was the explanation for the dramatic experience he had when approaching Damascus. A light from heaven flashed around him and he found himself smitten to the ground. Lying there in the dust of the highway Saul heard a voice saying, *"Saul, Saul, why do you persecute me?"* The next words that crossed Saul's lips were surprising, [5]*"Who are you, Lord?"* Immediately Saul knew that his crimes were known to God,

[5]"Who are you, Lord?" Saul asked. "I am Jesus, whom you are persecuting," he replied. [6]"Now get up and go into the city, and

you will be told what you must do." [7]The men travelling with Saul stood there speechless; they heard the sound but did not see anyone.

[8]Saul got up from the ground, but when he opened his eyes he could see nothing. So they led him by the hand into Damascus. [9]For three days he was blind, and did not eat or drink anything. Acts 9:5-9

The brightness of the light from heaven had blinded Saul so that he could see nothing. He was led by the hand like a blind man into Damascus, and he remained in that condition for three days and was unable to eat or drink.

[10]In Damascus there was a disciple named Ananias. The Lord called to him in a vision, "Ananias!" "Yes, Lord," he answered.

[11]The Lord told him, "Go to the house of Judas on Straight Street and ask for a man from Tarsus named Saul, for he is praying. [12]In a vision he has seen a man named Ananias come and place his hands on him to restore his sight."

[13]"Lord," Ananias answered, "I have heard many reports about this man and all the harm he has done to your saints in Jerusalem. [14]And he has come here with authority from the chief priests to arrest all who call on your name. Acts 9:10-14

Three men in Acts have the name Ananias: Ananias of Jerusalem (Acts 5), Ananias of Damascus (Acts 9) and Ananias the high priest (Acts 23).

Was this Ananias a native of Damascus? If so, how had he heard the gospel and become a believer in Jesus? The important thing is that when God spoke to him in a vision he was alert. What God had to say to him and wanted him to do came as quite a shock (vv. 10-12).

Most of us would probably have reacted as Ananias did. It would be like God asking one of us to go and speak in Jesus' name to Colonel Gaddafi of Libya, or the Iraqi dictator Saddam Hussein, or Osama bin Laden, the founder the Islamist militant group al-Qaeda in their heyday. We would swallow very hard and ask God a few questions. 'Lord, do you not know this man's reputation? You know what he did to your people in Jerusalem and he is this city to do the same foul work.'

> [15]*But the Lord said to Ananias, "Go! This man is my chosen instrument to carry my name before the Gentiles and their kings and before the people of Israel.* [16]*I will show him how much he must suffer for my name."* Acts 9:15-16

So Ananias went to where Judas lived on Straight Street. Sure enough, Saul knew that Ananias would be coming! God's providence is astonishing! His timing is always right.

Perhaps Ananias did a lot of deep thinking on his way to Straight Street, and by the time he got there something of the amazing purpose of God for Saul of Tarsus had sunk in. Watch Ananias as he and Saul meet for the first time.

First, Ananias placed his hands on Saul. Then he said something that was like a new language to Saul: *"Brother Saul"*. Next he spoke the name that completely bridged the gap between the two men.

> *"The Lord—Jesus, who appeared to you on the road as you were coming here—has sent me so that you may see again and be filled with the Holy Spirit."*
>
> [18]*Immediately, something like scales fell from Saul's eyes, and he could see again. He got up and was baptised,* [19]*and after taking some food, he regained his strength. Saul spent several days with the disciples in Damascus.* Acts 9:17-19

As Ananias and Saul looked into each other's eyes, I think they saw the grace of God in each other. They were brothers in Christ. What a transformation of the former persecutor of Christians!

THANK YOU, HEAVENLY FATHER:

For those among Your people who are like Ananias, an encourager of others, especially of those who are new believers in Jesus;

For Your sovereign grace to Saul of Tarsus, who to the end of his days regarded himself as the chief of sinners;

For Saul's conversion experience: it was the 'most unforgettable moment' of his entire life;

For the term that Ananias used when he and Saul met for the first time: *'Brother Saul';* giving Saul a warm and meaningful welcome into the family of God;

For the potential that You saw in Saul of Tarsus: believer, preacher, teacher, church planter, a witness before kings, and apostle to the Gentiles;

IN JESUS' NAME, AMEN

22. Acts 9: 19 - 22

SAUL PREACHING IN DAMASCUS

[19]Saul spent several days with the disciples in Damascus. [20]At once he began to preach in the synagogues that Jesus is the Son of God.

[21]All those who heard him were astonished and asked, "Isn't he the man who caused havoc in Jerusalem among those who call on this name? And hasn't he come here to take them as prisoners to the chief priests?" Acts 9: 19-21

I imagine that the news spread like a prairie fire that Saul of Tarsus had been converted. Imagine the introductions that took place as the believers in the Damascus area gathered together to meet him. Imagine the thanksgiving and praise that expressed the church's gratitude to God for this miracle of grace. Saul was with the disciples for several days.

[20]At once he began to preach in the synagogues that Jesus is the Son of God. Acts 9:20

This is a very significant and eloquent sentence. What better or more convincing evidence could Saul have given than to preach in the synagogues that Jesus is the Son of God? An old hymn that Irish Baptists used to sing over 130 years ago puts it like this:

What think you of Christ? is the test
To try both your state and your scheme;
You cannot be right in the rest,
Unless you think rightly of Him.
As Jesus appears in your view,
As he is beloved or not;

So God is disposed to you,
And mercy or wrath is your lot.
(The Harcourt Hymnal, 1st Edition, 1887)

If any of the believers were nervous about how Saul might preach Christ in the synagogues then let them worry no more. Saul was right about Christ, He preached him as **'the Son of God'.**

That point about Saul is extremely important. New believers need to be taught who Jesus really is. Do they believe in the biblical Jesus, or a Jesus of their own imagination? If they are not sure about him, then there is a danger they will not be sure about anything to do with the Christian life.

All who heard Saul preach thought they were 'seeing things'! 'Wasn't this the man who killed Christians? Isn't that why he came here?'

> [22] *Yet Saul grew more and more powerful and baffled the Jews living in Damascus by proving that Jesus is the Christ (Messiah).* Acts 9:22

We have not all had a 'Damascus road experience' of Jesus. Please don't worry about that. The important thing is that *'one day, in a quiet place, we met the Master face to face'*.

THANK YOU, HEAVENLY FATHER:

For the benefits of Christian fellowship to a new believer in Jesus;

For the exceptional gifts that some new believers exhibit within a short time following their conversion;

For the evangelising zeal of some new believers; they put older believers to shame with their willingness to witness;

For the body of Christ, made up of believers of all nationalities, cultures and age-groups and all (men, women and children) one in Christ;

IN JESUS' NAME, AMEN

23. Acts 9:23 - 31

PAUL IS PERSECUTED IN DAMASCUS AND FLEES TO JERUSALEM AND TARSUS

> [23]*After many days had gone by, the Jews conspired to kill him,* [24]*but Saul learned of their plan. Day and night they kept close watch on the city gates in order to kill him.* [25]*But his followers took him by night and lowered him in a basket through an opening in the wall.* Acts 9:23-25

We wondered how long it would be until the Jews in Damascus would vent their anger on Saul, their former colleague. They hatched a conspiracy to kill him. Thankfully, Saul learned of their plan. All entries and exits to Damascus were watched by day and by night. But Saul had made many new friends in the Lord in Damascus and some of them arranged to lower him in a basket through an opening in the city wall.

> [26]*When he came to Jerusalem, he tried to join the disciples, but they were all afraid of him, not believing that he really was a disciple.*

> [27]*But Barnabas took him and brought him to the apostles. He told them how Saul on his journey had seen the Lord and that the Lord had spoken to him, and how in Damascus he had preached fearlessly in the name of Jesus.* [28]*So Saul stayed with them and moved about freely in Jerusalem, speaking boldly in the name of the Lord.* [29]*He talked and debated with the Grecian Jews, but they tried to kill him.* [30]*When the brothers learned of this, they took him down to Caesarea and sent him off to Tarsus.* Acts 9: 26-30

When he had left Jerusalem some time previously it was with authority from the High Priest to arrest and imprison Christians.

Now he is back in Jerusalem as one of them! It was to the followers of Christ that he came, not to the Sanhedrin. Their problem was that they were afraid of him, not believing that he really was a disciple. I'm sure we understand their reticence. However in the goodness of God there is another 'Ananias-figure' whom we have met before (4:36-37): Barnabas: 'Big-hearted Barnabas'. He took Saul and brought him to the apostles.

It is clear from his recommendation of Saul that he had made sure of his facts: *how Saul on his journey had seen the Lord and that the Lord had spoken to him, and how in Damascus he had preached fearlessly in the name of Jesus* (v.27).

This was the open sesame that Saul needed. *So Saul stayed with them and moved about freely in Jerusalem, speaking boldly in the name of the Lord (v. 28)*. This is not the first time that Luke reports on Saul's boldness in preaching. Saul even *talked and debated with the Grecian Jews, but they tried to kill him*. We may be right in thinking they were from the synagogue of the Freedmen (6:8-9ff).

> [31]*Then the church throughout Judea, Galilee and Samaria enjoyed a time of peace. It was strengthened; and encouraged by the Holy Spirit; it grew in numbers, living in the fear of the Lord*. Acts 9:31

Instead of a widespread rising of the Jews who were to be found in synagogues scattered around the country, there was actually a time of peace. It is said the church *'enjoyed it'* and well they might if it meant the reunion of families and friends who had been scattered in Acts 8:2 &4.

The Holy Spirit was also doing a beautiful work of strengthening and encouraging the church throughout Judea, Galilee and Samaria so that it grew in numbers, all good reasons to magnify God and live in awe of Him. Jesus' great programme in Acts 1:8 was getting well underway.

THANK YOU, HEAVENLY FATHER:

For the way in which the Holy Spirit transformed Saul's previous knowledge of the Old Testament Scriptures; as a result they shone with new light and he was able to preach with authority that Jesus Christ is the Son of God;

For the Holy Spirit's protection of Saul's life both in Damascus and Jerusalem and for raising up resourceful friends to take measures to save his life;

For the extraordinary boldness (confidence) that the Holy Spirit gave Saul so that he was free from fear in his Gospel preaching;

For Barnabas (another Ananias figure) who made a practice of encouraging others, particularly new believers;

IN JESUS' NAME, AMEN

24. Acts 9:32-43

PETER, AENEAS AND DORCAS

We welcome Peter back into the narrative. Luke says that he had been travelling about the country, and in the course of his journey he came to Lydda, where some believers lived. So we can look forward to three thrilling stories: one about the healing of Aeneas and Dorcas; one about a notable conversion when Cornelius, an Italian centurion in the Roman army, became a believer; and one about an amazing escape when Peter was rescued from prison and probable death (if Herod had had his way).

> [32]*As Peter travelled about the country, he went to visit the saints in Lydda.* [33]*There he found a man named Aeneas, a paralytic who had been bedridden for eight years.* [34]*"Aeneas," Peter said to him, "Jesus Christ heals you. Get up and tidy up your mat." Immediately Aeneas got up.*
>
> [35]*All those who lived in Lydda and Sharon saw him and turned to the Lord.* Acts 9:32-35

I've mentioned 'the alertness of an evangelist' several times in these notes and I mention it again at this point. When Peter arrived in Lydda he 'found' a man named Aeneas, a paralytic who had been bedridden for eight years. In the same way as he had behaved toward the man at the Beautiful Gate of the temple in Acts 3, Peter took the initiative again.

[34]*"Aeneas,"* Peter said to him, *"Jesus Christ heals you. Get up and tidy up your mat."* Immediately Aeneas got up. Unlike modern healing crusades etc, etc, there was a complete absence of razzmatazz or hype! There was no glory for Peter, but rather glory for Peter's Lord. What a confident expression: *"Aeneas, Jesus Christ heals you."*

Not only was Aeneas rejoicing in new strength and wholeness of life, others who were present became believers: [35] *All those who lived in Lydda and Sharon saw him and turned to the Lord.* That is to say that many of the local people became believers in Jesus.

> [36]*In Joppa there was a disciple named Tabitha (which, when translated, is Dorcas), who was always doing good and helping the poor.* [37]*About that time she became sick and died and her body was washed and placed in an upstairs room.*
>
> [38]*Lydda was near Joppa; so when the disciples heard that Peter was in Lydda, they sent two men to him and urged him, "Please come at once!"*
>
> [39] *Peter went with them, and when he arrived he was taken upstairs to the room. All the widows stood around him, crying and showing him the robes and other clothing that Dorcas had made while she was still with them.* Acts 9:36-39

There was a choice lady by the name of Tabitha (or Dorcas), who lived in Joppa. She was a disciple of Jesus and was always doing good and helping the poor. Sadly, Dorcas died, and there was great lamentation over her death. Peter was sent for to come from Lydda and help in any way he could. Of course Peter came immediately he was sent for.

When he arrived her body was prepared for her funeral and many of the women were pleased to show him the many items of clothing that Dorcas had made. Once more, after a moment's consideration, Peter knew what he must do.

> [40]*Peter sent them all out of the room; then he got down on his knees and prayed. Turning towards the dead woman, he said, "Tabitha, get up." She opened her eyes, and seeing Peter she sat up.*
>
> [41]*He took her by the hand and helped her to her feet. Then he called the believers and the widows and presented her to them alive.* Acts 9:40-41

Peter's pastoral methods here are so Christlike. He had seen Jesus minister to sick folk and even dead people and raise them to life and health. Peter spoke to her and said, *'Tabitha, get up'* and she opened her eyes, saw him and sat up. He took her by the hand and helped her to her feet.

I don't think that Dorcas knew she had been dead because Peter had dealt so naturally and thoughtfully with her. He called the believers and widows and presented her to them alive.

> [42]*This became known all over Joppa, and many people believed in the Lord.* Acts 9:42

Such good news could not be kept a secret; soon people all over Joppa believed in the Lord.

Peter spent some further time in that city, lodging with a man called Simon, a tanner by trade. The raw materials for Simon's business were the hides of dead animals, which he converted into leather: an occupation despised by the Jews. Living cheek by jowl with Simon might have been difficult, to put it mildly!

> *Peter stayed in Joppa for some time with a tanner named Simon.* Acts 9:43

The nature of Simon's business didn't annoy Peter, who happily lodged in his house. The local synagogue probably shunned Simon.

THANK YOU, HEAVENLY FATHER:

For Peter's usual alertness to the opportunity to be a servant of Christ, and the man God used to raise Dorcas;

For the useful life that Dorcas had led for many years, so that at her death there were many thankful people testifying to her friendship and help;

For Peter's ability to meet and minister to people in various levels of society;

IN JESUS' NAME, AMEN

25. Acts 10:1 - 23

CORNELIUS CALLS FOR PETER

[1]At Caesarea there was a man named Cornelius, a centurion in what was known as the Italian Regiment. [2]He and all his family were devout and God-fearing; he gave generously to those in need and prayed to God regularly. [3]One day at about three in the afternoon he had a vision. He distinctly saw an angel of God, who came to him and said, "Cornelius!"

[4]Cornelius stared at him in fear. "What is it, Lord?" he asked. The angel answered, "Your prayers and gifts to the poor have come up as a memorial offering before God. [5]Now send men to Joppa to bring back a man named Simon who is called Peter. [6]He is staying with Simon the tanner, whose house is by the sea."

[7]When the angel who spoke to him had gone, Cornelius called two of his servants and a devout soldier who was one of his attendants. [8]He told them everything that had happened and sent them to Joppa. Acts 10:1-8

Cornelius enters Luke's narrative about the spread of the Gospel. He was a Roman centurion in the Italian Regiment. He is a most interesting person because *he and all his family were devout and God-fearing; he gave generously to those in need and prayed to God regularly*. To say that he was God-fearing means that he had ceased to practise his pagan religion and had become a worshipper of Jehovah, the Living God, the God of the Jews. He doesn't seem to have had a copy of the Hebrew Scriptures, or even a part of them, nor had he any contact with a Christian preacher up to this point in his life. God gave him a vision in which an angel came to him and called him by name, *'Cornelius!'*

This happened one day at about three o'clock in the afternoon. Despite being a little shocked at the appearance of the angel,

Cornelius managed to ask *'What is it, Lord?'* He received a very specific answer to his question.

> *'Your prayers and gifts to the poor have come up as a memorial offering before God.* [5] *Now send men to Joppa to bring back a man named Simon who is called Peter.* [6] *He is staying with Simon the tanner, whose house is by the sea.'* Acts 10:4-6

This was how a most significant meeting in the history of the Christian church was arranged. When the angel who had spoken to Cornelius had gone, he called two of his servants and a devout soldier who was one of his attendants.

> [8] *He told them everything that had happened and sent them to Joppa to find Peter and request him to come to his home.* Acts 10:8

It was about noon the next day when the deputation from Cornelius was entering Joppa. About the same time Peter had gone up on to the roof of his house. He was hungry and ready for his mid-day meal. While he was waiting for his meal he fell into a trance. This time Peter was given a vision from God.

> [11] *He saw heaven opened and something like a large sheet being let down to earth by its four corners.* [12] *It contained all kinds of four-footed animals, as well as reptiles of the earth and birds of the air.*
>
> [13] *Then a voice told him, "Get up, Peter. Kill and eat."* [14] *Surely not, Lord!" Peter replied. "I have never eaten anything impure or unclean."* [15] *The voice spoke to him a second time, "Do not call anything impure that God has made clean."*
>
> [16] *This happened three times, and immediately the sheet was taken back to heaven.* Acts 10:11-16

In the course of the vision a sheet containing all kinds of animals, both clean and unclean, was let down from heaven and a voice called on Peter to *'Kill and eat.'* Even in a trance Peter's Jewish food laws were so deeply ingrained in his system that he replied. [14] *Surely not, Lord! I have never eaten anything impure or unclean."* The voice spoke a second time. *"Do not call anything impure that God has made clean."* This was repeated a third time and the sheet was taken back to heaven.

That had given Peter something to think about. While he was meditating on the meaning of the vision the men from Cornelius had arrived at his door and were calling for him. (v. 17-18).

> [19]*While Peter was still thinking about the vision, the Spirit said to him, "Simon, three men are looking for you.* [20]*So get up and go downstairs. Do not hesitate to go with them, for I have sent them."*
>
> [21]*Peter went down and said to the men, "I'm the one you're looking for. Why have you come?"* [22]*The men replied, "We have come from Cornelius the centurion. He is a righteous and God-fearing man, who is respected by all the Jewish people. A holy angel told him to have you come to his house so that he could hear what you have to say."* [23]*Then Peter invited the men into the house to be his guests. The next day Peter started out with them, and some of the brothers from Joppa went along.* Acts 10:19-23

Peter invited the men into his house to be his guests. They stayed with him overnight and next morning they set off for Caesarea with the assurance that all the circumstances that had brought them together were from the Lord.

THANK YOU, HEAVENLY FATHER:

For the varied ministries of the Holy Spirit: there is no where he cannot go, and no one to whom he cannot speak;

For the readiness of Cornelius to receive Peter and hear what he had to say;

For the readiness of Peter to obey the clear guidance of the Holy Spirit;

For the significance of the above three observations in today's world; no country is *'a closed country'* to the Holy Spirit;

IN JESUS' NAME, AMEN

26. Acts 10:23 - 48

PETER AT CORNELIUS' HOUSE

> [23]*Then Peter invited the men into the house to be his guests. The next day Peter started out with them, and some of the brothers from Joppa went along.*

> [24]*The following day he arrived in Caesarea. Cornelius was expecting them and had called together his relatives and close friends.* [25]*As Peter entered the house, Cornelius met him and fell at his feet in reverence.* [26]*But Peter made him get up. "Stand up," he said, "I am only a man myself."* [27]*Talking with him, Peter went inside and found a large gathering of people.* Acts 10:23-27

Luke is a superb storyteller and writer. The narratives in his Gospel and the Acts are fascinating reading. Is any modern writer his equal?

Following an overnight stay with Peter, his guests and he plus some of the brothers from Joppa set out for Caesarea. When they arrived at Cornelius' house they found that their arrival was expected and that Cornelius had invited his relatives and close friends to come to his house to meet Peter. On entering the house Cornelius prostrated himself at Peter's feet, thinking that was the appropriate way to welcome a man of God. But Peter made him get up. *"Stand up,"* he said, *"I am only a man myself" (v. 26).*

Following a brief chat with Cornelius, Peter entered the house and said a few introductory words to those who were gathered.

> [28]*You are well aware that it is against our law for a Jew to associate with a Gentile or visit him. But God has shown me that I should not call any man impure or unclean.* [29]*So when I was sent for, I came without raising any objection. May I ask why you sent for me?* Acts 10:28-29

That was the right question to ask and Cornelius was delighted to answer it.

> [30]*Cornelius answered: "Four days ago I was in my house praying at this hour, at three in the afternoon. Suddenly a man in shining clothes stood before me* [31]*and said, 'Cornelius, God has heard your prayer and remembered your gifts to the poor.*
>
> [32]*Send to Joppa for Simon who is called Peter. He is a guest in the home of Simon the tanner, who lives by the sea.'* [33]*So I sent for you immediately, and it was good of you to come.*
>
> *Now we are all here in the presence of God to listen to everything the Lord has commanded you to tell us."* Acts 10:30-33

If every church or congregation on Sunday morning were to address their preacher as Cornelius addressed Peter, it would be like an electric shock for them. They might preach as they never did before!

In Peter's next words we begin to see the purpose of the vision that God gave to him in Joppa.

> [34]*Then Peter began to speak: "I now realise how true it is that God does not show favouritism* [35]*but accepts men from every nation who fear him and do what is right.*
>
> [36]*You know the message God sent to the people of Israel, telling the good news of peace through Jesus Christ, who is Lord of all.*
>
> [37]*You know what has happened throughout Judea, beginning in Galilee after the baptism that John preached—* [38]*how God anointed Jesus of Nazareth with the Holy Spirit and power, and how he went around doing good and healing all who were under the power of the devil, because God was with him.* Acts 10:34-38

Peter was breaking new ground for the gospel. He didn't have any other apostles with him to consult about the appropriate behaviour in these totally new circumstances. Twenty-four hours ago he had received 'a short, sharp, shock' type lesson about his narrow-minded Jewish prejudices. These must be abandoned in the service of the Gospel.

Peter acknowledges that God had taught him a lesson that he, as a Jew and a Christian, needed to learn. It had already transformed his thinking about how to present the gospel to Gentiles:

> "*I now realise how true it is that God does not show favouritism* [35]*but accepts men from every nation who fear him and do what is right.*" Acts 10:34-35

Peter was making it clear to this Gentile audience that this was the framework out of which he was speaking to them.

He then moved on to draw on the audience's knowledge of Jesus – he could not be sure how much they knew about him.

He referred to Jesus' ministry since his baptism by John,

> '*How God anointed Jesus of Nazareth with the Holy Spirit and power, and how he went around doing good and healing all who were under the power of the devil, because God was with him.*' Acts 10:37–38.

When Peter said '*We are witnesses of everything he did in the country of the Jews and in Jerusalem,*' he was referring to the apostles of Jesus. Peter then followed with the important facts of the death, burial and resurrection of Jesus (v. 39).

> *They killed him by hanging him on a tree,* [40] *but God raised him from the dead on the third day and caused him to be seen.*
>
> [41] *He was not seen by all the people, but by witnesses whom God had already chosen—by us who ate and drank with him after he rose from the dead.* [42]*He commanded us to preach to the people and to testify that he is the one whom God appointed as judge of the living and the dead.*
>
> [43]*All the prophets testify about him that everyone who believes in him receives forgiveness of sins through his name.*" Acts 10:39-43

All the saving facts of Jesus' life, death and resurrection were included in Peter's message (vv. 39-43) at which point something dramatic happened.

> [44]*While Peter was still speaking these words, the Holy Spirit came on all who heard the message.*
>
> [45]*The circumcised believers who had come with Peter were astonished that the gift of the Holy Spirit had been poured out even on the Gentiles.* [46]*For they heard them speaking in tongues and praising God.*
>
> *Then Peter said,* [47]*"Can anyone keep these people from being baptised with water? They have received the Holy Spirit just as we have."* [48]*So he ordered that they be baptised in the name of Jesus Christ.*
>
> *Then they asked Peter to stay with them for a few days.* Acts 10:44-48

In the previous study I remarked, *'This was how a most significant meeting in the history of the Christian church was arranged.'* It was the upshot of God speaking to a Roman Centurion in Caesarea and to an apostle of his who was in Joppa.

This is the 'Gentile' Pentecost! It took place on a different date, but it was the same Holy Spirit who was poured out on those who believed.

Peter had some preparation for this scene, but the Jewish believers who had come with him from Joppa had not. What convinced them that what they had witnessed was of God?

> [45]*The circumcised believers who had come with Peter were astonished that the gift of the Holy Spirit had been poured out even on the Gentiles.* [46]*For they heard them speaking in tongues and praising God.* Acts 10:45-46

They recognised common factors between (what is conveniently called) the Jerusalem (or Jewish) Pentecost and this, the Gentile Pentecost.

Peter is the leader in the gathering and gives biblical and pastoral teaching to the new believers. Luke says, '*he ordered that they be baptised in the name of Jesus Christ.'* After this Peter spent some further time at Caesarea.

THANK YOU, HEAVENLY FATHER:

For this great event in the history of the Christian church, when Jews and Gentiles were seen to be one in Christ Jesus, united by their common faith and the indwelling Holy Spirit;

For the sensitivity of Peter to the Holy Spirit's prompting and instruction, and for his courage to act on the lesson that he had been taught;

For the way in which the Holy Spirit had prepared the hearts of Cornelius and his extended family circle to hear and to believe the gospel preached by Peter;

For the reality of Christian unity, a work of the Holy Spirit, which modern believers seem to value lightly, if at all;

IN JESUS' NAME, AMEN

27. Acts 11: 1 to 18

PETER EXPLAINS HIS ACTIONS TO THE CHURCH IN JERUSALEM

[1]The apostles and the brothers throughout Judea heard that the Gentiles also had received the word of God. [2]So when Peter went up to Jerusalem, the circumcised believers criticised him [3]and said, "You went into the house of uncircumcised men and ate with them."

[4]Peter began and explained everything to them precisely as it had happened:

[5] "I was in the city of Joppa praying, and in a trance I saw a vision. I saw something like a large sheet being let down from heaven by its four corners, and it came down to where I was. [6] I looked into it and saw four-footed animals of the earth, wild beasts, reptiles, and birds of the air. [7]Then I heard a voice telling me, 'Get up, Peter. Kill and eat.' [8] 'I replied, 'Surely not, Lord! Nothing impure or unclean has ever entered my mouth.' [9]The voice spoke from heaven a second time, 'Do not call anything impure that God has made clean.' [10]This happened three times, and then it was pulled up to heaven again

[11]"Right then three men who had been sent to me from Caesarea stopped at the house where I was staying. [12]The Spirit told me to have no hesitation about going with them. These six brothers also went with me, and we entered the man's house. [13] He told us how he had seen an angel appear in his house and say, 'Send to Joppa for Simon who is called Peter. [14]He will bring you a message through which you and all your household will be saved.'

[15] "As I began to speak, the Holy Spirit came on them as he had come on us at the beginning. [16]Then I remembered what the Lord had said: 'John baptised with water, but you will be baptised with the Holy Spirit.' [17]So if God gave them the same gift as he gave us, who believed in the Lord Jesus Christ, who

> *was I to think that I could oppose God?"* [18] *When they heard this, they had no further objections and praised God, saying, "So then, God has granted even the Gentiles repentance unto life."* Acts 11:1-18

The Christian Church took a great step forward on the day that the Holy Spirit was poured out on the Gentile believers in the home of Cornelius in Caesarea. I remember thinking of the loneliness of Peter when this was taking place because he was the only apostle present, and a great responsibility rested on him. He had participated in the 'Jewish Pentecost' in Acts 2, and in the 'Samaritan Pentecost' in Acts 8 but for such experiences to be granted to him three times in one lifetime was exceptional. It wasn't a surprise to Peter when his apostles and brothers voiced their criticism of his behaviour (v. 3). However, I have the impression that he had rehearsed his response many times while travelling back to Jerusalem.

Peter explained how the Holy Spirit had spoken to him through a vision of various clean and unclean foods (vv. 4-10). As a Jew, Peter had refused to eat any of the food displayed before him. While he was thinking about this three men from Cornelius had called at the house where he was staying, introduced themselves and invited him to come with them to Caesarea (vv. 11- 14).

Peter reported on the warm welcome he had received in Caesarea, how he had preached the gospel to the Cornelius' family and how the Holy Spirit had been poured out in that home and on that family circle (as at Samaria and at Jerusalem).

Peter had thought himself clear about the ministry and leading of the Holy Spirit and concluded *'if God gave them the same gift as he gave us, who believed in the Lord Jesus Christ, who was I to think that I could oppose God? (vv. 5-14)".*

Now the question was: **Will the believers at Jerusalem accept Peter's testimony?**

THANK YOU, HEAVENLY FATHER:

For Peter's obedient response to the vision that you gave him in Joppa, so that he was willing to set aside his Jewish prejudices and enter heartily into the evangelisation of the Gentiles;

For the openness of Cornelius in the presence of Peter, receiving him as God's messenger;

For the sovereignty of the Holy Spirit working in whomever and wherever he wills to draw sinners to Jesus;

IN JESUS NAME, AMEN

28. Acts 11:19-26

APOSTLES FROM JERUSALEM VISIT THE CHURCH AT ANTIOCH

We need to cast our minds back to the scattering of the church in Jerusalem and Saul's relentless campaign of persecution against it (Acts 8). All except the apostles were scattered throughout Judea and Samaria. Saul went from house to house in Damascus arresting believers and having them thrown into prison. We take up that story in Acts 11:19.

Those who had been contemporaries of Stephen, the first Christian martyr, had fled as far as possible from Jerusalem until they reached Phoenicia, Cyprus and Antioch in Syria. As they journeyed they evangelised people whom they met on the road, but for some reason they confined this witness only to Jews. Alas, their Jewish prejudice restricted their gospel preaching. However, in the good providence of God, believing men from Cyprus and Cyrene went to Antioch and began to speak to Greeks also, telling them the good news about the Lord Jesus,

> [20]*Some of them, however, men from Cyprus and Cyrene, went to Antioch and began to speak to Greeks also, telling them the good news about the Lord Jesus.* [21]*The Lord's hand was with them, and a great number of people believed and turned to the Lord.* [22]*News of this reached the ears of the church at Jerusalem, and they sent Barnabas to Antioch.* Acts 11:20-22

No one can accuse the early apostles of neglect of duty or any lack of single mindedness. When news of both Jewish and Gentile conversions at Antioch reached Jerusalem the believers there sent the apostle Barnabas to that city.

> *When he arrived and saw the evidence of the grace of God, he was glad and encouraged them all to remain true to the Lord with all their hearts. He was a good man, full of the Holy Spirit and faith, and a great number of people were brought to the Lord.* Acts 11:23-24

Luke gives us a helpful reminder of the fitness of Barnabas for the Lord's work. He was a fine strategist.

> [25]*Then Barnabas went to Tarsus to look for Saul, and when he found him, he brought him to Antioch. So far a whole year Barnabas and Saul met with the church and taught great numbers of people. The disciples were called Christians first at Antioch.* Acts 11:25

THANK YOU, HEAVENLY FATHER:

For Your patience with us when are slow to accept new things that the Holy Spirit does in Your work;

For the fact that there are such fine men as Barnabas in the church of Jesus Christ whose love for souls is like that of their Master;

IN JESUS' NAME, AMEN

29. Acts 11: 27-30

PROPHETS FROM JERUSALEM VISIT THE CHURCH AT ANTIOCH

> [27]*And in these days prophets came from Jerusalem to Antioch.* [28]*Then one of them, named Agabus, stood up and showed by the Spirit that there was going to be a great famine throughout all the world, which also happened in the days of Claudius Caesar.* Acts 11:27-28

I expect that the presence of experienced believers in the church at Antioch went a long way in persuading the entire group of the wisdom, indeed the biblical wisdom, of responding positively to this known and present need.

Isn't it astonishing, despite the distances between them and the non-existence of 'IT' in those days, how quickly news travelled in the world of the first century AD?

> [29]*The disciples, each according to his ability, decided to provide help for the brothers living in Judea. This they did, sending their gift to the elders by Barnabas and Saul.* Acts 11:29

Not only did they establish lines of communication; within a matter of days these links had also become supply lines as believers, living in areas to which the gospel had newly come, collected and dispatched goods to prepare for days of famine in Judea and Jerusalem (vv. 27 – 30).

A quotation has suggested itself as a conclusion to this section. I cannot get away from it, so here it is: ***"Look . . . see how these Christians love one another!"*** That tribute was paid by Tertullian, a lawyer in the 1st century AD.

THANK YOU, HEAVENLY FATHER:

For Peter's courage and confidence in your guidance so that he did not hesitate to take the Gospel to the Family of Cornelius;

For the sovereign working of Your Holy Spirit as he moved freely in that family circle where so many folk were hearing the gospel of Jesus for the first time;

For the satisfaction of the leaders of 'the mother church' in Jerusalem in recognising a true work of the Holy Spirit in the planting of the new church in Antioch in Syria.

For the spontaneous care and generosity of the members of the young Gentile church in Antioch that they so readily began to contribute goods to send to their Jewish counterparts in the Church at Jerusalem and Judea when they knew that famine was coming there;

IN JESUS' NAME, AMEN

30. Acts 12: 1 to 19

PETER MIRACULOUS ESCAPE FROM PRISON

[1]Now about that time Herod the king stretched out his hand to harass some from the church. [2]Then he killed James the brother of John with the sword.

[3]And because he saw that it pleased the Jews, he proceeded further to seize Peter also. Now it was during the Days of Unleavened Bread.

[4] So when he had arrested him, he put him in prison, and delivered him to four squads of soldiers to keep him, intending to bring him before the people after Passover. Acts 12:1-4

Perhaps the thought had occurred to you that when we moved out of Luke's gospel leaving behind the heady days of resurrection that marked its ending that suddenly everything would 'flop' when Jesus would leave his church on earth and return to heaven. Not so.

Had there been one dull day since Acts 1:1 until Acts 12:1?

Hadn't the Lord's work continued without significant loss of momentum?

Hadn't there been three 'Pentecosts' (if we may put it that way for a moment), one in Jerusalem, one in Samaria and one in Caesarea and the growth of the Christian church continued as believers were added to the Lord? Yes, there were days of suffering for Stephen. Others lost their goods and homes. Saul the persecutor became Saul the preacher of the gospel. There had been a special meeting in Jerusalem attended by representatives of various churches, to receive a report from the apostles and evangelists about the Lord's work.

This was a meeting not marked by a dull agenda and boredom but by thanksgiving and praise for the new churches at Caesarea and in Syrian Antioch. If we could transport some of those folk from Jerusalem in Acts 11 & 12 and bring them to a Business Meeting of a local church in the UK or the USA, or bring them into a Denominational Annual Meeting that has been organised to death, would they look at us and wonder if we had ever been saved?

I wouldn't be at all surprised if one of them would ask us 'Don't you people over here believe in the Holy Spirit?'

Ah, but the devil hadn't gone away, you know! He put it in King Herod's mind to mount another wave of persecution against believers and many were arrested. Herod had James the brother of John murdered. He saw that his actions pleased the Jews and so he seized Peter as well and put him in custody. No doubt a modern-day security firm had recently serviced the facilities in the holding cells. Herod had Peter put in a cell, in the care of four squads of four guards (around the clock). He would be safe there until after Passover. His trial was something to look forward to (12:1-4).

> [5]*Peter was therefore kept in prison, but constant prayer was offered to God for him by the church.* [6]*And when Herod was about to bring him out, that night Peter was sleeping, bound with two chains between two soldiers; and the guards before the door were keeping the prison.* Acts 12:5-6

Did you notice the church's secret weapon? It is the most powerful weapon that the Christian church possesses. If it is not being used, whose fault is it? It can be focussed on a particular issue 24 hours per day. And when God answers nothing can stand in his way. V. 5 is a great motto that can motivate individual, lonely believers every day that they live anywhere on earth. Meanwhile, it was time for God to work. The church turned to prayer, which is the only power which the powerless possess.

[7] Now behold, an angel of the Lord stood by him, and a light shone in the prison; and he struck Peter on the side and raised him up, saying, "Arise quickly!" And his chains fell off his hands.

[8]Then the angel said to him, "Gird yourself and tie on your sandals"; and so he did. And he said to him, "Put on your garment and follow me." [9]So he went out and followed him, and did not know that what was done by the angel was real, but thought he was seeing a vision.

[10]When they were past the first and the second guard posts, they came to the iron gate that leads to the city, which opened to them of its own accord; and they went out and went down one street, and immediately the angel departed from him. [11]And when Peter had come to himself, he said, "Now I know for certain that the Lord has sent His angel, and has delivered me from the hand of Herod and from all the expectation of the Jewish people."
Acts 12:7-11

The pressures against Christians were great, but the power of God that was for them was greater. Peter would have been a bright man indeed had he not needed to blink a few times to get a grip on what was happening to him. He needed to be hurried, *'Arise quickly!'* As he and the angel spoke the chains fell off Peter's hands. *"Gird yourself and tie on your sandals, Peter"*, and he did so.

Peter followed the angel through two guard posts and then through the iron gate that led into the city street. It opened itself without any human agency. And Peter found himself alone, on a Jerusalem street, in the middle of the night.

[11]And when Peter had come to himself, he said, "Now I know for certain that the Lord has sent His angel, and has delivered me from the hand of Herod and from all the expectation of the Jewish people." [12] So, when he had considered this, he came to the house of Mary, the mother of John whose surname was Mark, where many were gathered together praying. [13]And as Peter knocked at the door of the gate, a girl named Rhoda came to answer. [14]When she recognised Peter's voice, she was

> *so overjoyed she ran back without opening it and exclaimed, "Peter is at the door!"* Acts 12:11-14

If we didn't know better we might think that some of the people in the prayer meeting in Mary's house that night had Irish blood in their veins. It sounds like 'an Irish wake' after tongues have been well lubricated. The people are praying, Peter is knocking, Rhoda runs to open the door, she hears Peter's voice and recognises it but she doesn't open the door. 'You're out of your mind,' they tell her. But Peter keeps knocking and when they open the door, they are astonished. People used to pay good money to listen to comedy like that!

> [15]*"You're out of your mind," they told her. When she kept insisting that it was so, they said, "It must be his angel."* [16]*But Peter kept on knocking, and when they opened the door and saw him, they were astonished.*

> [17]*Peter motioned them to be quiet and described how the Lord had brought him out of prison. And he said, "Go, tell these things to James and to the brethren." And he departed and went to another place.* Acts 12:15-17

Meanwhile, there was consternation in the palace of Herod.

> [18]*Then, as soon as it was day, there was no small stir among the soldiers about what had become of Peter.* [19]*But when Herod had searched for him and not found him, he examined the guards and commanded that they should be put to death. And he went down from Judea to Caesarea, and stayed there.* Acts 12:18-19

Herod doesn't seem to be too bothered. But then he was a man who lived by his moods, one day up and the next day down, and when he was neither up nor down, look out, not even Herod knows what he will do next. At least four guards, or perhaps all sixteen, were executed on the whim of Herod as a result of Peter's escape.

Alas, in many corridors of power around the world it is the Herods who are in control and the Christians who suffer. However, we Christians know that with God on their side His people will win;

THANK YOU, HEAVENLY FATHER:

For your sovereign control of everything You have made;

For the weapon of prayer that You have entrusted to Your people in their fight with the world, the flesh and the devil;

For the way in which the devil frequently over-reaches himself in his assaults on Your Son and on Your People;

For those who are saved: to them Christ is the power of God and the wisdom of God. For the foolishness of God is wiser than man's wisdom, and the weakness of God is stronger than man's strength (1 Cor. 1:24-25);

IN JESUS' NAME, AMEN

31. Acts 12: 19 - 25
HEROD'S DEATH

> [19]*But when Herod had searched for him and not found him, he examined the guards and commanded that they should be put to death. And he went down from Judea to Caesarea, and stayed there.*

Isn't Herod a tyrant? In modern times the man who comes to mind as his equal in cruelty and instability is the late Idi Amin in Uganda. Sadly there were too many others like him in the African countries. After his death many thousands of women and children were discovered in mass graves. They had been murdered on his orders.

In v. 19 some of Herod's guards were murdered on a whim of Herod. Can't you see him dusting the sand off his hands and stepping into his chariot, ordering the driver to take him to Caesarea?

He hasn't gone many miles before he has another quarrel to settle.

> [20] *Now Herod had been very angry with the people of Tyre and Sidon; but they came to him with one accord, and having made Blastus the king's personal aide their friend, they asked for peace, because their country was supplied with food by the king's country.*

People from these coastal towns were waiting for his arrival. It appears that by some means they had persuaded a man called Blastus to be their intermediary and to speak to Herod on their behalf.

> *They asked for peace, because they depended on the king's country for their food supply.*

They desired to live in peace with Herod, because their country benefitted greatly from Herod's country of Galilee, where there was plenty of corn to be had year on year.

Herod had determined to make this a big event; he would rant and rave and strut and sweat and create an impression such as only an egotistic man can do.

> [21]*So on a set day Herod, arrayed in royal apparel, sat on his throne and gave an oration to them.* [22]*And the people kept shouting, "The voice of a god and not of a man!"*
>
> [23]*Then immediately an angel of the Lord struck him, because he did not give glory to God. And he was eaten by worms and died.* Acts 12:21-23

Pause for a moment and think. See how God turned this scene upside down. Acts 12 began with the death of James, Peter the leading apostle was in prison and Herod was on the rampage.

Within half a dozen verses Herod was struck down by a divine hand and died, Peter had been released from prison and the word of God was triumphing.

I have been privileged to visit the USA many times since 1980. When travelling through the country I enjoy finding **'HISTORICAL MARKERS'** by the highway. I think that Luke included 'Historical Markers' in his second book. You may find more – or less. They serve as reminders of what God has done in our lives and in the lives of generations of faithful men and women who passed this way before us. Think of each of these sixteen markers for a moment and give hearty thanks to God for each and all of them.

[1] Acts 2:1-13	The Advent of the Holy Spirit;
[2] Acts 2:42-47	The features of a Spirit-filled church;
[3] Acts 2:47	The daily growth of the church;
[4] Acts 4:12	Jesus Christ is the only Saviour of sinners;
[5] Acts 4:19-20	The indefatigable resolution of Peter and John when they persisted in preaching;
[6] Acts 4:31	Unforgettable answers to the church's prayers;

[7] Acts 4:32-37	The mutual sharing of believers in meeting each other's needs;
[8] Acts 5:12-16	Numerous healings and conversions in Jerusalem;
[9] Acts 5:17-42	Peter's miraculous release from prison;
[10] Acts 6:1-7	The appointment of the deacons; the conversions of many priests;
[11] Acts 7:1-8:59	The defence and martyrdom of Stephen;
[12] Acts 8:4-25	The Samaritan Pentecost;
[13] Acts 9:1-31	The Conversion of Saul of Tarsus;
[14] Acts 10:1-11:18	The Gentile Pentecost in Caesarea;
[15] Acts 11:19-30	The New Church in Antioch
[16] Acts 12:24-25	The continued growth of the church; the restoration of John Mark, the young preacher and missionary.

> *[24]But the word of God grew and multiplied. [25]And Barnabas and Saul returned from Jerusalem when they had fulfilled their ministry, and they also took with them John whose surname was Mark.* Acts 12:24-25

When Barnabas and Saul believed their ministry at Caesarea was fulfilled for the present time, John Mark, the son of Mary Mark of Jerusalem, accompanied them on their next mission. That is another story.

THANK YOU, HEAVENLY FATHER:

For this chapter of encouragement; You always know when your people need cheering up;

For the fact that 'there are more things wrought by prayer than this world dreams of';

For the downfall of Herod; this man reaped spiritually what he sowed, he sowed to the flesh and of the flesh he reaped corruption;

For the fellowship that Christian workers experience in the Lord's service;

IN JESUS' NAME, AMEN

iii. Acts 13:1 - 28:31

YOU SHALL BE MY WITNESSES TO THE ENDS OF THE EARTH ACTS 13:1 – 15:35

PAUL'S FIRST MISSIONARY JOURNEY

32. Acts 13:1-3

BARNABAS AND SAUL SENT OUT FROM THE CHURCH AT ANTIOCH

THIS IS ANTIOCH IN SYRIA, THE CAPITAL OF SYRIA.

> [1]*In the church at Antioch there were prophets and teachers: Barnabas, Simeon called Niger, Lucius of Cyrene, Manaen (who had been brought up with Herod the tetrarch) and Saul.*
>
> [2]*While they were worshipping the Lord and fasting, the Holy Spirit said, "Set apart for me Barnabas and Saul for the work to which I have called them."*
>
> [3]*So after they had fasted and prayed, they placed their hands on them and sent them off.* Acts 13:1-3

So far as first impressions go we have a picture of the church at Antioch in our minds. The first word that comes to mind is *'young'*. Another word is *'small':* its first influx of members in any numbers came from Jerusalem following the persecution of that church by Saul of Tarsus (11:19). Another fact is that *'it was exceptionally gifted'* having a number of prophets and teachers in the membership *(13:1)*.

We could truthfully describe it as *'surprisingly mature'* because men from Jerusalem took the gospel there (11:20). There was evidence *'of the grace of God in the lives of the members'* (22-24). Another term could be *'it was well instructed in the faith of the gospel'* (vv. 25-26). Barnabas and Saul had spent a year with the church helping it to become spiritually strong. *'Eager to care for their fellow believers in Jerusalem and Judea'* (27-30); they wasted no time in sending material help to their mother church.

Sometimes young churches hold back from a missionary vision, pleading their size as a reason for not accepting the responsibility to send out members in the Lord's mission field. If this response is allowed to prevail, then it may prevent the church from honouring the Lord.

Let's take special note of how the Holy Spirit guides a local church (of any size) about committing their members to the Lord's work. How did the Spirit do it in Antioch?

> [2] *While they were worshipping the Lord and fasting, the Holy Spirit said, "Set apart for me Barnabas and Saul for the work to which I have called them."* Acts 13:2

Now I must ask an embarrassing question. Think of your church prayer meeting. Out of a total of 60 minutes – or perhaps 75 – how much time is actually spent praying? What special arrangements are made to ensure that the maximum number of people can participate audibly? Or is your church prayer meeting dead, if only it had the sense to stiffen!

You see, however they ran the prayer meetings in Antioch those present became aware of the voice of the Lord speaking right there in the meeting. Did it take place as long as it takes us to read the second half of v. 2? Perhaps, we don't know exactly. I think it looks as if the members present for prayer were not only talking to the Lord in prayer, but were listening to the Lord in prayer as well.

The word from the Holy Spirit was: [2] *"Set apart for me Barnabas and Saul for the work to which I have called them."*

There was no missionary committee; no visas to be obtained from various governments through whose countries the missionaries would pass, no cultural orientation, no language training. Possibly their possessions were what they stood up in.

In today's world these points of reference are essential; otherwise prospective missionaries may find themselves in a prison cell, if not on the next aircraft on their way home again, having been deported from the country in which they had hoped to be evangelists and church planters.

The essential fact about the church at Antioch was this: it felt compelled to proceed immediately and therefore, with fasting and prayer and the laying on of hands, it sent Barnabas and Saul on their first missionary journey together, and young John Mark travelled with them.

Stand amazed at them if you want to, but the divine compulsion that they felt was undeniable.

Another factor may be relevant – it is possible that the three missionary colleagues represented three age-groups. Saul may have been the eldest of the three and John Mark, the youngest, with Barnabas closer to Saul in age than to Mark. A lot of missionary learning would take place when all three were 'in harness' in the towns and cities of Asia Minor, rather than sitting in lectures in a seminary back at home.

You will know from my background of more than 50 years in the Baptist ministry that I have accumulated some wisdom about missionary work. Therefore I am not saying that all or anything that I mentioned above is 'anathema'.

I am saying with great emphasis that for three men of such diverse backgrounds and experience to work together for the glory of God there needed to be godly submission to one another, along with a strong sense of stewardship to the sending church in Antioch. Early missionaries had a lot of learning to do; today we don't know it all yet, either! Modern missionaries are not renowned for being the most submissive to leadership.

To put your hand in the hand of Jesus and say, *'Here am I, send me,'* is to open your mouth very wide.

Don't say those words to Him, unless you have heard His call. If so, may God's richest blessing be yours, until you see Jesus face to face in heaven.

THANK YOU, HEAVENLY FATHER:

That when Jesus calls me I must follow, follow Him today;

That you do not send us to serve anywhere alone; make us grateful for the helpers you are giving us, and to love and respect them as we love and serve our Lord;

For the faithful folks at home who, when wishing us God's blessing on going to the mission field, are faithful stewards of what you have given them and so they faithfully support and pray for us.

For your economy: it never fails; the finances that are needed in your work are already in the pockets of your people.

IN JESUS' NAME, AMEN

33. Acts 13:4-12

BARNABAS, SAUL AND JOHN MARK ON CYPRUS

An Island in the Eastern Mediterranean Sea

[4]The two of them, sent on their way by the Holy Spirit, went down to Seleucia and sailed from there to Cyprus. [5]When they arrived at Salamis, they proclaimed the word of God in the Jewish synagogues. John was with them as their helper.

[6]They travelled through the whole island until they came to Paphos. There they met a Jewish sorcerer and false prophet named Bar-Jesus, [7]who was an attendant of the proconsul, Sergius Paulus.

The proconsul, an intelligent man, sent for Barnabas and Saul because he wanted to hear the word of God.

[8]But Elymas the sorcerer (for that is what his name means) opposed them and tried to turn the proconsul from the faith.

[9]Then Saul, who was also called Paul, filled with the Holy Spirit, looked straight at Elymas and said, [10]"You are a child of the devil and an enemy of everything that is right! You are full of all kinds of deceit and trickery. Will you never stop perverting the right ways of the Lord? [11]Now the hand of the Lord is against you. You are going to be blind, and for a time you will be unable to see the light of the sun." Immediately mist and darkness came over him, and he groped about, seeking someone to lead him by the hand.

[12]When the proconsul saw what had happened, he believed, for he was amazed at the teaching about the Lord. Acts 13:4-12

This is a good point to refer back to Acts 1:8 and to the 'rule of thumb' outline that Jesus gave the apostles about the work He had for them to do following his ascension. Jesus had prophesied that the apostles would be '*his witnesses in Jerusalem, and in all Judea and Samaria, and to the ends of the earth.*'

Peter and the apostles, based in Jerusalem, had promoted the gospel in and around the great city of Judaism (1:12–8:1); Philip the evangelist plus Peter and John had evangelised in Judea and Samaria (8:4-11:19); next comes the point where the churches would be guided by the Holy Spirit to take the gospel to the rest of the world. The church at Antioch was first to respond to the Lord's direction to take the gospel *to the ends of the earth'* (Acts 13:1-3).

A look at a map of the Near East in the first century AD will help us grasp the progress of the gospel up to this point in Acts. Beginning at Jerusalem and proceeding north (not forgetting Judea slightly to the south), then further north through Samaria (not forgetting Caesarea) to Damascus (Acts 9). Keep going north to Syrian Antioch (Acts 13) from where Saul and Barnabas and John Mark were sent out on a missionary journey by the church there. They went to the seaport of Seleucia and from there sailed to Cyprus. So we begin to see (even in layman's terms) how the gospel had proceeded from Jerusalem to Syrian Antioch, before turning further left and south to the Island of Cyprus. So we might say that the gospel followed an anti-clockwise route beginning at Jerusalem.

The church at Antioch was the first to catch the vision of taking the gospel overseas (in contrast to being limited to the Palestinian and Syrian mainland).

> [5]*When they arrived at Salamis, they proclaimed the word of God in the Jewish synagogues. John was with them as their helper.* Acts 13:5

We can almost catch a sniff of the briny air on the quayside at Salamis, a commercial port on the eastern end of the island. The gospel was arriving in Cyprus for the first time. The three men didn't have to pray long about where they ought to begin evangelising. Off they went to find a Jewish synagogue–and found more than one!

Had we been worshippers at the synagogue that morning, what would have been our reaction of the arrival of these Jews who were preaching about Jesus? Perhaps we might have been indifferent, leaving the synagogue after worship as we had always done. There is no record of a negative response on the part of the synagogue leaders. We imagine that our three friends thanked God and took courage.

> [6]*They travelled through the whole island until they came to Paphos. There they met a Jewish sorcerer and false prophet named Bar-Jesus,* [7]*who was an attendant of the proconsul, Sergius Paulus. The proconsul, an intelligent man, sent for Barnabas and Saul because he wanted to hear the word of God.* [8]*But Elymas the sorcerer (for that is what his name means) opposed them and tried to turn the proconsul from the faith.*
> Acts 13:6-8

Their initial reconnaissance of the island brought them to Paphos at the western end of the island–a journey of about ninety miles. They wouldn't have felt entirely 'lost' because Barnabas was a native of Cyprus.

Luke has already introduced Sergius Paulus (v. 7) through reference to two members of the household staff, a Jewish sorcerer called Elymas, and a false prophet called Bar-Jesus.

Although the group were meeting as complete strangers, we are fascinated to learn that the Holy Spirit had given Sergius Paulus a spirit of enquiry about the Gospel.

Stand back for a moment and think: Sergius Paulus wants to hear the word of God and had sent for Barnabas and Saul for that purpose (v. 7). Right there the devil has one of his agents, Elymas the Jewish sorcerer (a magician) about whom Luke says, *who opposed them and tried to turn the proconsul from the faith (v. 8)*. So Sergius Paulus saw the visitors as prospective friends and spiritual helpers, whereas

Elymas saw them as a threat to his prestige in the community and to his livelihood.

Paul viewed the behaviour of Elymas as a serious attack by the devil and he confronted Elymas Magus (in Cyprus) as Peter had confronted Simon Magus (in Samaria, 8:20ff).

This is the point in Paul's life at which Luke divulges that Saul was also called Paul. Here Paul is in a non-Jewish context and therefore he doesn't call Paul 'Saul' again. Next he tells us something of the utmost importance:

> [9]*Then Saul, who was also called Paul, filled with the Holy Spirit, looked straight at Elymas and said,* [10]*"You are a child of the devil and an enemy of everything that is right! You are full of all kinds of deceit and trickery. Will you never stop perverting the right ways of the Lord?* [11]*Now the hand of the Lord is against you. You are going to be blind, and for a time you will be unable to see the light of the sun." Immediately mist and darkness came over him, and he groped about, seeking someone to lead him by the hand.* Acts 13:9-11

I think it is evident that Sergius Paulus could see that Paul's initiative, boldness, and outspokenness in condemning Elymas were all from God. What happened next? Dr. Luke used two medical terms to describe what God had done to Elymas in this swift act of judgment: *Immediately mist and darkness came over him, and he groped about, seeking someone to lead him by the hand.*

Perhaps Paul recalled how he had been smitten by blindness on the Damascus road when he met the Risen Christ for the first time.

> [12]*When the proconsul saw what had happened, he believed, for he was amazed at the teaching about the Lord.* Acts 13:12

There in the State Apartments of the Roman Pro-Consul, the Holy Spirit went into combat with the evil one and overthrew him; Paul the apostle of Jesus confounded the Jewish sorcerer, and the gospel triumphed over the occult.

I imagine that when the group went their separate ways later that day, the visitors left with a standing invitation to call again at any time. This initial fruit of the gospel in Cyprus would be well-pastored.

THANK YOU, HEAVENLY FATHER:

For the astonishing guidance of the Holy Spirit in superintending the meeting of Paul, Barnabas and John Mark, with the Pro Consul Sergius Paulus;

For this visual aid to all who are the servants of the Lord that a godly sensitivity to the Holy Spirit is an essential ingredient in our work for the Lord;

For Your forgiveness when our 'blundering' efforts in ministering to others have led to further confusion; Lord, have mercy.

IN JESUS' NAME, AMEN

34. Acts 13: 13 to 52
IN PISIDIAN ANTIOCH

Pisidia: a small Roman province in S. Asia Minor, near Phrygia

> [13]*From Paphos, Paul and his companions sailed to Perga in Pamphylia, where John left them to return to Jerusalem.* [14]*From Perga they went on to Pisidian Antioch. On the Sabbath they entered the synagogue and sat down.* [15]*After the reading from the Law and the Prophets, the synagogue rulers sent word to them, saying, "Brothers, if you have a message of encouragement for the people, please speak."* Acts 13:13-15

Paul and Barnabas (and Mark, of course) had sailed due north from Cyprus and arrived on the Asian mainland. Paul was back in his native land. Barnabas had left his behind (Acts 4:36). Perga was an ancient Greek city and a busy seaport in the region of Pamphylia, now in Antalya province on the southwestern coast of Turkey (on the Mediterranean Sea).

Luke slips in a personal note when he reveals that John Mark left them in Perga and returned to Jerusalem (v. 13). He doesn't disclose any reason for this parting between the young man and his senior colleagues, therefore speculation is useless. Even if we try 'reading between the lines' (as we say) we find no further clues. Let's withhold judgment until we get to Chap. 15:37-39, when the serious consequences of his leaving begin to appear.

We know that when Paul and Barnabas were about to set out on a second missionary journey (15:38) the two of them were sharply divided about whether to take John Mark with them.

> [38]*Paul did not think it wise to take him, because he had deserted them in Pamphylia and had not continued with them in the work.*

> [39]*They had such a sharp disagreement that they parted company. Barnabas took Mark and sailed for Cyprus,* [40]*but Paul chose Silas and left, commended by the brothers to the grace of the Lord.* [41]*He went through Syria and Cilicia strengthening the churches.* Acts 13:38-41

We are happy to learn from Paul's second letter to Timothy that he had changed his mind about young Mark. Paul asks Timothy to *'get Mark and bring him with you, because he is helpful to me in my ministry'* (2 Tim. 4:11).

We need to recognize that there are two sides to this story: on one hand we are distressed to see that the providence that made John Mark available became an excuse for Christian quarrelling; and on the other hand we need to be thankful that four missionaries went out to evangelize instead of only two.

From Perga they went on to another Antioch, this time in Pisidia (v. 14).

I have good friends who live in Danville, VA. Before I visited them for the first time I opened a large road map of the USA to see where they lived. I soon gave up because I couldn't find a town called Danville anywhere.

However, before writing this paragraph I did a search on my computer by asking the question *'How many cities in the USA have the name Danville?'*I got 1,300 results! So you will be pleased to know that the Antiochs in Asia Minor are no trouble to us at all. Well, maybe not, because I have learned since that Alexander the Great built 16 cities all called Antioch, in honour of his father. We won't go into them.

The First Sabbath in Antioch Acts 13:13-43

What took Paul and Barnabas to Antioch? There was a synagogue there, and observing the proper protocol for visitors they entered the building and sat down (v. 14). In synagogue fashion the scrolls were taken down from the tabernacle behind the pulpit and the appointed portions for the day were read. We may presume that our friends joined in the reading.

Next, again in synagogue fashion, the rulers of the synagogue made a request to the visitors: *"Brothers, if you have a message of encouragement for the people, please speak."*

> [16]*Standing up, Paul motioned with his hand and said: "Men of Israel and you Gentiles who worship God, listen to me!"* Acts 13:16

We can see Paul responding to the invitation in a very dignified fashion – the synagogue service wasn't a place for telling jokes but rather getting the attention of everyone present with his first sentence. People would quickly recognise him as an experienced speaker.

Luke is recording the major part of what Paul had to say that morning. His theme was how God had delivered his people from the land of Egypt; how he had endured them for about forty years in the wilderness; how he overthrew seven nations in Canaan and gave that land to his people, the Israelites, as their inheritance. All of which took about 450 years (vv.16-20).

Every mind in the synagogue was in gear, engaging with Paul as he preached. God had given judges to rule his people until the time of Samuel the prophet. Then the people wanted a king and he gave them Saul the son of Kish of the tribe of Benjamin who ruled 40 years (v. 20 -21). After removing Saul, God made David the King of Israel because he said of him *'I have found David son of Jesse a man after my own heart; he will do everything I want him to do' (v. 22).*

Then taking a great leap of about 1000 years down the centuries Paul came to the point of his sermon:

> [23]**"From this man's descendants God has brought to Israel the Saviour Jesus, as he promised.** [24]*Before the coming of Jesus, John preached repentance and baptism to all the people of Israel.* [25]*As John was completing his work, he said: 'Who do*

you think I am? I am not that one. No, but he is coming after me, whose sandals I am not worthy to untie.' Acts 13:23-25

Here is the first point of application in Paul's sermon:

[26] "Brothers, children of Abraham, and you God-fearing Gentiles, it is to us that this message of salvation has been sent. Acts 13:26

Paul presumed that the folks in the Antioch synagogue knew how the Jews had treated Jesus. He was going to remind them anyhow.

[27]The people of Jerusalem and their rulers did not recognise Jesus, yet in condemning him they fulfilled the words of the prophets that are read every Sabbath.

[28]Though they found no proper ground for a death sentence, they asked Pilate to have him executed. [29]When they had carried out all that was written about him, they took him down from the tree and laid him in a tomb.

[30]But God raised him from the dead, [31]and for many days he was seen by those who had travelled with him from Galilee to Jerusalem. They are now his witnesses to our people. Acts 13:27-31

Here is a second major point in Paul's sermon:

[32] "*We tell you the good news*: What God promised our fathers [33]he has fulfilled for us, their children, by raising up Jesus. *As it is written in the second Psalm: 'You are my Son; today I have become your Father.'*

[34]The fact that God raised him from the dead, never to decay, is stated in these words: 'I will give you the holy and sure blessings promised to David.' [35]So it is stated elsewhere: 'You will not let your Holy One see decay.'

[36]"For when David had served God's purpose in his own generation, he fell asleep; he was buried with his fathers and his body decayed. [37]But the one whom God raised from the dead did not see decay.' Acts 13:32-37

Here is a third major point in Paul's sermon:

> [38]"Therefore, my brothers, I want you to know that through Jesus the forgiveness of sins is proclaimed to you. [39]*Through him everyone who believes is justified from everything you could not be justified from by the law of Moses. [40]Take care that what the prophets have said does not happen to you: [41]" 'Look, you scoffers, wonder and perish, for I am going to do something in your days that you would never believe, even if someone told you.'* "Acts 13:38-41

Luke records that the visit of his friends to Antioch was deeply appreciated.

> [42] ***As Paul and Barnabas were leaving the synagogue, the people invited them to speak further about these things on the next Sabbath.***
>
> [43]*When the congregation was dismissed, many of the Jews and devout converts to Judaism followed Paul and Barnabas, who talked with them and urged them to continue in the grace of God.* Acts 13:42-43

The Second Sabbath in Antioch Acts 13:44-52

> [44]*On the next Sabbath almost the whole city gathered to hear the word of the Lord. [45]When the Jews saw the crowds, they were filled with jealousy and talked abusively against what Paul was saying.* Acts 13:44-45

We wondered when opposition would raise its ugly head and what form it would take. Answer: it came in the form of sheer jealousy (v. 43). Crowds like these had never been a feature of synagogue life on other Sabbaths. The local people were also vocal: 'This visiting rabbi is an able speaker and preacher, but we have no room and no need for the likes of him here'. Now the lines were clearly drawn.

> [46]*Then Paul and Barnabas answered them boldly:* "We had to speak the word of God to you first. *Since you reject it and do not consider yourselves worthy of eternal life,* we now turn to

> the Gentiles. [47]*For this is what the Lord has commanded us: " 'I have made you a light for the Gentiles, that you may bring salvation to the ends of the earth.' "* Acts 13:46-47

This was music to many Gentile ears in Antioch. Such a day of blessing had never been seen in that city before.

> [48]*When the Gentiles heard this, they were glad and honoured the word of the Lord; and all who were appointed for eternal life believed.* [49]*The word of the Lord spread through the whole region.* Acts 13:48-49

Did you spot another of Luke's **HIGHWAY MARKERS**? There it is in v.48.

Not all of the synagogue members were supporters of Paul and his preaching of God's way of salvation. They incited God-fearing women of the higher social class and also leading men of the city. Soon the population had turned against Paul and Barnabas and expelled them from the region around Antioch.

Paul was a man of experience and this wasn't the first time he had experienced persecution. He had even come to expect it. So the two servants of the Lord shook the dust off their feet and took the road to Iconium. Were they down-hearted?

> *And the disciples were filled with joy and with the Holy Spirit.* Acts 13:52

Where was Iconium? It was about 100 miles east of Pisidian Antioch and was served by a good road system.

THANK YOU, HEAVENLY FATHER:

For the preaching of the gospel of Jesus Christ in the power of the Holy Spirit; and especially for those occasions when people have their Bibles open to read the word for themselves;

For Paul's familiarity with Jewish worship and his continued respect for all things Jewish which enabled him to behave as a Jew when seeking to win Jews; and as a Gentile when seeking to win Gentiles;

For the hunger for the Word of God, and for the Living Word, that the Holy Spirit can create in the hearts of sinners so that they long to know Jesus;

IN JESUS' NAME, AMEN

35. Acts 14: 1-7
IN ICONIUM

THE ANCIENT CAPITAL OF LYCAONIA

> [1]*At Iconium Paul and Barnabas went as usual into the Jewish synagogue. There they spoke so effectively that a great number of Jews and Gentiles believed.*

One thing is abundantly clear: the blessing of the Lord was with Paul and Barnabas. It is astonishing how Christian service is transformed by this realisation. I was privileged to have a godly man who served as an Elder in one of the churches I pastored. Many Irish readers may remember James McManus. He would come to me, take my hand in a warm handshake and say, 'God bless you, the Lord is with you.' I tell you, one of James' benedictions was worth a thousand sermons.

We see Paul's strategy right away – they *'went as usual into the Jewish synagogue.'* The Lord was with them: '*There they spoke so effectively that a great number of Jews and Gentiles believed.*' We rejoice to receive a report like this.

> [2]*But the Jews who refused to believe stirred up the Gentiles and poisoned their minds against the brothers.* [3]*So Paul and Barnabas spent considerable time there, speaking boldly for the Lord, who confirmed the message of his grace by enabling them to do miraculous signs and wonders.* [4]*The people of the city were divided; some sided with the Jews, others with the apostles*. Acts 14:2-4

Perhaps you have heard someone ridicule a preacher for his poor preaching – or for preaching too long – or preaching above people's heads – or for driving people away. Perhaps you have been guilty of such foolish talking yourself.

Well now, let's do a bit of personal work here. In the above paragraph, comprising vv. 2 to 4, how do you account for various responses to the gospel?

The Jews who refused to believe – were doing what Jews do; they were sinning against the truth. Who will you blame for that?

The Gentiles who allowed the Jews to poison their minds against the preachers – they knew even less about the gospel than did the Jews – and believed the lies they were told. Who will you blame for that?

Paul and Barnabas spent considerable time there speaking boldly for the Lord, who confirmed the message of his grace by enabling them to do miraculous signs and wonders. Who will you thank for that?

When are we going to understand that when the gospel is preached in the power of the Holy Spirit there is spiritual warfare going on? Instead of being one of the preacher's critics why don't you become one of the preacher's intercessors? Instead of doing the devil's work, what about doing the Lord's work?

> [5]*There was a plot afoot among the Gentiles and Jews, together with their leaders, to ill-treat them and stone them.* [6]*But they found out about it and fled to the Lycaonian cities of Lystra and Derbe and to the surrounding country,* [7]*where they continued to preach the good news.* Acts 14:5-7

They found out about the plot and they fled. They were wise men. Christians don't seek martyrdom; their lives are precious and therefore like other human beings they do not run into danger. When God spares his servants from suffering and injury they are thankful, but if God permits their martyrdom, like Stephen they enter his eternal presence with joy. It is happening everyday somewhere in the world where oppressive regimes murder believers in Jesus, leaving widows and orphans to fend for themselves when husbands and fathers are taken from them.

Does this mean that Christian relatives cease all gospel work and withdraw from the frontline? The answer is 'No'. Like Paul and Barnabas they continue to preach the good news.

THANK YOU, HEAVENLY FATHER:

For all those in every land who are hearing the gospel in their own language and in their own culture; may Your Holy Spirit clarify the gospel message and reveal Jesus to them;

For all who are our supporters in kind and our intercessors in spiritual warfare when we are serving in the frontline where Jesus is needed most;

For those who are actively opposing the gospel; may the enormity of their sinful behaviour become clear to their consciences and may they seek forgiveness and salvation from the hands of the Saviour;

For those who are new believers in every land and culture; that the Holy Spirit will be their teacher enabling to them read and understand the Scriptures, and if they do not own a single page of Scripture may You supply this need in a miraculous way;

For health and strength for all Your servants, and the provision of all their needs by Your bountiful hand;

IN JESUS' NAME, AMEN

36. Acts 14: 8-20

IN LYSTRA AND DERBE

LYSTRA: A Roman Colony. The home city of Timothy

DERBE: In S. W. Lycaonia, Asia Minor

> [8]*In Lystra there sat a man crippled in his feet, who was lame from birth and had never walked.* [9]*He listened to Paul as he was speaking. Paul looked directly at him, saw that he had faith to be healed* [10]*and called out, "Stand up on your feet!" At that, the man jumped up and began to walk.* Acts 14:8-10

Saul and Barnabas didn't begin their visit in Lystra by going to the local synagogue–because it didn't have one. Arrangements, we might say, had been taken right out of their hands!

God had a needy man there, who was paying exceptional attention to Paul as he was speaking. Paul noticed the man and knew that the Holy Spirit was speaking to him. Looking into his face Paul *'saw that he had faith to be healed'*, and without further warning called out to him: *"Stand up on your feet!"* At that, the man jumped up and began to walk.

The public, gathered round, witnessed the miracle. The man who had never walked in his life because his inability to walk was congenital, had obeyed Paul's command to stand up on his feet. Paul hadn't touched him in order to convey any grace or power of movement. What was the explanation?

This miracle was a sovereign work of God. Miracles are not made to order. Paul didn't pray the evening before: 'Lord we hope to be in Lystra tomorrow morning, I'd like you to do a miracle for me about mid-day!'

Let's note the reaction of the local people. Why did they behave as they did?

> [11]*When the crowd saw what Paul had done, they shouted in the Lycaonian language,* ***"The gods have come down to us in human form!"*** [12]*Barnabas they called Zeus, and Paul they called Hermes because he was the chief speaker.* Acts 14:11-12

The crowd acted like this because Zeus and Hermes were the only gods they knew. This was an utterly pagan city. Archaeologists have found two inscriptions and a stone altar indicating that these two gods were worshipped as the local deities.

The people concluded that their gods had come down to them as men. If this were the case then history would have been repeating itself. Jupiter (*aka* Zeus) and his son Mercury (*aka* Hermes) once visited the hill country of Phrygia, disguised as mortal men. We needn't take that story any further.

The crowd had become fanatical.

> [13]*The priest of Zeus, whose temple was just outside the city, brought bulls and wreaths to the city gates because he and the crowd wanted to offer sacrifices to them.* Acts 14:13

It was only with the utmost difficulty that Paul and Barnabas prevented these pagan rituals taking place and the people worshipping these two servants of the living God as if they were gods.

> [14]*But when the apostles Barnabas and Paul heard of this, they tore their clothes and rushed out into the crowd, shouting:* [15]*"Men, why are you doing this? We too are only men, human like you. We are bringing you good news, telling you to turn from these worthless things to the living God, who made heaven and earth and sea and everything in them."* Acts 14:14-15

Those who are connoisseurs of good sermons will say from the sidelines: 'Why didn't Paul use a good text, roll up his sleeves and wade into that crowd. The one thing the crowd needs is a good strong gospel. Why doesn't he quote Isaiah 53:5 to them?' Paul was a wiser man than that.

The fact is that Paul could have quoted the entire Old Testament from Genesis to Malachi – and the people at Lystra wouldn't have understood a word of it. It would have sounded like a foreign language to them.

Having narrowly avoided being worshipped as gods, Paul and Barnabas used the simplest words they could speak. Listen carefully:

> [15]*"Men, why are you doing this? We too are only men, human like you. We are bringing you good news, telling you to turn from these worthless things to the living God, who made heaven and earth and sea and everything in them.*
>
> [16]*In the past, he let all nations go their own way.* [17]*Yet he has not left himself without testimony: He has shown kindness by giving you rain from heaven and crops in their seasons; he provides you with plenty of food and fills your hearts with joy."* [18]*Even with these words, they had difficulty keeping the crowd from sacrificing to them.* Acts 14:15-18

While Paul had gained the undivided attention of the citizens, the priest of Zeus and other officials, he had arrived at the point where he would tell the Lystrans how to know the living God. What happened next? Paul's witness was interrupted.

> [19]*Then some Jews came from Antioch and Iconium and won the crowd over. They stoned Paul and dragged him outside the city, thinking he was dead.* [20]*But after the disciples had gathered round him, he got up and went back into the city. The next day he and Barnabas left for Derbe.* Acts 14: 19-20

What difference is there between an unbelieving Jew and an unbelieving Gentile? Very little, because both of them hate Jesus Christ, the only mediator between God and men.

These enemies of the gospel weren't the slightest bit concerned about Paul's welfare; he was only a voice to be silenced. So they lifted stones off the road and stoned him, and dragged him outside the city, thinking he was dead.

That is not all. *'After the disciples had gathered around him'* presumably tending to his wounds and praying for his recovery, *'he got up and went back into the city.'* Who, if anyone, would give them hospitality for a night? Perhaps at least one family may have had the courage to do so.

The next day he and Barnabas left for Derbe (v. 28).

THANK YOU, HEAVENLY FATHER:

For moral courage such as Paul and Barnabas displayed in very difficult circumstances; they make us feel ashamed of our feeble stand for Jesus;

For the evangelising zeal of Paul and Barnabas; they had the alertness of evangelists;

For needy souls, like the man who listened so closely to the gospel now that it had come to him;

For those who are the enemies of the gospel, and who may not be far from the kingdom of God;

For Your infinite patience with mankind, not willing that any should perish but that all should come to repentance;

IN JESUS' NAME, AMEN

37. Acts 14: 21-28

THE RETURN TO LYSTRA AND DERBE

> [21]*They preached the good news in that city and won a large number of disciples. Then they returned to Lystra, Iconium and Antioch,* [22]*strengthening the disciples and encouraging them to remain true to the faith. "We must go through many hardships to enter the kingdom of God," they said.* Acts 14:21-22

The city referred to in v. 21 is Derbe. Their visit was marked by the conversion of '*a large number of disciples*'. Again, Paul and Barnabas, and all preachers ever since, can only bow gratefully before God and thank him for his sovereignty in salvation.

Our friends were resolved to revisit Lystra, Iconium and Antioch, which they did. Their message may have been rejected by many of the local people, but there were true believers in the community also, and so, for their sake they went back to '*strengthen the disciples and encourage them to remain true to the faith.*' That is a model of pastoral after-care when new births are recorded in the kingdom of God. Indeed they found it necessary to emphasise "*We must go through many hardships to enter the kingdom of God,*"

A new subject emerges in v. 23ff. It is an aspect of the pastoral care of the local church.

> [23]*Paul and Barnabas appointed elders for them in each church and, with prayer and fasting, committed them to the Lord, in whom they had put their trust.* Acts 14:23

No doubt that Paul would have given more teaching on the subject than is recorded here. (We have to wait until his first and second letters to Timothy are in circulation to learn more about Elders.) It wasn't a short meeting with speedy business when the elders were appointed. They were instructed from the Scriptures, and committed to the Lord's protection and enabling so that they would not fail in the heavy responsibility of pastoring the believers (v. 23).

> [24]*After going through Pisidia, they came into Pamphylia,* [25]*and when they had preached the word in Perga, they went down to Attalia.*
>
> [26]*From Attalia they sailed back to Antioch, where they had been committed to the grace of God for the work they had now completed.*
>
> [27]*On arriving there, they gathered the church together and reported all that God had done through them and how he had opened the door of faith to the Gentiles.* [28]*And they stayed there a long time with the disciples.* Acts 14:24-28

Here is a model of missionary work that has not yet passed its 'sell-by date'. They had been sent out from Antioch, and they reported back to the church there. They reported what God had done. They would have reported the hardships and disappointments too.

Then the whole meeting, missionaries and the sending church, would have praised the Lord together and rejoiced in the many triumphs of his grace in the lives of Jews and Gentiles alike.

THANK YOU, HEAVENLY FATHER:

For the fellowship we share in your service;

For the times of hardship and the times of blessing; we know that both serve your glory;

For the double ministry of evangelising and pastoring that is required in many churches, where for want of gifted men, the work cannot be shared and is not done adequately;

For the pleasure it is when you open the door of faith in an area that had previously been spiritually hard and difficult; the glory is altogether Yours;

IN JESUS' NAME, AMEN

38. Acts 15:1-21

THE COUNCIL AT JERUSALEM

[1]Some men came down from Judea to Antioch and were teaching the brothers: "Unless you are circumcised, according to the custom taught by Moses, you cannot be saved."

[2]This brought Paul and Barnabas into sharp dispute and debate with them. So Paul and Barnabas were appointed, along with some other believers, to go up to Jerusalem to see the apostles and elders about this question. Acts 15:1-2

We cannot forget, and we must not forget that the Gospel of Jesus Christ was intended for a whole world of sinners; it came first to the Jews and then to the Gentiles (Greeks etc.). So there will be situations arising where it is important to ask: are the people being addressed as Jews or Gentiles?

In v.1 the men from Judea were Jews, who had become believers in Jesus, but who were holding on to one of their Jewish rites (circumcision) to the extent that they taught that believers in Jesus were not properly saved unless they were circumcised.

It is no surprise that Paul and Barnabas were brought into sharp dispute and debate with them. At the heart of the whole matter was the question: **Is a person saved by faith alone in Jesus Christ alone through grace alone, or by faith in Jesus Christ plus circumcision?**

If matters had been allowed to go unchecked there might have been a Christian church with two streams of believers, the circumcised and the uncircumcised, or worse, two Christian churches both claiming direct succession from Jesus Christ with two ways of salvation. This shows how important it was that this matter be resolved.

> [2]*The believers in Antioch appointed Paul and Barnabas along with some other believers to go up to Jerusalem to see the apostles and elders about this question.* [3]*So the church sent them on their way, and as they travelled through Phoenicia and Samaria, they told how the Gentiles had been converted.* Acts 15:2-3

The deputation is sharing the good news of gospel advance as they travel. It is becoming even clearer that the Christian church is neither exclusively Jewish nor Gentile, but Jews and Gentiles who believe in Jesus Christ are saved without the necessity of circumcision. The rest of the churches needed to know this.

> [4]*When they came to Jerusalem, they were welcomed by the church and the apostles and elders, to whom they reported everything God had done through them.* Acts 15:4

Once the deputation from Antioch had settled in, formal discussion commenced right away:

> **[5]** ***Then some of the believers who belonged to the party of the Pharisees stood up and said, "The Gentiles must be circumcised and required to obey the law of Moses."*** **Acts 15:5**

This stated the business of what became known as the Jerusalem Council. Naturally enough it was a Jerusalem party who were the first to speak (v. 5). The majority of these believers had been Pharisees at one time

> [6]*The apostles and elders met to consider this question.* [7]***After much discussion, Peter got up and addressed them:*** *"Brothers, you know that some time ago God made a choice among you that the Gentiles might hear from my lips the message of the gospel and believe.* Acts 15:6-7

PETER WAS THE FIRST SPEAKER (vv. 6 – 11)

Peter spoke from his experience as a believer in Jesus and as an apostle of Jesus, and was listened to with respect. (What a model for modern churches to follow!).

> [7]***<u>After much discussion, Peter got up and addressed them</u>: "Brothers, you know that some time ago God made a choice among you that the Gentiles might hear from my lips the message of the gospel and believe.***
>
> [8]*God, who knows the heart, showed that he accepted them by giving the Holy Spirit to them, just as he did to us.* [9]*He made no distinction between us and them, for he purified their hearts by faith.*
>
> [10]*Now then, why do you try to test God by putting on the necks of the disciples a yoke that neither we nor our fathers have been able to bear?*
>
> [11]*No! We believe it is through the grace of our Lord Jesus that we are saved, just as they are."* Acts 15:7-11

In vv. 7-8 Peter is relating his experience of preaching on the Day of Pentecost (to a mainly Jewish audience) and then later of preaching in the house of Cornelius in Caesarea (to a mainly Gentile audience).

He has clear recall of what happened when he preached the gospel there.

> [8]*God, who knows the heart, showed that he accepted them by giving the Holy Spirit to them, just as he did to us.* [9]*He made no distinction between us and them, for he purified their hearts by faith.* Acts 15:8-9

So the testimony of the apostle Peter is that God placed no further burden or condition on the family of Cornelius other that simple faith in Jesus Christ.

Peter concluded his testimony with a question and a statement.

<u>His question was</u>: [10]*Now then, why do you try to test God by putting on the necks of the disciples a yoke that neither we nor our fathers have been able to bear?*

His concluding statement was: [11] *No! We believe it is through the grace of our Lord Jesus that we are saved, just as they are."* Acts 15:10-11

BARNABAS AND PAUL WERE NEXT TO SPEAK (V. 12)

> [12]***The whole assembly became silent as they listened to Barnabas and Paul*** *telling about the miraculous signs and wonders God had done among the Gentiles through them.* Acts 15:12

As some of the others who were present knew (and as we do), these two men had returned recently from a two year missionary journey. Some would have heard their news previously, and others were hearing it for the first time as they listened to these respected servants of the Lord. All that the two had to do to make a very strong impact on the entire assembly was to *'tell about the miraculous signs and wonders God had done among the Gentiles through them'*. Clearly they had been working to build churches comprising both Jewish and Gentile believers.

THEN JAMES SPOKE (vv. 13 – 21)

This is James, the Lord's brother. He was the last of his family circle to come to faith in Jesus as his God and Saviour. He became a respected leader of the church in Jerusalem after a short time.

> [13]***James spoke up: "Brothers, listen to me.*** [14]*Simon has described to us how God at first showed his concern by taking from the Gentiles a people for himself.*
>
> [15]***The words of the prophets are in agreement with this, as it is written:***

[The following notes are inserted to show how James' thoughts were shaping his recommendations.]

- James remembered and quoted a prophecy from Amos 9:11-12. He is thinking 'on his feet' as we say.

[16]" *'After this I will return and rebuild David's fallen tent. Its ruins I will rebuild, and I will restore it,* [17]*that the remnant of men may seek the Lord, and all the Gentiles who bear my name, says the Lord, who does these things'* [18] *that have been known for ages.*

- Basing his conviction on Peter's testimony and on Amos' prophecy, James continued:

[19]"*It is my judgment, therefore, that we should not make it difficult for the Gentiles who are turning to God.*

- It is not the Jewish ritual of circumcision that is at the heart of our discussion.
- Rather it is the question of living holy lives as Christians ought in today's world.
- We all know there are urgent issues on which all the churches need guidance.
- Jewish and Gentile believers could avoid offending each other's consciences and strengthen mutual fellowship by observing four principles.
- James is about to conclude his statement.

[20]***Instead we should write to them,*** *telling them* [1]*to abstain from food polluted by idols,* [2]*from sexual immorality,* [3]*from the meat of strangled animals and* [4]*from blood.*

- There is no need for Christians to write new laws.
- The laws of Moses regarding these matters are adequate and do not need changing.
- They are also widely known and have been for generations.
- Moses taught these things from our earliest days.

[21]*For Moses has been preached in every city from the earliest times and is read in the synagogues on every Sabbath."*
Acts 15:13-21

We need to pause here for a moment, because it looks as if James has introduced a second subject to the agenda.

Why? So far as he was concerned, the subjects he raised in v. 20 were not only important, but urgent. They take the form of four prohibitions.

- It is fair and accurate to say that when James added these secondary issues, he was thinking about relationships between Jewish/Gentile believers. In his view it was unnecessary to add anything on the subject of salvation and circumcision. In his view it was necessary to add some things that represented areas of offence, if not actually stress and tension, between fellow-believers.
- The next observation is to say that if James added the secondary issues to the agenda on his own initiative, Is it not strange that there wasn't a single objection raised by anyone present.
- In that case the decision to include these issues in the letter to the Churches was the unanimous decision of the Council.
- That means that we need to shift the emphasis off James and put it on everyone else – i.e. the entire Council.

Now the question is:

Why did the Council support the inclusion of these matters in the letter to the churches?

Commentators are not at their most helpful when explaining why these four issues were singled out for attention.

1 ***'Abstain from food polluted by idols' (v. 20 & 29).*** Don't eat meat that had been offered to idols, which is idolatry. This might not have troubled a Gentile, but it would have troubled a Jew. Therefore at a fellowship meal it would be well not to serve meat that had been offered to idols.

[2] ***'Abstain from sexual immorality' (vv. 20 & 29).*** Society was corrupted by licentiousness. Many cities were modern versions of Sodom and Gomorrah (Gen. 19). God's salvation delivered sinners from immorality, and God's holy law prohibited it. New believers need to learn what God blesses and what God abhors.

[3] ***'Abstain from the meat of strangled animals' (vv. 20 & 29).*** To this day there is a right way and a wrong way of slaughtering an animal. Abattoirs have to follow strict rules. To add to the difficulty Moslems and Jews follow different rules. For Jews 'Kosher' meat comes from clean animals that have been killed properly so that the blood has been drained from the carcase. James was asking that Gentile believers show consideration for the religious scruples of the Jews.

[4] ***'Abstain from blood' (vv. 20 & 29).*** In our culture the nearest English equivalent of this is *'a black pudding'*. I am not sure if they are as popular now as they once were. In difficult economic times they were the rough equivalent of steak for the working man. On a Friday the butcher would have rows of them hanging up in his shop. The wives of working husbands would be at his shop not later than 12 o'clock, to be sure of some still being on sale. The prohibition James is introducing is against *'eating blood.'* The Bible forbids this (Leviticus 17:10).

Paul's Letters to the Churches were written anything up to 10 years after the Jerusalem Council. In them he takes a more liberal view of meat offered to idols

(1 Cor. 8:4-8 *'An idol is nothing at all in the world and there is no God but one; we are no worse if we do not eat and no better if we do'*). In his view, it is still meat. It hasn't changed in any way. It will still feed a hungry man!

We need to be scrupulously honest and admit that James's concerns appear to be more about preventing Jewish inhibitions being offended than about defending theological principles. Three of the four prohibitions were food laws and one was a moral law. Jews and Gentile believers must both avoid sexual immorality.

After this the Jerusalem Council was able to reach a unanimous conclusion that has, in fact, settled the matter of salvation and circumcision for all time.

Believing Jews and Gentiles are one body in Christ through faith alone in Christ alone. The Council resolved to convey its decisions to the churches by letter and by deputation visits.

THANK YOU, HEAVENLY FATHER:

For the events that were instrumental in gathering the churches together in one place where they convened as a Council of Churches, and transacted the business of heaven and human hearts in a spirit of utter dependence on the Holy Spirit.

For the spirit of respect and patient waiting on one another while aspects of the business were presented as clearly as possible and evidently accepted without carnal quibbling.

For *'the good and pleasant thing'* it is when brethren dwell together in unity;

IN JESUS' NAME, AMEN

39. Acts 15: 22-35

THE COUNCIL'S LETTER TO GENTILE BELIEVERS

[22]Then the apostles and elders, with the whole church, decided to choose some of their own men and send them to Antioch with Paul and Barnabas. They chose Judas (called Barsabbas) and Silas, two men who were leaders among the brothers. [23]With them they sent the following letter: Acts 15: 22-23

The apostles and elders, your brothers, To the Gentile believers in Antioch, Syria and Cilicia: Greetings.

Not only did James do a magnificent job as president of the Council; the behaviour of the speakers and council members was impeccable.

The letter that follows is a model of brevity, considering the weighty matters that were being explained to the churches:

[24]We have heard that some went out from us without our authorisation and disturbed you, troubling your minds by what they said.

[25]So we all agreed to choose some men and send them to you with our dear friends Barnabas and Paul–[26]men who have risked their lives for the name of our Lord Jesus Christ. [27] Therefore we are sending Judas and Silas to confirm by word of mouth what we are writing.

[28]It seemed good to the Holy Spirit and to us not to burden you with anything beyond the following requirements: [29]You are to abstain from food sacrificed to idols, from blood, from the meat of strangled animals and from sexual immorality. You will do well to avoid these things. Farewell. Acts 15: 24-29

In v. 24 the writer refers to the doctrinal crisis that had arisen in the churches, but he doesn't feel it necessary to make further comment about it.

In v. 25 the writer explains that the Council was unanimous in deciding to issue a letter to the churches and to send Barnabas and Paul, and also Judas and Silas, to deliver the letter and pay pastoral visits to the churches.

In v. 28 the Council notes that it was convinced that the Holy Spirit had guided its deliberations and therefore no new requirements were being laid on the churches.

James had made the Council aware that four matters that offended Jewish and Gentile relationships (especially among believers) could be dealt with at this time, and the attendant problems removed (v. 29). The four matters are named in vv 20 – 24.

These standards had been taught in the reading of the Old Testament scriptures in the synagogues every Sabbath. We get the impression that they were known among Gentiles as well as Jews.

How was the letter received in the churches?

> [30]*The men were sent off and went down to Antioch, where they gathered the church together and delivered the letter.* [31]*The people read it and were glad for its encouraging message.* Acts 15:30-31

Judas and Silas stayed for some time to minister to the believers at Antioch. Then they were sent back to Jerusalem with the hearty blessings of their friends in Antioch (Some MSS do not have v. 34).

> [35]*But Paul and Barnabas remained in Antioch, where they and many others taught and preached the word of the Lord.* Acts 15:35

THANK YOU, HEAVENLY FATHER:

For the remarkable gift of leadership that the Holy Spirit had given James, (the last of the Lord's brothers to come to faith in Him) fitting him to be among the early leaders in the infant church.

For the efficiency of the participants at the Jerusalem Council – a beautiful blend of the grace of God and good business practice;

For the blessing that followed the pastoral visits to the churches by the deputation that was appointed to this task; they appear to have been welcomed in the churches and the spirit of fellowship that was generated was mutually beneficial.

IN JESUS' NAME, AMEN

Acts 15:36-18:22

Paul' Second Missionary Journey

40. Acts 15: 36-41

DISCORD BETWEEN PAUL AND SILAS

[36]Some time later Paul said to Barnabas, "Let us go back and visit the brothers in all the towns where we preached the word of the Lord and see how they are doing."

[37]Barnabas wanted to take John, also called Mark, with them, [38]but Paul did not think it wise to take him, because he had deserted them in Pamphylia and had not continued with them in the work.

[39]They had such a sharp disagreement that they parted company. Barnabas took Mark and sailed for Cyprus, [40]but Paul chose Silas and left, commended by the brothers to the grace of the Lord. [41]He went through Syria and Cilicia, strengthening the churches. Acts 15:36-41

A question that crops up perennially in Christian circles is '*What happens when good men differ?*' There has to be more than one answer to the question, because it never pops up in quite the same circumstances. In every area of life you may care to mention good men differ.

The phrase *'Some time later' (v. 36)* possibly covers the period over winter. So with the coming of spring the missionaries could be on the road again, pursuing another missionary journey.

These two men were mature, with experience of life and work behind them, who had even worked together in evangelism and encouraging the churches, but now they have reached an impasse.

WHY?

It was very simple. Barnabas wanted to take John Mark with them (he and John were cousins). But Paul did not think it wise to take him, because he had deserted them in Pamphylia and had not continued with them in the work.

The suggestion had come from Paul (v. 36). *"Let us go back and visit the brothers in all the towns where we preached the word of the Lord and see how they are doing."* One sentence later they are at loggerheads. Barnabas wanted to take John Mark with them. Paul said 'No way!'

If Luke wasn't present (this isn't one of the 'we' passages) then either Barnabas, or Paul, or even John Mark told him about what happened.

1. <u>There is no hint about who was right and who was wrong</u>. That the team should have broken up on a matter like this was an unspeakably sad fact.
2. <u>There is 'an old chestnut' here</u>: When this kind of issue arises, which is the greater duty: to place the interest of the individual or the work first?
3. <u>We know that Paul and Barnabas became colleagues again</u> (1 Cor. 9:6 & Col. 4:10). But we ask: What toll did the years of estrangement take of the two men?
4. <u>We know that Paul, in time, had come to appreciate Mark and also to depend on him</u> to the extent that he asked for him to come and minister to him toward the end of his life. (2 Tim. 4:11; cf. Col. 4:10; Philemon 24). If this represents a change of mind and attitude on the part of Paul, he never gives any hint that this was the case.
5. <u>We might like to know what effect Paul's refusal to take John Mark along made on the young man.</u> Again there is not a shred of evidence.
6. <u>On the plus side</u>, I have to admit and be thankful for the fact that four missionaries went out instead of two.

I'm going to make two comments:
these are my personal thoughts.

A. I think that Barnabas (big-hearted Barnabas) wasn't a fighter. He was a man of peace. If Paul's mind was made up not to take John Mark, then Barnabas wasn't going to make a bad matter worse, and certainly not at the cost of a break in fellowship. However, that could not be avoided.

The contention was so sharp between them that they departed asunder one from the other (v. 39 KJV).

B. We know that Paul was an academic and a deep thinker. He could cocoon himself within a problem or a line of thought (at least for a short time) and forget about other people. Perhaps you know people like this.

I think that Paul was that kind of man who having arrived at a decision or a course of action, followed his instincts and went where his thoughts took him. I believe that Paul made his decision about Mark like that, went on about his business, and thought no more about it.

In other words he didn't spend the rest of his life holding a private post-mortem on the decision every time it crossed his mind. I don't think it crossed his mind very often, if ever again.

I would like to say to Paul: 'You can do that for so many years and nobody may ever notice or object. But you may find yourself doing a lot of apologising in your later years for heartbreak and pain you caused others in your youth.'

Barnabas took Mark and sailed for Cyprus, [40]but Paul chose Silas and left, commended by the brothers to the grace of the Lord. [41] He went through Syria and Cilicia, strengthening the churches.

THANK YOU, HEAVENLY FATHER:

For Your infinite patience with us when we push ahead (rightly or wrongly) forgetting that other people are affected by our decisions;

For our colleagues in Your service; help us to respect them, pray and think along with them, not thinking more of ourselves that we ought to think;

For younger believers who are within our circle of friends and acquaintances, who look up to us, even imitate us, that we be *'ourselves'* when with them, never pretending to be what we know we are not;

For the harvest You give us from time to time in Your service and for the divine promise that in due time we shall reap if we faint not.

IN JESUS' NAME, AMEN

41. Acts 16:1-5

TIMOTHY JOINS PAUL AND SILAS

[1]He came to Derbe and then to Lystra, where a disciple named Timothy lived, whose mother was a Jewess and a believer, but whose father was a Greek. [2]The brothers at Lystra and Iconium spoke well of him. [3]Paul wanted to take him along on the journey, so he circumcised him because of the Jews who lived in that area, for they all knew that his father was a Greek.

[4]As they travelled from town to town, they delivered the decisions reached by the apostles and elders in Jerusalem for the people to obey. [5]So the churches were strengthened in the faith and grew daily in numbers. Acts 16: 1-5

Here is Paul – and another young disciple. This time it is Timothy, to whom Paul refers as 'my son in the faith' (1 Tim. 1:2). We rejoice with Paul that he was used by God in the conversion of Timothy.

Paul knew the family well because in 2 Timothy 1 he refers to Timothy's grandmother Lois and his mother Eunice as women of faith. We cannot find any clue about Timothy's age at conversion, except that from a very young age we know that he saw Christianity lived at home. His hometown was Lystra, his mother Lois was a Jewess and a believer, his father was a Greek. We do not know if his father was a believer, or if he was still alive at this time.

Timothy was known to the believers in Lystra and in Iconium and he had a good reputation among them. *'They spoke well of him' (v. 2)*. That is a striking testimony for a young believer to have. It was an early indication that there might be a place for him in the Lord's service in God's good time.

This impressed Paul very much on this visit to Lystra to the extent that he wanted to take him along on the journey (v. 3). There is something in v. 3 that non-Jewish minds may wonder about.

> [3]*Paul wanted to take him along on the journey, so he circumcised him because of the Jews who lived in that area, for they all knew that his father was a Greek.* Acts 16:3

If circumcision was not essential to salvation (as the Jerusalem Council had pronounced in Acts 15) why then did Paul circumcise Timothy because of all the Jews who lived in that area?

Paul is thinking of Timothy's usefulness on the missionary team. He would not be a passenger on the team, but a worker, perhaps in Mark's place, just as Silas had taken Barnabas' place. Timothy's Jewish-Greek parentage would open doors to him in both communities.

The question in Paul's mind was: **To what extent can Timothy be considered a Jew?** He had been brought up in the Scriptures as if his home was a Jewish home, brought up by his mother in the Jewish faith, but he had never been circumcised. The reason for Paul's action was because '*of the Jews who lived in the area, for they all knew that his father was a Greek.*'

Fine for Paul, but Timothy had to submit to this painful ritual (baby boys were usually circumcised when they were eight days old e.g. Jesus: Luke 2:21; and Saul: Phil 3:5).

In Paul's view there was no way that Timothy could present the gospel to Jews, talk his way around the matter of circumcision, and get away with it.

Timothy was acceptable to God by faith alone in Christ alone without circumcision, but he was not acceptable to Jews because he had not been circumcised.

If we refer to 1 Timothy 4:14 and 2 Timothy 1:6 we learn that Paul and the Elders in Lystra 'ordained' Timothy to the gospel ministry by laying their hands on him which underscores the fact that they agreed with Paul about Timothy's fitness to be an evangelist among Jews.

For the sake of completeness please refer to various scriptures that underscore the giftedness of Timothy e.g. 1 Timothy 4:14-16; 2 Timothy 2:15; and Philippians 2:19-23. The last reference in this list really glows with the level of appreciation that Paul has for Timothy. *'I have no one else like him, who takes a genuine interest in your welfare. For everyone looks out for their own interests, not those of Jesus Christ.'*

Whatever we may feel or think about Paul's logic at this distance in time, I think we have to suspend judgement, and rather anticipate meeting this young, warm-hearted, genuine and sincere pastor of the church of Jesus Christ.

THANK YOU, HEAVENLY FATHER:

For the significant roles that Timothy's mother and grandmother had in his Christian upbringing, which in Your economy, was a major part of his preparation for the Lord's work;

For the input of Paul and Silas, and the approval of the elders at Lystra, when it appeared to all that Timothy was ready to be commended to the work;

For the incalculable influence of godly parents in our lives; they were people of their time, but they had a wisdom that was not of this world. Even in the matter of teaching us good manners, how to behave ourselves in church and how to respect elderly people they were preparing us for pastoral ministry. We give you our heartfelt thanks.

IN JESUS' NAME, AMEN

42. Acts 16:6-10

PAUL' VISION OF THE MAN OF MACEDONIA

> [6]*Paul and his companions travelled throughout the region of Phrygia and Galatia, having been kept by the Holy Spirit from preaching the word in the province of Asia.*
>
> [7]*When they came to the border of Mysia, they tried to enter Bithynia, but the Spirit of Jesus would not allow them to.* [8]*So they passed by Mysia and went down to Troas.* Acts 16:6-8

We get an impression of how the minds of Paul and Silas were working. They had it in mind to focus on the province of Asia, but it became clear, probably by a process of elimination, that this was not God's will at that time. They had made it as far as Troas, a seaport in northwest Asia Minor.

Being sensible men they were wise enough to pause so that the Lord could clarify his will to them. Things would look different in the morning. This was the case. They passed Mysia and went down to Troas (v. 8).

> [9] *During the night Paul had a dream in which God gave him a vision in which he saw a man of Macedonia standing and begging him.* ***"Come over into Macedonia and help us.***
>
> [10] *After Paul had seen the vision, we got ready at once to leave Macedonia, concluding that God had called us to preach the gospel to them.* Acts 16:9-10

Pardon me for asking, but I am a little bit puzzled. Did the spirit of prayer unite the men or were they not in the habit of disagreeing with Paul? There wasn't much 'dialog-ing' (if I may invent a word) so far as I can see.

Setting out from Troas the mainland of Macedonia lay straight ahead on the opposite shore. After passing the small island of Samothrace, Philippi lay west by north. Samothrace was roughly the halfway point.

Macedonia was an early name for Greece. From the later years of the 5th century BC the land of Macedonia came under strong Greek influence. Vv. 10 -12 report that after several days at sea they landed at Neapolis and travelled to Philippi, a Roman colony and the leading city of that district of Macedonia.

This would be a convenient point at which to obtain a good Bible dictionary with maps and look up Paul's Missionary Journeys – the maps all cover the greater Mediterranean area and surrounding territories. (You will reap the benefits of such a book for the rest of your life. It will be an excellent investment of money and time. Buy the best you can afford.)

First, please notice that the Aegean Sea lies between Macedonia in the West and Troas in Asia Minor in the East. The significance of making this journey from Troas to Philippi was to cross from the continent of Asia to the continent of Europe!

I hope that readers who are of European extraction will rejoice with me before God for this great advance of the gospel from Asia to Europe. Greater things were to follow the initiative of Paul and Silas in bringing the gospel to Europe. Centuries later the Protestant Reformation would be cradled in the continent of Europe and its influence would go out across the world.

Please note also that Luke wrote about *'them'* in vv. 1-5 and since v. 6 has been writing about *'we'*. Apparently he had rejoined then at Troas (v. 10). There are four of these so called 'we sections' in this book. They are found in 16:10-17; 20:5-15; 21:1-18; & 27:1-28:16. I imagine that the minds of all three were now focused on the future and what God was going to do. I am sure that none of them would allow minor matters or personal feelings to interfere with that prospect.

Before we move to another section perhaps it may help someone to point out how Paul's guidance came to him.

God had given him a restless passion. Think about the numerous efforts that Paul (and Silas) had made to discover what direction they should go next. They were committed men for whom serving the Lord was a privilege and a priority. Discovering and doing His will were paramount. They only had peace when they knew they were doing God's will.

God had given him a strong physique. Paul was a small man they tell us, perhaps slightly deformed. Nevertheless, he seems to have been a man of iron, who could endure what others would have found impossible. Recall his being stoned and left for dead at Iconium (14:19-20). Friends cared for him, and after a night's rest he got up and went back into the city. Your health will be a factor of guidance in the light of where the Lord may want you to serve him.

God had given him good partners. John Mark wouldn't have stood a chance had he still been with them. Rough travelling and continual physical challenges were not for him. (I hope I am not thinking of him unkindly). When we imagine the three men in the boat on the journey to Philippi, men of faith and fortitude, men of character and commitment we can only look forward to what God is going to do in them and through them on this, Paul's Second Missionary Journey.

'How will I know God's will?' is a question that is frequently asked. A layman's answer is 'When all the lights are at green'. Most folks asking the question have a number of factors in their minds; currently some lights are red, some are amber, some are green.

Red means 'wait', amber means 'not yet but get ready' and green means 'go.'

THANK YOU, HEAVENLY FATHER;

For the way Your Spirit selects and assembles a team of men for the fulfilling of Your will in any particular purpose or period of time; we remember that not many were wise by human standards; not many were influential, not many of noble birth were called; You chose the weak things of the world to shame the strong;

For the multitude of ways in which you communicate Your will and with it the conviction that 'the Lord has spoken'; 'This is the way, walk in it.'

For the unfolding of history whereby nations and men become Your instruments to change the face of the world map, setting nations up, bringing nations down, and all the while extending and establishing the kingdom of heaven among men;

For the cameo of the kingdom that Paul and Silas and Luke exhibited to an ungodly world; to Your name be the glory, now and forever.

IN JESUS' NAME, AMEN

43. Acts 16:11-15

LYDIA'S CONVERSION AT PHILIPPI

[11]From Troas we put out to sea and sailed straight for Samothrace, and the next day on to Neapolis.

[12]From there we travelled to Philippi, a Roman colony and the leading city of that district of Macedonia. And we stayed there several days.

[13]On the Sabbath we went outside the city gate to the river, where we expected to find a place of prayer. We sat down and began to speak to the women who had gathered there.

[14]One of those listening was a woman named Lydia, a dealer in purple cloth from the city of Thyatira, who was a worshipper of God. The Lord opened her heart to respond to Paul's message.

[15]When she and the members of her household were baptised, she invited us to her home. "If you consider me a believer in the Lord," she said, "come and stay at my house." And she persuaded us. Acts 16: 11-15

Luke is still travelling with them; did you notice his use of the word 'we'? As I read through the block of five verses I rejoiced again at Luke's gift of story-telling. Every word is a working word. They landed at Neapolis, the seaport of Philippi. Their 150 mile journey had lasted two days. He builds fact upon fact like a bricklayer building a wall.

There is a strong possibility that there was no synagogue in Philippi, because the only religious meeting that our friends could find was totally comprised of women. A quorum of ten men was necessary before a synagogue could be constituted. Paul and his friends went along to the women's prayer meeting. It had convened outside the city gate, by the river. This was where they found the meeting, sat down and began to speak to the women who had gathered there.

Did you notice Luke's storytelling gift? First he began with the city, then he selected the women's prayer meeting, then the three men joined the group and got talking to the women. The story opens like the heart of a flower to the sun.

Next Luke focussed on Lydia. He had discovered her name. It was Lydia. He had discovered her occupation She was a seller of purple cloth. It is probable that she held a franchise in Philippi for a cloth manufacturer in Thyatira.

Luke discovered that she had become a worshipper of God, believing and behaving like a Jew without having become one. Luke was a keen observer of people, and so he noticed something else about Lydia: *'The Lord opened her heart to respond to Paul's message.'* Once that point was reached Luke's pen must have streaked across his papyrus. If he had never learned shorthand in his youth, I am sure he sorely wished that he had.

> [15]*When she and the members of her household were baptised, she invited us to her home. "If you consider me a believer in the Lord," she said, "come and stay at my house." And she persuaded us.* Acts 16:15

Let's complete this study by taking a step back, and by asking a question. Why was Lydia found at the prayer meeting?

Luke says ***'She worshipped God.' (v.14).***

> There was a deep awareness of the living God in her mind and heart and a great desire to know Him.

Luke says: ***'The Lord opened her heart to heed the things spoken by Paul' (v.14).***

> I leave you to imagine the feelings of this woman on hearing for the first time how she could know the living God through

His Son, Jesus Christ. Imagine her hearing about how her sinful heart could be cleansed, that her sins could be forgiven and she could become a child of God through repentance and faith in Jesus Christ.

<u>Luke says</u>: *'She and her household were baptised'* (v.15)

This means that Paul not only preached and explained the gospel, but spoke to her about immediately confessing Christ by being baptised in obedience to Christ's command. Lydia obeyed without hesitation.

The household would likely have included her servants and perhaps other mature members of her family. Whether it included children is a point that can neither be proved nor disproved from this text.

<u>Luke says</u>: *'She invited us to her home, saying, 'If you have judged me faithful to the Lord, come to my house and stay.' And she constrained us' (persuaded us).* (v.15)

Can't you see this woman's face and hear the excitement in her voice? Can't you see her eager obedience to Christ's commandment to be baptised? Can't you hear the sincerity of her welcome to Paul and Silas? She is full of the joy of salvation.

She has gone further in one day than many modern Christians have gone in a lifetime of Christian profession–because of her simple faith and hearty obedience to Christ.

Many modern believers have a lot of catching up to do if they are ever to know the joy that this woman found in believing.

THANK YOU, HEAVENLY FATHER;

For all the circumstances You had to bring under control to have all these people in Philippi on that particular week-end;

For Paul, who did the preaching; for Luke who filled the role of reporter; for Lydia who provided the hospitality and for Silas providing support in whatever ways his help was needed.

For the fact that Jesus alone has the words of eternal life;

IN JESUS' NAME, AMEN

44. Acts 16:16-40

PAUL AND SILAS IN PRISON

> [16]*Once when we were going to the place of prayer, we were met by a slave girl who had a spirit by which she predicted the future. She earned a great deal of money for her owners by fortune-telling*. Acts 16:16

The scenario of vv. 16-40 is the imprisonment of Paul and Silas (and perhaps Timothy and Luke) in Philippi. Within that narrative there are two others: the deliverance of the slave girl and the conversion of the Philippian jailer; two powerful stories of the grace of God.

The Slave Girl.

The phrase 'a slave girl' accurately describes her circumstances. She had an evil spirit by which she foretold the future. But her life, such as it was, was not her own nor had it been for as long as she was controlled by the demon. Her two masters, whose names we do not know nor need to know were exploiting her demon possession and were making lots of money by parading her round from place to place as some kind of novelty.

Significantly, when she met Paul and the others she recognised them instantly and identified them without hesitation or fear.

The Visiting Preachers

> [16]*This girl followed Paul and the rest of us, shouting,* [17]*'These men are the servants of the most high God, who are telling you the way to be saved'.* [18]*She kept this up for many days. Finally Paul became so troubled that he turned round and said to the spirit, "In the name of Jesus Christ I command you to come out of her!" At that moment the spirit left her.* Acts 16:16-18

A single command spoken in the name of Jesus Christ was sufficient to deliver her from demon possession and give her life back to her again.

The owners of the slave girl.

> [19]*When the owners of the slave girl realised that their hope of making money was gone, they seized Paul and Silas and dragged them into the market-place to face the authorities.* Acts 16:19

The authorities in Philippi

> [20]*They brought them before the magistrates and said, "These men are Jews, and are throwing our city into an uproar* [21]*by advocating customs unlawful for us Romans to accept or practise."* Acts 16:20-21

The ruling of the Magistrates

> [22]*The crowd joined in the attack against Paul and Silas, and the magistrates ordered them to be stripped and beaten.* [23]*After they had been severely flogged, they were thrown into prison, and the jailer was commanded to guard them carefully.* [24]*Upon receiving such orders, he put them in the inner cell and fastened their feet in the stocks.* Acts 16:22-24

This was shocking treatment altogether, most of it uncalled for in relation to the alleged crime. The issue over which the citizens were rioting had nothing to do with the processes of common Law, rather two 'circus managers' had lost their income since their slave was set free by Jesus Christ.

So much for Roman Law.

We had occasion to draw attention to it previously when meditating on the way the Roman soldiers treated Jesus, mocking and torturing him (Luke 22: From his arrest to his crucifixion). We had occasion to remark on it when the apostles were first arrested and punished by the Jewish Council (Acts 4 & 5 esp. 5:41-42). The word 'brutal' comes to mind and seems rather tame to describe the cruelty of the soldiers' behaviour.

In the Prison at Midnight.

> [25]*About midnight Paul and Silas were praying and singing hymns to God, and the other prisoners were listening to them.* [26]*Suddenly there was such a violent earthquake that the foundations of the prison were shaken. At once all the prison doors flew open, and everybody's chains came loose.* Acts 16: 25-26

Late on the previous day God had seemed invisible, if not absent altogether. The visitors were praying and singing hymns to God. The other prisoners were listening to them (unless any of them were deaf!). This clause is one of Luke's details in recording this most unusual scene. I told you, Luke misses nothing! What was unusual about it? One of my American pastor friends would use three simple words: **'God showed up!'**

> [26]*Suddenly there was such a violent earthquake that the foundations of the prison were shaken. At once all the prison doors flew open, and everybody's chains came loose.*

> [27]*The jailer woke up, and when he saw the prison doors open, he drew his sword and was about to kill himself because he thought the prisoners had escaped.* [28] *But Paul shouted, "Don't harm yourself! We are all here!"* Acts 16:26-28

So far as the jailer was concerned the prison was falling down. The prisoners' chains were loosed. The jailer realised that he would be better off dead than alive when morning would come, and he would be asked to account for the escape of the prisoners and pay for his neglect of duty with his life. Thankfully, in the mêlée, the jailer heard Paul's shout, somewhere somebody found a light and so the poor man, at his wit's end, fell down before Paul and Silas, asked, ***'Sirs, what must I do to be saved? (v. 30)'***

The Message that the Jailer and his extended family believed:

> [31]*So they said, "Believe on the Lord Jesus Christ, and you will be saved, you and your household."* [32]*Then they spoke the word of the Lord to him and to all who were in his house.* [33]*And he took them the same hour of the night and washed their stripes. And immediately he and all his family were baptized.* [34]*Now when he had brought them into his house, he set food before them; and he rejoiced, having believed in God with all his household.* Acts 16:31-34

The Release of the Preachers:

> [35]*And when it was day, the magistrates sent the officers, saying, "Let those men go."* [36]*So the keeper of the prison reported these words to Paul, saying, "The magistrates have sent to let you go. Now therefore depart, and go in peace."* [37]*But Paul said to them, "They have beaten us openly, uncondemned Romans, and have thrown us into prison. And now do they put us out secretly? No indeed! Let them come themselves and get us out."* Acts 16: 35-37

Why couldn't Paul have buttoned his lip for once in his life? Why couldn't he have gone quietly? Actually there were sound reasons for Paul's stubbornness:

The prisoners were Roman citizens; they had not broken any part of Roman law. They had been flogged (severely beaten) as if they were not Roman citizens, which was contrary to Roman law. The magistrates had made a spectacle of them yesterday. The magistrates thought they could get them out of town quietly today. The prisoners were not going to go quietly. 'Let the magistrates on whose orders we were mistreated yesterday, come down and let us out themselves.'

The magistrates in their robes came down to the prison, spoke respectfully to the prisoners and simply and quietly requested them to leave the city.

Paul behaved as he did because he knew that if Roman law could be broken and citizens of Rome be maltreated once, and the wrong be allowed to go unchallenged, it could happen again. So Paul was thinking ahead. He was thinking of other Christians who might find themselves in the same position.

At least in Philippi, the statute book would show that Roman citizens were never to be maltreated again within that jurisdiction.

What happened next?

We thank God for Lydia, this recently converted Christian woman, who had the gift of hospitality, and was unstinting in using it!

> *After Paul and Silas came out of the prison, they went to Lydia's house, where they met with the brothers and encouraged them. Then they left.* Acts 16:40

THANK YOU, HEAVENLY FATHER:

For the courage of Paul and his companions when under pressure;

For the deliverance of this young woman who for too long, had lived in bondage to the devil;

For Paul's believing and authoritative use of the name of Jesus Christ to rebuke the demon that was controlling the young woman;

For the Holy Spirit (silently and unobserved) restraining an angry crowd who had been incited to riot;

For the Christian evangelists suffering from a severe beating, praying and singing hymns to God at midnight, to Your glory and as a witness to the other prisoners;

For the Holy Spirit restraining the prisoners from escaping, preserving the jailer's life from sentence to death following a court martial, and for the salvation of all his extended family;

For the gospel testimony of the jailer and his family, in professing their faith in Jesus Christ through baptism, and providing a meal for Paul and his friends;

IN JESUS' NAME, AMEN

45. Acts 17:1-9
IN THESSALONICA

[1]Now when they had passed through Amphipolis and Apollonia, they came to Thessalonica, where there was a synagogue of the Jews.

In reading the place names in this section please remember that we are still in Greece. From Philippi take the road south, visiting the coastal towns as you go and you will come to Thessalonica. Actually you will have walked 100 miles. Paul made the local synagogue his first stop. He preached there for three Sabbath days.

His message was of first importance:

[2]Then Paul, as his custom was, went in to them, and for three Sabbaths reasoned with them from the Scriptures, [3]explaining and demonstrating that the Christ had to suffer and rise again from the dead, and saying, "This Jesus whom I preach to you is the Christ." Acts 17:2-3

The method in Paul's Preaching.

A few chapters ago when Paul was in Lystra, he found himself in a totally pagan city. In fact the priest of the local religion mistook Paul and Silas as two of the gods, Zeus and Hermes, who had become incarnate. It was only with the utmost difficulty that the priest and some of his fellow-idolaters were prevented from worshipping Paul and Silas. Paul didn't even open a Biblical scroll there, nor did he quote the Scriptures – because either method would have made no sense to the listeners. There was little or no knowledge of the gospel there. In the end local Gentile unbelievers, incited by Jews from Antioch and Iconium, stoned Paul and dragged him out of the city leaving him for dead.

Thessalonica had a synagogue where Paul was invited to preach for three Sabbaths. What was his preaching method here? The answer is in v. 2.

> *For three Sabbaths (he) reasoned with them from the Scriptures, [3]explaining and demonstrating that the Christ had to suffer and rise again from the dead, and saying, "This Jesus whom I preach to you is the Christ."* Acts 17:3

I believe that Paul was right to vary his preaching methods, not for the sake of variety but for the sake of clarity, in other words clear communication. In Athens Paul didn't quote Scripture, but he preached Christ just the same.

We have to admit that he preached Christ, whether he was quoting directly from the Scriptures or not. In other words his message was moulded by the Scriptures on every occasion.

The fruit of Paul's Preaching:

If this was his first visit to Thessalonica his reputation must have preceded him. So far as we know, it was Paul and his band of helpers who had brought the gospel to this busy city and seaport. Luke is eager to give us some good news because he writes:

> *[4]And some of them were persuaded; and a great multitude of the devout Greeks, and not a few of the leading women, joined Paul and Silas.* Acts 17:4

I love Luke's choice of words: e.g. 'persuaded, 'a great multitude of the devout Greeks and not a few of the leading women joined Paul and Silas.' The reason for spending three weeks preaching in the synagogue was that Paul had adopted the policy of preaching to the Jews first, as in Pisidian Antioch (13:44-52). When Jews believed Paul thanked God, but where they rejected the gospel then Paul turned to the Gentiles.

Opposition to Paul's Preaching.

To arrive at a right impression we must note that there was active opposition to Paul and his message.

> [5]*But the Jews were jealous; so they rounded up some bad characters from the market-place, formed a mob and started a riot in the city. They rushed to Jason's house in search of Paul and Silas in order to bring them out to the crowd.* Acts 17:5

We learn here that you cannot trust a riotous crowd to be concerned about the truth: it was not truth but lies that fuelled their fury against the preachers. Nor does a riotous crowd have any respect for private property or the safety of the occupants, and even less for a person's character. They rushed to Jason's house in an attempt to lay hands on the preachers. When they couldn't find the preachers they seized Jason and some other believers and brought them before the city officials. A riotous crowd has scant respect for Christian profession: Jason and his friends were well-known local believers. The crowd blamed Jason for welcoming the preachers in the first place, and for the message they preached. The crowd exaggerated the facts of the message being preached:

> [7]*"They are all defying Caesar's decrees, saying that there is another king, one called Jesus."* [8]*When they heard this, the crowd and the city officials were thrown into turmoil.* [9]*Then they put Jason and the others on bail and let them go.* Acts 17:7-9

Despite all the evidence on the plus side, the lying about Paul's preaching continued. Jesus didn't preach against Caesar; He preached about the kingdom of God. He had not come to preach political revolution, but rather to preach the crown-rights of Jesus Christ, who is Lord of All.

We cannot really be sure why the crowd stopped their rioting and trouble making at this point. It seems that their failure to find the 'troublemakers' who had come to the city, rendered further protest futile. The city officials hardly knew what to do, but they flexed their political muscles and had Jason and his friends bound over in a sum of money to keep the peace. This meant that various parties to this bail had to meet certain conditions: Jason and his companions probably had to undertake that Paul and Silas would leave town and not return, with severe penalties if the agreement were broken. If that happened then Jason and others who had raised the bail money would forfeit the lot.

A visit that began with three Sabbaths' fruitful preaching in the synagogue, that resulted in numerous conversions (vv. 2-4), ended some time later with the visiting evangelists being legally banned from returning there again, with a valued brother in the Lord standing bail as a guarantee that the agreement would be kept (v. 9).

THANK YOU, HEAVENLY FATHER:

For the truth that it is *'in You that we live and move and have our being.'* We are safely kept by Your almighty hand;

For the knowledge that when our enemies *'accuse us and say all manner of things against us falsely for Jesus' sake'* You know the whole truth about us;

For the indefatigable zeal and courage of Paul and his companions in the work of evangelism;

IN JESUS' NAME, AMEN

46. Acts 17:10-15

IN BEREA

[10]As soon as it was night, the brothers sent Paul and Silas away to Berea. On arriving there, they went to the Jewish synagogue. Acts 17:10

This town had a synagogue which had a different way of doing things. I think you might have felt a freshness in the air as soon as you entered through the door. This was the first point of contact for Paul and Silas when they had to find a safe haven from the persecuting Jews at Thessalonica. This wasn't a run-of-the-mill synagogue. In fact it was significantly different.

[11]Now the Bereans were of more noble character than the Thessalonians, for they received the message with great eagerness and examined the Scriptures every day to see if what Paul said was true. Acts 17:11

I wonder how some of our sleepy congregations would cope with this practice if it were introduced in our services. One would hope that it would result in a spirit of wakefulness and thoughtfulness. Here is something we didn't expect to happen: it proved to be a very effective form of evangelism.

[12]Many of the Jews believed, as did also a number of prominent Greek women and many Greek men. Acts 17:12

If only the Jews in Thessalonica could have minded their own business: but no, they wouldn't allow the Berean Jews that liberty. If only they had listened as carefully when Paul was with them, the rest of the chapter might have read differently. Here is the latest news flash from Thessalonica:

> [13]*When the Jews in Thessalonica learned that Paul was preaching the word of God at Berea, they went there too, agitating the crowds and stirring them up*. Acts 17:13

The Berean Jews were concerned for the safety of Paul and Silas and Timothy. They immediately sent Paul to the coast, but Silas and Timothy remained at Berea.

> [14]*The brothers immediately sent Paul to the coast, but Silas and Timothy stayed at Berea.* [15]*The men who escorted Paul brought him to Athens and then left with instructions for Silas and Timothy to join him as soon as possible*. Acts 17: 14-15

In this way the three friends were preserved from harm and were united again in Athens.

THANK YOU, HEAVENLY FATHER:

For the ministry of Your Holy Spirit who teaches us to be as wise as serpents and harmless as doves when other oppose us;

For the individual leader, or family in the Berean synagogue whose influence had trained the others to search the Scriptures daily for themselves;

For the fresh thinking in the synagogue at Berea, and the high quality of spiritual life to be found there.

For the love that Paul was shown by the Berean Jews when Jews from Thessalonica came to oppose and even abuse him; Thank You also for your good hand overseeing the escape arrangements they made. Thank You for his safe journey to Athens;

IN JESUS' NAME, AMEN

47. Acts 17:16-34

IN ATHENS

Anyone who knows even a little bit about Greece is also likely to know that Athens was a beautiful city. It was built on Mount Acropolis to honour its patron goddess Athene.

It was in Athens around 500BC that the world's first experiment in direct democracy developed as a method of government. Centuries later Sir Winston Churchill, Britain's Wartime leader, is reported to have answered those who criticised democracy by saying, 'Democracy is the worst form of human government, until you have tried the others.'

It can be irritating at times to hear people bragging about being democrats, that they live under a democratic government and so on. They are not quite correct, because their statement hides a misunderstanding. The popular concept in people's minds is really 'direct' democracy. There is no such thing. The early Greek experiment had to be modified. Nowadays the word 'democracy' means 'government by the people'. Is this the case? Most Western nations are parliamentary democracies, which is a very different thing. In other words, the citizens elect members of parliament to serve for a period of years, so that they can rule on our behalf. They think of themselves and we speak of them as the representatives of the people. Do they always deliver what they promise at election-time, and do they always do what we would like them to do at all other times? Whatever your opinion, when you think of democracy, think of Greece.

Back to Athens: this vast city had buildings and monuments that were unrivalled anywhere in the world. Athens was literally a forest of idols and monuments. There were more gods in Athens that in the rest of the country. There were innumerable temples, shrines, statues and altars. A Roman satirist said that *'it was easier to find a god there than a man.'* Paul noticed as he made his way into the city that they even had an altar 'To the Unknown God.' This altar was a kind of eternal insurance policy in case there was an important 'god' whom they did not know really existed and therefore had ignored. The Greeks decided to honour him anyway.

Paul's first impression of the city made him sad

> [16]*While Paul was waiting for them in Athens, he was greatly distressed to see that the city was full of idols*. Acts 17:16

Paul was a man whose Bible and whose conscience said that Jesus Christ is Lord. What other emotion will a man feel who has surrendered himself and all his powers to serve the Son of God and sees a city given to idolatry? A similar question is: Why did Jesus weep so sorely over a city like Jerusalem?

At this point Paul hadn't begun to preach in the city. He was on a private reconnaissance walk around it. He didn't have to be quiet for long because he soon found the local synagogue. As it turned out he had plenty of preaching opportunities in the synagogue and also in the local market-place every day.

> [17]*So he reasoned in the synagogue with the Jews and the God-fearing Greeks, as well as in the market-place day by day with those who happened to be there*. Acts 17:17

If there were believers in Jesus who belonged to the synagogue, we would expect that he received a welcome from them. If there were no believers there then Paul would have been glad to meet unbelieving Jews to whom he would teach the gospel of Christ. As always his message was *the good news about Jesus and the resurrection (v. 18b)*

A new experience was waiting for Paul and his friends

> [18]*A group of Epicurean and Stoic philosophers began to dispute with him. Some of them asked, "What is this babbler trying to say?" Others remarked, "He seems to be advocating foreign gods." They said this because Paul was preaching the good news about Jesus and the resurrection.* Acts 17:18

These Epicurean and Stoic philosophers were the representatives of university life in Athens. The city had a reputation for having the most important university in the ancient world. We presume that Paul was shown proper courtesy as he and the group he had just met made their way to a meeting of the Areopagus. Who or what was the Areopagus?

The Areopagus was a hill in Athens which was dedicated to the honour of the god Ares or Mars. Areopagus was also the name of the Council that met on Mars' Hill, a court dating back to legendary times. Therefore Paul was brought here to be examined regarding his teaching. The result is that in 2014 the Areopagus is still remembered as the place where Paul preached, but many people in today's world would not even know as much as that about it. Christianity lives on, but the strength of these two philosophies that challenged Paul is scant today. So far as we know Christianity had not had such a sophisticated hearing up to this point.

> [19]*Then they took him and brought him to a meeting of the Areopagus, where they said to him,* ***"May we know what this new teaching is that you are presenting? [20] You are bringing some strange ideas to our ears, and we want to know what they mean."*** [21]*(All the Athenians and the foreigners who lived there spent their time doing nothing but talking about and listening to the latest ideas.)* Acts 17:19-21

I have to say that Paul has been criticised most unfairly for the sermon he delivered to the Areopagus. Critics say that he didn't read a verse of Scripture, that he didn't preach the cross. Just for a moment look back at v. 18 which specifically says that '*Paul was preaching the good news about Jesus and the resurrection'*. Before we are finished this study we shall be surprised at how much gospel he packed into his sermon. And there is also a thrilling final verse still to come.

Paul's Sermon on Mars' Hill (vv. 22 – 34)

Paul's opening sentence was masterly. In a couple of dozen words he had gone right to the heart of the Athenian way of life and begun to dissect it. We are sure that the Holy Spirit had ignited Paul's mind and given him the words to speak.

> [22]*Paul then stood up in the meeting of the Areopagus and said: "Men of Athens! I see that in every way you are very religious.* [23]*For as I walked around and looked carefully at your objects of worship, I even found an altar with this inscription: TO AN UNKNOWN GOD. Now what you worship as something unknown I am going to proclaim to you.* Acts 17:22-23

Here is an alert evangelist. He had been using his eyes as he entered the city and found the illustration he would use if he ever got the opportunity to preach here: *"Men of Athens! I see that in every way you are very religious."*

Not only had all the temples and statuary caught his attention, he had even found a quotable quote on one of the altars. He would use it too.

Paul is preaching with divine enabling. 'I know you have many gods,' he is saying, 'and you are even fearful of leaving one out because you haven't yet heard who he is. It is about him that I want to speak.'

'Now what you worship as something unknown
I am going to proclaim to you.'

I imagine that Paul, with that last sentence had gained the attention of everyone within the sound of his voice in the Areopagus that day.

WHO IS THE UNKNOWN GOD?

[24] "The God who made the world and everything in it is the Lord of heaven and earth and does not live in temples built by hands.

We are mistaken when we think of God as being like us (v. 24).

He is the creator of the universe. By contrast we are his creatures, he made us.

[25]*And he is not served by human hands, as if he needed anything, because he himself gives all men life and breath and everything else*. Acts 17:25

The God who made the world and everything in it is the Lord of heaven and earth, and is totally independent of us, his creatures (v. 25).

We do not sustain God; he sustains us and gives us everything that we need for our daily lives.

He is not served by human hands because he himself gives all men life and breath and everything else (v. 25).

God is not made richer because we erect statues and monuments, and other memorials to the dead. These things mean nothing to him.

God is the sovereign ruler of all nations.

From one man He made every nation of men that they should inhabit the whole earth; and He determined the times set for them and the exact places where they should live (V. 26). Why are ethnic groups scattered around the world as they are today? Genesis 11:8 – 9 is a good place to begin searching for the answer.

Paul is answering the Epicureans at this point in his message because they believed that the gods were so far distant and remote as to take No interest in, or have influence on human affairs (v. 27). So Paul affirms: **For in him we live and move and have our being** (v. 28).

There were very clever men listening to Paul who didn't believe any part of what he had shared so far. In fact Paul was to some extent ahead of his hearers because in v. 28 he clinched the first part of that verse with a quotation from one of their own poets who said in relation to God, *'We are his offspring.'*

(Attributed to Epimenides of Cnossos in Crete).

> [29]*"Therefore since we are God's offspring, we should not think that the divine being is like gold or silver or stone—an image made by man's design and skill.* Acts 17:29

If what I am teaching you about the Unknown God is the truth, what then is the meaning of all the idols and shrines in this great city?

Your best artists and sculptors have been mistaken down the centuries of this city's history and have made images of the Unknown God which are contrary to what God has revealed about himself.

You might ask:

'Why hasn't God done something about our blasphemy?'

Well you might ask – because there is an answer.

> [30]*In the past God overlooked such ignorance, but now he commands all people everywhere to repent.* Acts 17:30

And how and where will He call mankind to judgement?

Listen carefully:

> [31]*For he has set a day when he will judge the world with justice by the man he has appointed. He has given proof of this to all men by raising him from the dead."* Acts 17:31

This was as far as Paul got in his message: he had still had more to tell the Athenians about God's appointed judge of mankind; he had still to explain to them the reasons for the incarnation, life and death of God's Son; and of course the good news of his triumphant resurrection.

I wonder if there was a strong Jewish representation in the crowd at the Areopagus that day. There was a strong negative reaction from the audience when Paul mentioned resurrection. Was it the Jews who were sneering? A sneer could be heard rattling its way from many throats around the arena. But others said: **'We want to hear you again on this subject.'**

Please do not miss the closing verse of this very moving report written by Luke:

> ***33 At that, Paul left the Council. 34 A few men became followers of Paul and believed. Among them was Dionysius, a member of the Areopagus, also a woman named Damaris, and a number of others.***

Paul the preacher had concentrated on sowing the seeds of truth, and God the Holy Spirit was responsible for the fruit that followed.

We close our Bibles on Acts 17 with profound thanksgiving to God because it records one of the greatest opportunities of Paul's whole ministry, the presentation of the gospel to the world-famous, supreme council of Athens, the Areopagus.

THANK YOU, HEAVENLY FATHER:

For the use of the facilities at the synagogue at Thessalonica and Berea, before opposition arose to hinder the gospel;

For the resourcefulness of Paul when addressing a pagan audience; he could refer to their idolatry manifest in all the statuary in Athens and their fear of an unknown god. He had the general knowledge that enabled him to make a spiritual point by using a quotation from one of their own poets.

For the name of Jesus being preached and heard in the Areopagus in Athens.

IN JESUS' NAME, AMEN

48. Acts 18:1-22
IN CORINTH

[1]After this, Paul left Athens and went to Corinth. [2]There he met a Jew named Aquila, a native of Pontus, who had recently come from Italy with his wife Priscilla, because Claudius had ordered all the Jews to leave Rome. Paul went to see them, [3]and because he was a tentmaker as they were, he stayed and worked with them. [4]Every Sabbath he reasoned in the synagogue, trying to persuade Jews and Greeks. Acts 18:1-4

God Has His People in Many Places

We begin to get the impression that a significant number of men and women were circulating in the Roman world evangelising wherever they went.

Here we are meeting Aquila and Priscilla (v. 2.) who were husband and wife. We presume that they were Italian by nationality and had lived in Rome until an Edict of Claudius (the fourth Roman Emperor) had ordered all Jews to leave Rome. A good point about Claudius is that he gave to Jews throughout the Empire the right of religious worship, but later, as we have just been informed, he banished all Jews from Rome. The Roman historian Suetonius hints at reasons for this dispersion. Suetonius wrote about riots in Rome instigated by a man called Chrestus (sounds a bit like Christian, doesn't it?) involving Christians and strict Jews. Rather than taking time to sort through this sectarian strife, and thus arriving at a legal settlement, Claudius simply ordered all Jews to leave Rome. The famine foretold by Agabus at the time of Saul's conversion took place in the reign of Claudius (Acts 11:28).

Paul heard about Aquila and Priscilla, two people who like himself, had only recently come to Corinth; he went to visit them, *'and because he was a tentmaker as they were, he stayed with them and worked with them.'*

These two had an extraordinary working knowledge of the scriptures and so they were a tremendous help to Apollos (v. 24) and no doubt many others. They got him back on the rails, so to speak, and by the end of this chapter Apollos is confidently commended to the Lord's work, one of his gifts being knowledge and ability to teach the Scriptures.

So from then on the weekly programme for all three was tent-making through the week and preaching in the synagogue every Sabbath (vv.2-4).

Soon Silas and Timothy arrived from Greece, and from that point onwards Paul devoted himself exclusively to preaching, *'testifying to the Jews that Jesus was the Christ (v. 5).'*

In the early chapters of Acts Luke used to insert **HISTORICAL MARKERS** to point to what God had done in various places. I expect that you have noticed that it is now more often the case that the Jews have become Paul's avowed opponents (as in Philippi, Thessalonica, Berea and now, at Corinth).

> [6]*But when the Jews opposed Paul and became abusive, he shook out his clothes in protest and said to them, "Your blood be on your own heads! I am clear of my responsibility. From now on I will go to the Gentiles."* Acts 18:6

It is interesting that when one door closes the Lord often opens another one. When Paul could not preach in the synagogue in Corinth, he discovered that a believer by the name of Titius Justus, lived next door. What happened next is even more typical of how God works. The synagogue was closed to Paul, but read on.

> [8]*Crispus, the synagogue ruler, and his entire household believed in the Lord; and many of the Corinthians who heard him believed and were baptised.* Acts 18:8

I imagine there was hearty thanksgiving to the Lord in Paul's lodgings with Aquila and Priscilla and with his colleagues Silas and Timothy as they bowed before the Lord in wonder, love and praise.

God had many people in Corinth

> [9]*One night the Lord spoke to Paul in a vision: "Do not be afraid; keep on speaking, do not be silent.* [10]*For I am with you, and no-one is going to attack and harm you, because* ***I have many people in this city."*** [11]*So Paul stayed for a year and a half, teaching them the word of God.* Acts 18:9-11

We need to pause here for a moment to think about what is expressed in what God said to Paul: first: **'I have many people'**, and then second: **'in this city.'**

The God of Creation and Providence and Redemption can look at a city like Corinth and say about it: **'I have many people in this city.'**

We used to be in that position. We did not yet belong to Christ, but God looked on as if we already belonged to Him through His Son, and could see the time when we would belong to Him.

I haven't the space or even the information I need to help you understand the kind of city that Corinth was. It was a cesspit of immorality. What went on in that city both by day and by night can hardly be printed in a Christian book.

I believe that I must be honest and realistic, and by dealing with the sordid facts about Corinth using as few words as possible, bring unlimited and eternal glory to the God of our salvation. Corinth was a city of wealth, luxury and immorality. To be 'Corinthian' was to live a life of profligacy and debauchery. The Corinthians were devoted to Aphrodite, the goddess of love. Her worshippers came from all over the ancient world. Her temple on the Acrocorinthus had over 1000 priestesses of vice not found in other shrines in Greece. Every night they descended on the Acrocorinth to ply their trade in the worship of Aphrodite. One could buy anything in Corinth if he had the money. Homosexuality was rampant. Knowing what he knew about this city, could Paul be unafraid, and accept God's assurance that he will not be harmed, **because God had many people in this city (v. 10)?**

How would this change your attitude to those for whose salvation you are praying? The majority of Christian workers know this text well – because they have been claiming it for years.

It seemed as if the Lord had no sooner given Paul this encouraging vision of many people in Corinth who were unbelievers at the present time but who would in God's good time become believers, when the Jews revolted against Paul and brought him into the Court of Gallio.

> [12]*The Jews made a united attack on Paul and brought him into court.* [13]*"This man," they charged, "is persuading the people to worship God in ways contrary to the law."* Acts 18:12-13

Just as Paul was about to speak (he didn't want to lose an opportunity to witness to the Jews), Gallio got a word in first. It shows that he was a wise old owl. He made a clear statement indicating what he thought about the behaviour of everyone involved in this uprising.

> [14]*Just as Paul was about to speak, Gallio said to the Jews, "If you Jews were making a complaint about some misdemeanour or serious crime, it would be reasonable for me to listen to you.*
>
> [15]*But since it involves questions about words and names and your own law—settle the matter yourselves. I will not be a judge of such things."*
>
> [16]*So he had them ejected from the court.* [17]*Then they all turned on Sosthenes the synagogue ruler and beat him in front of the court. But Gallio showed no concern whatever.* Acts 18:14-17

Gallio ruled that there was no point of Roman law before the court; that he would have no part in ruling on religious matters affecting the Jews, at which point he had the court cleared. In fact Gallio by his decision and actions had passed a favourable verdict on the Christian faith and established a significant legal precedent. Romans who were Christians were protected by the law. Rome had not forbidden the apostles to preach. Paul stayed in Corinth for at least a year and a half.

Nevertheless, the Jews wanted somebody to blame, and so they turned on Sosthenes the synagogue ruler (as if he were to blame) and gave this unfortunate man a hammering in full view of the court. Luke says that Gallio showed no concern whatever. Why should he? It wasn't his problem.

A further word about Sosthenes, the new ruler of the synagogue (who succeeded Crispus v. 8). It is possible that he became a Christian because a Sosthenes is included in Paul's salutation to the Church at Corinth.

> *Paul, called to be an apostle of Christ Jesus by the will of God, and our brother Sosthenes*. (1 Corinthians 1:1).

Apart from this conjecture we have no further evidence of his later life either as a Jew or a Christian.

> [18]*Paul stayed on in Corinth for some time. Then he left the brothers and sailed for Syria, accompanied by Priscilla and Aquila. Before he sailed, he had his hair cut off at Cenchrea because of a vow he had taken.*
>
> [19]*They arrived at Ephesus, where Paul left Priscilla and Aquila. He himself went into the synagogue and reasoned with the Jews.* [20] *When they asked him to spend more time with them, he declined.*
>
> [21]*But as he left, he promised, "I will come back if it is God's will." Then he set sail from Ephesus.* [22]*When he landed at Caesarea, he went up and greeted the church and then went down to Antioch*. Acts 18:18-22

Luke gives us up-to-date news of the movements of missionaries. Paul stayed on in Corinth for some time. We think it may not have been for too long, because soon Paul gives the impression that he was a man in a hurry.

He left to go to Syria by sea taking Silas and Timothy with him, accompanied by Priscilla and Aquila (v. 18).

Before he sailed Paul had his hair cut off at Cenchrea (the port of Corinth) because of a vow he had taken. It is thought that for personal reasons Paul had resolved to take a Nazarite vow. In the Old Testament Samson and Samuel, and (in the New Testament) John the Baptist were associated with the practice of taking such vows. Jesus was a Nazarite from birth (Luke 1:15). There will be more about this when Paul arrives in Jerusalem (Acts 21:17-26).

They sailed on to Ephesus (v. 19), where Paul had left Priscilla and Aquila. As always he went into the synagogue and reasoned with the Jews. They asked him to spend more time with them, but he declined. As he was leaving he promised that he would come back to Ephesus, if God so willed.

His journey continued to Caesarea, where he went inland and greeted the church in Jerusalem. He made that a brief visit and proceeded to Antioch (in Syria). This ended Paul's Second Missionary Journey (v. 22).

THANK YOU, HEAVENLY FATHER:

For loving us from all eternity and then saving us through Your Son's sacrificial death on Calvary;

For the bonds of Christian love that bind believers together; 'though sundered far, by faith we meet around a common mercy-seat'.

For delivering Your servants from dangers seen and unseen, from principalities and powers so that nothing in all creation is able to separate us from the love of God that is in Christ Jesus;

For wisdom for Your servants when they find themselves in new situations;

For every heart and life in which the Holy Spirit is at work, revealing Jesus to unbelievers on whom You have set Your love;

IN JESUS' NAME, AMEN

Acts 18:23 - 21:16

Paul's Third Missionary Journey

49. Acts 18: 23-28

MISSIONARY ARRIVALS & DEPARTURES

After spending some time in Antioch, Paul set out from there and travelled from place to place throughout the region of Galatia and Phrygia, strengthening all the disciples. Acts 18:23

PAUL

This third missionary journey took Paul to Corinth (18:18), Syrian Antioch (18:22), to Galatia and Phrygia (Asia Minor) (18:23), and to Ephesus (19:1) where he spent two years and three months teaching and preaching.

Stage two begins in v. 23: *he travelled from place to place throughout the region of Galatia and Phrygia*. He must have had the constitution of an ox! Well, yes, but he also found himself battling with weakness on occasions. We need to learn that the best of men are only men at best, but God's strength is made perfect in weakness.

This is where we need to get out our Bible Dictionary and spend a while browsing over the maps of Paul's missionary journeys. In this way we shall soon be able to think our way around Bible lands. All of this makes Bible Study increasingly interesting. After over 50 years in the gospel ministry I wish I knew my Bible better, because then I would know Jesus better too.

APOLLOS

[24]Meanwhile a Jew named Apollos, a native of Alexandria, came to Ephesus. He was a learned man, with a thorough knowledge of the Scriptures. Acts 18:24

The story continues. I'm very fond of this little narrative, because it enforces a lesson that is not always easy to learn, especially when a colleague takes you aside and tells you some of your faults. We hate to be criticised. It depends on who the critic is, and whether they care about us enough to say uncomfortable things.

I remember walking with a colleague along a country road in the Midlands of Ireland–about 48 years ago–when I said something that 'jarred' with him. (I had used the wrong part of the verb 'to be'.) We may use colloquialisms sometimes, but not all the time.

He didn't stop there; he was only starting at that point! He was right, and I am grateful to him to this day. To this day I hear his rebuke, but I am not angry at him. Nor does he have to apologise to me. What was my problem? Simply this: you can take a boy out of the country, but you cannot take the country out of the boy! I had to cast off some bad habits learned in childhood, colloquial expressions and suchlike; they were commonplace, but because I heard them every day I didn't know how out of place they sounded.

If somebody is tearing you apart because they are in a bad temper that is one thing (they owe you an apology at an appropriate time), but what does Proverbs 27:6 mean when it says, 'Wounds from a friend can be trusted' (NIV)? Think about that.

I think that Apollos received a warm welcome to Ephesus. He and Priscilla and Aquila became firm friends in a short time. This man was well-educated and alongside that qualification he had another that was if anything even more important in the work he was doing; he had a thorough knowledge of the Scriptures. More than this he must have been an interesting speaker:

> [25]*He had been instructed in the way of the Lord, and he spoke with great fervour and taught about Jesus accurately, though he knew only the baptism of John.*
>
> [26]*He began to speak boldly in the synagogue. When Priscilla and Aquila heard him, they invited him to their home and explained to him the way of God more adequately.* Acts 18:25-26

Aquila and Priscilla loved to hear him preach **but** – something in this man's theology wasn't quite right. For one thing he knew only the baptism of John the Baptist; therefore he preached only the baptism of John. He had not been instructed about believer's baptism and therefore his preaching fell flat, because there was no connection to the death and burial and resurrection of Jesus in his faith as a believer. The same would have been true of his preaching. They took him to their home and explained the way of God more adequately.

Thankfully he listened. I wonder if he lived to be an old man. If he did, I would venture to say that he thanked the Lord often for the good friends that he had made in Ephesus. The counsel of Aquila and Priscilla made a difference to his ministry. So much so, that the other brothers in Ephesus had sufficient confidence in him and sent him to southern Greece.

> [27]*When Apollos wanted to go to Achaia, the brothers encouraged him and wrote to the disciples there to welcome him. On arriving, he was a great help to those who by grace had believed.* [28]*For he vigorously refuted the Jews in public debate, proving from the Scriptures that Jesus was the Christ.* Acts 18:27-28

O God, send us more of your servants with gifts like those of Aquila, Priscilla and Apollos.

THANK YOU, HEAVENLY FATHER:

For Your Holy Spirit, the great Teacher, who takes the things of Christ and makes them real to us;

For the wonderful change that has taken place in our lives since Jesus came into our hearts;

For the home of Aquila and Priscilla, and how they used it to further the work of Your kingdom, by providing a place to live for Paul and helping Apollos grow in grace and the knowledge of Jesus Christ;

For the help that Apollos ministered to believers ever since his experience in Ephesus (v. 27).

IN JESUS' NAME, AMEN

50. Acts 19: 1 - 22

PAUL IN EPHESUS

[1]While Apollos was at Corinth, Paul took the road through the interior and arrived at Ephesus. There he found some disciples [2]and asked them, "Did you receive the Holy Spirit when you believed?" They answered, "No, we have not even heard that there is a Holy Spirit."

[3]So Paul asked, "Then what baptism did you receive?" "John's baptism," they replied. [4]Paul said, "John's baptism was a baptism of repentance. He told the people to believe in the one coming after him, that is, in Jesus."

[5]On hearing this, they were baptised into the name of the Lord Jesus.

[6]When Paul placed his hands on them, the Holy Spirit came on them, and they spoke in tongues and prophesied. [7]There were about twelve men in all. Acts 19:1-7

Sometimes we have been amazed at how quickly news of the Lord's work spread from place to place in the New Testament world. In this case we are surprised at how long it took for news of the cessation of John's baptism to reach twelve disciples in Ephesus.

Something caused Paul to put a leading question to them (v. 2).He asked them, "Did you receive the Holy Spirit when you believed?" They answered, "No, we have not even heard that there is a Holy Spirit."

Sermons have been preached on Acts 19:2 that should have been torn up and incinerated as soon as they were written! I say that with some feeling because I had the sad experience as a boy of about 13 years of age, wrestling with the question recorded in this verse. I was afraid to go to sleep at night in case I didn't have the Holy Spirit.

A godly aunt of mine had given me some sermons of the late W. P Nicholson to read. That was where this negative, doubt-creating influence came from. The KJV translation didn't help, but seemed to support the difficulty with its wording: 'Have you received the Holy Ghost since ye believed?' (v. 2)

Paul's question has been used by 'holiness' preachers to raise a doubt in the minds of new believers. Their purpose is to raise a hunger for the Holy Spirit in the new believers. Strange as it might seem, this is erroneous teaching.

Paul was pursuing a completely opposite purpose: namely to establish the fact that every believer in Jesus receives the Holy Spirit at conversion. Paul patiently pastored them and told them what they had somehow missed hearing. He asked them, 'Then what baptism did you receive?' 'John's baptism,' they replied.

> [4]*Paul said, "John's baptism was a baptism of repentance. He told the people to believe in the one coming after him, that is, in Jesus."* [5]*On hearing this, they were baptised into the name of the Lord Jesus.*
>
> [6]*When Paul placed his hands on them, the Holy Spirit came on them, and they spoke in tongues and prophesied.* [7]*There were about twelve men in all.* Acts 19:4-7

I'm not going to designate this as 'the Ephesian Pentecost' because only twelve believers were involved; in other words the effect of it was very parochial compared to what happened in Jerusalem (2:1-16), Samaria (8:14-17) and in the home of Cornelius in Samaria (10:4-46).

> [8]*Paul entered the synagogue and spoke boldly there for three months, arguing persuasively about the kingdom of God.* Acts 19:8

We are beginning to get the impression that this is going to be a fast-moving chapter. It must have re-arranged the programme of the local synagogue if Paul went there every day for three months arguing persuasively about the kingdom of God. Not everyone was a supporter of Paul and his preaching. There were those who opposed him.

> [9]*But some of them became obstinate; they refused to believe and publicly maligned the Way. So Paul left them. He took the disciples with him and had discussions daily in the lecture hall of Tyrannus.* Acts 19:9

Another two years' evangelistic lectures, sermons etc. were made possible when the lecture hall of Tyrannus became available. The benefit of the prolonged period of daily witness is noted at the end of v. 10:

[10] *This went on for two years, so that all the Jews and Greeks who lived in the province of Asia heard the word of the Lord.* This evidently means that Jews from a wide area found opportunity to attend to Paul's ministry.

> [11]*God did extraordinary miracles through Paul,* [12]*so that even handkerchiefs and aprons that had touched him were taken to the sick, and their illnesses were cured and the evil spirits left them.*
>
> [13]*Some Jews who went around driving out evil spirits tried to invoke the name of the Lord Jesus over those who were demon-possessed. They would say, "In the name of Jesus, whom Paul preaches, I command you to come out."* Acts 19:11-13

That is a grand statement in v. 11: God did extraordinary miracles through Paul. The picture is balanced by v. 13 which records that some Jews thought they could imitate what Paul was doing. They thought nothing of using the name of Jesus, without having the authority to do so. Failing to realise the power of that name, especially if used blasphemously, they 'didn't know what hit them' when the demons turned on them and they were badly injured. Here follows a case in point.

> [14]*Seven sons of Sceva, a Jewish chief priest, were doing this.* [15]*One day the evil spirit answered them, "Jesus I know, and I know about Paul, but who are you?"* [16]*Then the man who had the evil spirit jumped on them and overpowered them all. He gave them such a beating that they ran out of the house naked and bleeding.* Acts 19:14-16

Did this in any way take away from the Name of Jesus? No. There was a sense of God that was almost tangible. The power of Jesus' name was felt in various ways.

> [17]*When this became known to the Jews and Greeks living in Ephesus, they were all seized with fear, and the name of the Lord Jesus was held in high honour.*
>
> [18]*Many of those who believed now came and openly confessed their evil deeds.*
>
> [19]*A number who had practised sorcery brought their scrolls together and burned them publicly. When they calculated the value of the scrolls, the total came to fifty thousand drachmas.* [20]*In this way the word of the Lord spread widely and grew in power.* Acts 19:17-20

God had vindicated himself in the preaching of the Gospel. Many needs were represented in that crowd and the Holy Spirit was busy in ministering as He moved from person to person. **'God had showed up.'** People were renewing their Christian profession in ways that hurt, and involved considerable financial loss. There was honest confession of sin. The articles used in sorcery, their colourful and complicated scrolls, once considered very valuable, were all cast into the fire. Someone calculated the commercial value of these things at in the region of several million US dollars in today's money. I cannot imagine how this claim can be substantiated. One thing is clear: this was 'dedication' with a capital 'D'.

Here is another grand statement: [20]*In this way the word of the Lord spread widely and grew in power.*

Luke has just enough space to squeeze in Paul's latest travel plans:

> [21]*After all this had happened, Paul decided to go to Jerusalem, passing through Macedonia and Achaia. "After I have been there," he said, "I must visit Rome also."* [22]*He sent two of his helpers, Timothy and Erastus, to Macedonia, while he stayed in the province of Asia a little longer.* Acts 19: 21-22

We cannot pause here to review Paul's extensive travel since his conversion in Acts 9 – but my readers can do this: so many miles by sea, so many on foot. We don't read of Paul using mules or donkeys (do we?). So the work of God continues: religious people as well as pagan people need to be evangelised, and new believers need to be established in the faith.

THANK YOU, HEAVENLY FATHER:

For the mix of people that are present when the gospel is being preached: the risen Lord is there, the Holy Spirit is there, the Devil is there, sincerely repentant believers are there, some who play with the devil are there, and many others are in the valley of decision. O God, who is sufficient for these things?

For the continuing need for pastoral work in every gathering of people; some have been wrongly taught and need to understand the gospel clearly. O God You know who they are. May the Holy Spirit draw them to Jesus.

For the power of the Word of God in word and in speech; that makes us wise for salvation;

IN JESUS' NAME, AMEN

51. Acts 19: 23 - 41
THE RIOT AT EPHESUS

[23]About that time there arose a great disturbance about the Way.

[24]A silversmith named Demetrius, who made silver shrines of Artemis, brought in no little business for the craftsmen. [25]He called them together, along with the workmen in related trades, and said: "Men, you know we receive a good income from this business. [26]And you see and hear how this fellow Paul has convinced and led astray large numbers of people here in Ephesus and in practically the whole province of Asia. He says that man-made gods are no gods at all. [27]There is danger not only that our trade will lose its good name, but also that the temple of the great goddess Artemis will be discredited, and the goddess herself, who is worshipped throughout the province of Asia and the world, will be robbed of her divine majesty." Acts 19:23-27

This man Demetrius didn't need to be 'wound up'- he was a self-starter. He didn't need notes either: he had a clear grasp of what he wanted to say against Paul and in support of Diana (or Artemis) the goddess of the Ephesians. He had a clear grasp of what Paul said about idols. He says that man-made gods are no gods at all (v. 26).

Calling on all the guild-members in Ephesus (as a Trade Union would rally its members today) he spelled out the cost to their livelihood as silversmiths in Ephesus. There may already have been a falling off in the sale of silver statues and so on; he was adamant that given time the temple of the goddess would be discredited and through a decline in worship be robbed of her divine majesty. Demetrius watched a wave of anger flow over the 'union members'. They began shouting 'Great is Artemis of the Ephesians!' Soon the whole town was in an uproar (v. 28).

The angry crowd grabbed Gaius and Aristarchus, two Greek companions of Paul and dragged them into the theatre (v. 29). Paul could hardly be restrained from going in there himself to speak on their behalf – but the rest of the disciples would not allow him to go in. Even some officials of the province, friends of Paul, sent him a message to the same effect (v. 30-31). There was such confusion that most of the people didn't know why they were there (v. 32).

The Jews tried to put Alexander forward as their spokesman, but the crowd was not prepared to listen to a Jew and so he had no opportunity to speak because for about two hours the crowd continued shouting 'Great is Artemis of the Ephesians (v. 33-34).

Thankfully, there was one man present that day who knew how to appeal to the frenzied crowd. His name is not given, but the office he held in local government is mentioned: he was the Town Clerk of Ephesus (v. 35). He spoke a lot of common sense.

1. The world knows that the city of Ephesus is the guardian of the temple of the great Artemis and of her image which fell from heaven (v. 35). These are undeniable facts of our local history, so there is no need for you to do anything except to be quiet and not do anything rash (v. 36).
2. The town clerk was a man of principle and therefore spoke the truth about any matter before him, in this case the men whom the crowd wanted to harm. 'You brought these men here, though they have neither robbed temples nor blasphemed our goddess' (v. 37).
3. If Demetrius and his fellow craftsmen have a grievance against anybody, the courts are open and there are the proconsuls. They can press charges (v. 38).
4. If there is anything further you want to bring up, it must be settled in a legal assembly (v. 39).

5. The fact of the matter is that we (i.e. all gathered here) are in danger of being charged with rioting because of today's events. In that case we would not be able to account for this commotion, since there is no reason for it (v. 40).
6. After he had said this, he dismissed the assembly (v. 41).

Well, what do we make of all that? Demetrius behaved as Union Leaders sometimes do: he spoke first and thought afterwards. The town clerk, whatever his name (I wish we knew it), was evidently a man of maturity and when he spoke people listened.

He reminds me of Shakespeare's Shylock, the young Jewish moneylender in 'The Merchant of Venice'. He was described as a 'Daniel come to judgment' for the skill of his legal arguments.

Finally, we would be very blind if we failed to see the hand of God in the whole incident from beginning to end. He kept the apostle and his companions from danger; he equipped a pagan Ephesian with extraordinary wisdom so that his speech caught the attention of everyone in the vast theatre. The whole matter appears to have cooled down, almost as quickly as it had heated up in the mind of Demetrius.

THANK YOU, HEAVENLY FATHER;

For Your ways and Your thoughts, always above and beyond ours: we worship You;

For preserving the lives of Paul and his companions from dangers seen and unseen;

For keeping us from being intimidated by the darkness all around us: keep us looking to Jesus, the author and finisher of our faith;

For our immortality until our work is done: thank You for this thought; thank You for your hand sustaining and blessing us, and giving us such success as You see is appropriate for us;

IN JESUS' NAME, AMEN

52. Acts 20:1-12

VV. 1-6 THROUGH MACEDONIA AND GREECE

> [1]*When the uproar had ended, Paul sent for the disciples and, after encouraging them, said good-bye and set out for Macedonia.* Acts 20:1

A map of Greece shows that Macedonia is the northern half of the country and Achaia is the southern section. When Paul left Athens he may have travelled by sea for at least some of the way to arrive in Achaia. His pastoral visits must have been greatly appreciated by the believers. V. 2 simply says 'finally he arrived in Greece. That name can be used of the whole country combining Macedonia and Achaia where he stayed for three months.

He had it in mind to go on to Syria, but a Jewish plot was discovered just as he was about to set sail for Syria, and so he turned back through Macedonia (3). We made reference a few studies ago to the numerous Christian people (single and married) who were itinerant evangelists in various countries. Here is a sample of those who were in Europe at that time:

> [4]*He was accompanied by Sopater son of Pyrrhus from Berea, Aristarchus and Secundus from Thessalonica, Gaius from Derbe, Timothy also, and Tychicus and Trophimus from the province of Asia.*

> [5]*These men went on ahead and waited for us at Troas.* [6]*But we sailed from Philippi after the Feast of Unleavened Bread, and five days later joined the others at Troas, where we stayed seven days.* Acts 20:4-6

This geographical note solves our problem: we were wondering how did Paul and the others get to Asia? The answer is that they sailed from Philippi (in Europe) and five days later arrived in Troas (in Asia). It thrills me when the Bible comes alive with the mention of places that I know well, and especially in this case where the gospel came to the Continent where I have lived all my life. More importantly, the men mentioned in v. 4 were the fruits of his evangelistic labours since he first entered the Lord's work. Luke had rejoined the party (see the pronoun 'we' from v. 5 onwards). So there was a party of say eight or nine altogether.

vv. 7 – 11 Eutychus Raised From the Dead at Troas

> *On the first day of the week we came together to break bread. Paul spoke to the people and, because he intended to leave the next day, kept on talking until midnight. [8]There were many lamps in the upstairs room where we were meeting. [9]Seated in a window was a young man named Eutychus, who was sinking into a deep sleep as Paul talked on and on. When he was sound asleep, he fell to the ground from the third storey and was picked up dead. [10]Paul went down, threw himself on the young man and put his arms around him. "Don't be alarmed," he said. "He's alive!"*
>
> *[11]Then he went upstairs again and broke bread and ate. After talking until daylight, he left. [12]The people took the young man home alive and were greatly comforted.* Acts 20:7-11

People who fall asleep in church sometimes have embarrassing moments: they may talk (or even sing) in their sleep, or fall out of their seat if their body has defied the centre of gravity – or, as here, a young man fell asleep sitting in a window-frame and then fell three storeys to the street below, where he was picked up dead.

If this happened in a Western church would the pastor be sued for putting the man to sleep, and thus endangering his life and safety? It would not surprise me!

In Troas Paul went down to the street, threw himself on the young man and put his arms around him, 'Don't be alarmed,' he said, 'He's alive!'

And we all say **'Thank You, Heavenly Father.'**

There is a more important value in this short section: it provides a window on a young church at worship in 1st century Troas.

When everyone had assembled again in that Upper Room, the worship concluded with the Breaking of Bread. It was late at night, so let's not argue that this is the purpose of the Sunday morning meeting. There is something even more important than that.

My firm conviction is that in Acts 2:42-47 we are given a list of the essential ingredients of Christian worship, including the observance of the ordinances of baptism and the Lord's Supper and such service as the Gospel requires.

That was how the Jerusalem Church organised themselves; other New Testament churches organised themselves under the superintendancy of the Holy Spirit. The church you attend will make similar arrangements. Other churches are not 'wrong' if they don't do it in exactly the same way you do in your place of worship.

After the above brief points about the Breaking of Bread I expect that many of my readers will agree with me that we need a breath from the Holy Spirit to sweep through 'our place' before the Lord comes again.

Paul didn't preach by the sundial, or an hourglass, he preached by the calendar. He preached until daylight, and then left. Here is a beautiful end-piece:

> [12]*The people took the young man home alive and were greatly comforted.*

THANK YOU, HEAVENLY FATHER:

For the various ways in which the Holy Spirit brought the young churches into being;

For how those infant churches were superintended by the Holy Spirit in their worship and their witness to the world of their time;

For the Breaking of Bread services that are convened in every culture of the world where you have Your people; O Lord greatly refresh Your people;

IN JESUS' NAME, AMEN

53. Acts 20:13-38

PAUL'S FAREWELL TO THE EPHESIAN ELDERS

Evidently Luke is in the advance party because he is using his special word 'we' to tell us so. He is about to describe the coastal voyage that enabled Paul to catch up with his colleagues at Miletus.

> [13]*We went on ahead to the ship and sailed for Assos, where we were going to take Paul aboard. He had made this arrangement because he was going there on foot.*
>
> [14]*When he met us at Assos, we took him aboard and went on to Mitylene.*
>
> [15]*The next day we set sail from there and arrived off Kios. The day after that we crossed over to Samos, and on the following day arrived at Miletus.* Acts 20:13-15

Paul felt a strong tug towards Ephesus; the thought had been with him for a long time – but he abandoned it to save time in the province of Asia because he was in a hurry to reach Jerusalem, if possible, by the day of Pentecost.

However the tug that he felt was sufficient for him to send a message to the elders at Ephesus asking them to meet him at Miletus (v. 17). As usual Paul was a few thoughts ahead of everybody else and had a speech ready to deliver to them.

> [18]*When they arrived, he said to them: "You know how I lived the whole time I was with you, from the first day I came into the province of Asia.*
>
> [19]*I served the Lord with great humility and with tears, although I was severely tested by the plots of the Jews.*

[20]You know that I have not hesitated to preach anything that would be helpful to you but have taught you publicly and from house to house.

[21]I have declared to both Jews and Greeks that they must turn to God in repentance and have faith in our Lord Jesus. Acts 20:18-21

He spoke to them about the dedication that is necessary in the Lord's work

He had been a 'double-barrelled' preacher; that is he preached to the religious unsaved and to the pagan unsaved. Most of his evangelistic preaching was like that. His reference to declaring the message to both Jews and Greeks was made with total honesty, because he preached to them wherever they were to be found.

He spoke to them with firsthand knowledge of the dangers inherent in the Lord's work

He had suffered physically as an apostle and evangelist. (Can you recall any of those hardships?) He believed that the Holy Spirit was ministering to him about suffering for the Lord's sake and saying that 'prison and hardships are facing me.'

[22]And now, compelled by the Spirit, I am going to Jerusalem, not knowing what will happen to me there. [23]I only know that in every city the Holy Spirit warns me that prison and hardships are facing me. [24]However, I consider my life worth nothing to me, if only I may finish the race and complete the task the Lord Jesus has given me—the task of testifying to the gospel of God's grace. Acts 20:22-24

He identified the duties and disciplines of the Christian ministry

Once he had gone from them the elders who had been his co-pastors needed to be watchful as never before, always on guard. It would have been impossible to pack any more warning or wisdom into vv. 26 to 31, than Paul did.

[26]Therefore, I declare to you today that I am innocent of the blood of all men.

[27]For I have not hesitated to proclaim to you the whole will of God.

[28]Keep watch over yourselves and all the flock of which the Holy Spirit has made you overseers. Be shepherds of the church of God, which he bought with his own blood.

[29]I know that after I leave, savage wolves will come in among you and will not spare the flock. [30]Even from your own number men will arise and distort the truth in order to draw away disciples after them. [31]So be on your guard!

Remember that for three years I never stopped warning each of you night and day with tears. Acts 20:26-31

You can almost feel the apostle's heartbeat as he is speaking; ***'savage wolves will come in among you'.*** Furthermore ***'Even from your own number men will arise and distort the truth in order to draw away disciples after them.'*** Paul knew that there is nothing more vulnerable than a young church.

There was a sad parting coming in a matter of hours when he would say a fond farewell to the Ephesian elders on the shore at Miletus. He is convinced that he would not see them again on this earth. He had so much to say: so much to pack into a short time. If we are not careful we are in danger of overlooking the most precious thoughts of all: Notice how Paul spoke about the church. Never forget whose church it is, the church in which the Lord has placed us to serve him.

[28]Keep watch over yourselves and all "the flock of which the Holy Spirit has made you overseers". Be shepherds of "the church of God, which he bought with his own blood." Acts 20:28

Paul – its time you weren't here!

At last he went on board the vessel; his final words were these:

> [32] *"Now I commit you to God and to the word of his grace, which can build you up and give you an inheritance among all those who are sanctified.* [33] *I have not coveted anyone's silver or gold or clothing.* [34] *You yourselves know that these hands of mine have supplied my own needs and the needs of my companions.*
>
> [35] *In everything I did, I showed you that by this kind of hard work we must help the weak, remembering the words the Lord Jesus himself said: 'It is more blessed to give than to receive.'*
>
> [36] *When he had said this, he knelt down with all of them and prayed.* [37] *They all wept as they embraced him and kissed him.* [38] *What grieved them most was his statement that they would never see his face again. Then they accompanied him to the ship.* Acts 20:32-38

What a word of farewell – and every word of it true. Have we ever known another human being whose life was filled with self-forgetful service to others? Yes, we have! Paul had learned those words from Jesus his Lord and Saviour. Paul always put Jesus first.

THANK YOU, HEAVENLY FATHER:

For the ties that bind our hearts in Christian love: the fellowship of kindred minds is like to that above;

For the influence of a good man on his colleagues and all to whom he ministers: make us truly grateful for this variety in those who minister to us in Your name;

For the evaluation of a good man's life work: we cannot possibly know the whole story, that is known only to You;

For the fact that all things are but loss compared with the excellence of the love of God in Jesus Christ our Saviour;

IN JESUS' NAME, AMEN

54. Acts 21: 1-16

ON TO JERUSALEM

Reading the opening verses of this chapter reminds me of the thousands of travellers queuing to go through the US Customs & Immigration Hall at Newark International Airport, New York. It is the first port of entry for passengers (flying on United Air from Belfast) and, of course, by carriers from other parts of Europe. Every year when we pass through we are convinced that the lines get longer. The last time we went through it took us two and a quarter hours – and there were many small children in the lines, and not all of them in strollers. Think of all the travel plans that had been put together. Think of all the luggage that passengers just cannot leave at home. Think of the weary parents, Then add an extra feature in Paul's time (behind verses 1-6) There were no computerised flight schedules; instead there was total dependence on wind and weather if the journeys were ever to be completed.

The stages of the journey:

> [1]*After we had torn ourselves away from them, we put out to sea and sailed straight to Cos. The next day we went to Rhodes and from there to Patara.* [2]*We found a ship crossing over to Phoenicia, went on board and set sail.* [3]*After sighting Cyprus and passing to the south of it, we sailed on to Syria. We landed at Tyre, where our ship was to unload its cargo.* Acts 21:1-3

That was a heart-rending farewell at Miletus (v. 1). They sailed to Cos, an island off the coast of Asia. There was a large Jewish settlement there at the time of Paul's Missionary Journeys. They could see Cyprus in the distance but passed on the south side of it. A day later they went to Rhodes and on to Patara. Rhodes had become a small town where several trade routes passed through. Rhodes was the centre of a sun-cult, the famous colossus being a statue of Helios. Rhodes and Patara were seaports in the shelter of Asia Minor coast on the Mediterranean Sea. The next port of call was Tyre on the Syrian Coast. There the ship discharged its cargo.

The highlights of the journey:

> [4]*Finding the disciples there, we stayed with them seven days. Through the Spirit they urged Paul not to go on to Jerusalem.* [5]*But when our time was up, we left and continued on our way. All the disciples and their wives and children accompanied us out of the city, and there on the beach we knelt to pray.* [6]*After saying good-bye to each other, we went aboard the ship, and they returned home.* Acts 21:4-6

Whatever risks were involved in travel by land and sea, there was a great 'added extra' for travelling Christians. When the ship tied up in Tyre some other believers were there and so the two groups became as one and had seven days of fellowship and refreshment. Some in the group knew of Paul's resolve to get to Jerusalem by Pentecost; yet others in his party were nervous about him going there at all (v. 4). Both groups (Paul and the others) believed they were reflecting the mind of the Holy Spirit (vv. 4 & 12).

It must have been a memorable scene on the beach at Miletus when all the disciples and their wives and children knelt on the beach to pray. That would have been a Christian witness – perhaps a powerful one. We imagine one part of the company going on board ship and the other part going back to their homes.

The final stage of the journey:

Luke continues reporting (again we spot his 'signature in the text'–the little word 'we'). The ship headed for Tyre, via Ptolemais, where there were more disciples to greet. They had a full day to spend with them. The following day the ship headed for Caesarea, the magnificent city that Herod built as the port for Jerusalem.

Philip the deacon (one of the seven), here also called the evangelist, lived in Caesarea. The travellers had hospitality with Philip and his four daughters who prophesied (v. 8).

Another man whom we met on a previous occasion, Agabus the prophet, came down from Judea. He brought bad news for Paul. He took Paul's belt, and tied his own hands and feet with it. Then he prophesied, 'The Holy Spirit says, in this way the Jews of Jerusalem will bind the owner of this belt and will hand him over to the Gentiles (vv. 10-11)'.

The end of the journey:

> Luke reports: [12]*When we heard this, we and the people there pleaded with Paul not to go up to Jerusalem.* [13]*Then Paul answered, "Why are you weeping and breaking my heart? I am ready not only to be bound, but also to die in Jerusalem for the name of the Lord Jesus."* Acts 21:12-13

Some friends who lived in Caesarea decided to go with Paul to Jerusalem, taking him to the home of a disciple called Mnason. This man was a Cypriot and a disciple of Jesus (v.15-16).

Before we move on to the next section, let's pause a moment to think about v. 14. It reflects two opinions about Paul going to Jerusalem. He believed that it was God's will for him to go there. Perhaps the majority of the others held the opposite point of view. I expect you can spot the issue here: it is simply that they cannot both be right.

Luke thinks of a 'shorthand' way of representing the situation and used an economy of words: [14] *When he (Paul) would not be dissuaded, we gave up and said, "The Lord's will be done."*

When praying for guidance about anything, we lay before the Lord the sum of our knowledge of the matter. Other believers, holding an opposite point of view will do the same. The issue is not 'Who is right'. The issue is: **'Are we willing for the Lord's will to be done?'** This principle of prayer demands transparent honesty before God on our part.

Only the Lord knows our heart's desire. Listen to Paul in Acts 20:22, *"And now, compelled by the Spirit,* ***I am going to Jerusalem****, not knowing what will happen to me there."*

Despite prayer and discussion in both Tyre and Caesarea, Paul could not be persuaded to change his mind.

> [4]*Finding the disciples there, we stayed with them seven days.* ***Through the Spirit they urged Paul not to go on to Jerusalem.*** Acts 21:4

Next Agabus arrives from Judea: he takes Paul's belt off him, ties his own hands and feet with it and then makes a prophecy.

> [11]*Coming over to us, he took Paul's belt, tied his own hands and feet with it and said, "The Holy Spirit says,* ***'In this way the Jews of Jerusalem will bind the owner of this belt and will hand him over to the Gentiles.'"*** [12] *When we heard this, we and the people there pleaded with Paul not to go up to Jerusalem. Then Paul answered,* [13] ***"I am ready not only to be bound, but also to die in Jerusalem for the name of the Lord Jesus."*** Acts 21:11-13

Please note that the issue here is not a trivial matter (such as: what colour shall we paint the prayer room?), it is a matter affecting the life, and possible death, of one of the Lord's servants. It was a substantial matter.

I'm not sure where these concluding paragraphs will take us, but one thing I already know and am sure of: we are not going to say that the Holy Spirit contradicted himself. That is never the case.

What shall we conclude about Paul? He was a man of strong intellect, convictions and will: the predictions of suffering in Jerusalem did not deter him.

What shall we conclude about the majority of the believers? They held Paul in high regard, they valued him, and they could not imagine not having him with them. Their urging of Paul not to go to Jerusalem was an instinctive plea fuelled by the fruit of the Spirit in their hearts, they loved and valued him – and drew back from any thought of his death. It may, at base, have been a mildly selfish appeal. I would rather base it on their love for God's servant.

What shall we conclude about our friend Luke? He had rejoined the group, and it was inevitable that he should get involved in this discussion. So let's go back to where we began in 14: *When he would not be dissuaded, '**we**' gave up and said, **"The Lord's will be done."***

When Luke wrote these words he was not telling us that he had abandoned his confidence in prayer and intercession. Not at all. He was admitting that there are times and issues when a subject can be too vast for the outcome to be determined by the emphases of believers' prayers. At that point we trust the Lord where we cannot see him. There are some things we do not know, are not entitled to know, will never know until we get to heaven. In the meantime we can confidently pray with Luke, and without any loss of confidence in the wisdom of our Heavenly Father: **'The Lord's will be done.'**

The whole issue of Paul's life or death was in the hands of God, and never more so than when Luke wrote that sentence.

Think of it, it was too great a matter to be determined by the prayers of believers. Someone might say: 'that's an easy option–it just means that we sit back and do nothing.' I believe that response is mistaken.

Whenever we pray, 'The Lord's will be done' then it is our duty to live as obediently as we know how to the directions and assurances of the Scriptures. What do you know? The Lord's will is done! Then we seek His guidance for whatever is next in his will.

THANK YOU, HEAVENLY FATHER:

For journeying mercies (perhaps an old fashioned term nowadays): it gathers up all our need before God in prayer before we undertake a journey, whether long or short;

For friends who travel with us in Your service: thank You for their fellowship;

For favourable travelling conditions by land, sea and in the air;

For those we meet on our journey to whom we can speak a friendly word, a word of comfort, perhaps Your Holy Spirit will give is special word from Your Word, just for them;

For the ministry and the mystery of prayer in all its forms, adoration, confession, thanksgiving and supplication and intercession;

IN JESUS' NAME, AMEN

55. Acts 21:17-26

PAUL'S ARRIVAL AT JERUSALEM

Some years had passed and Paul had travelled thousands of miles since he and James, leader of the Jerusalem Church had last met, and in the meantime significant Church history had been made.

The growth and unity factors in the churches

When Paul and Barnabas, Judas and Silas were sent to visit all the churches and deliver the 'Letter from Jerusalem' (Acts 15:23-29) they were well received. A remarkable unity existed in the churches but could have been disrupted so easily. For instance, there was the potential for two Christian Churches to develop: one Jewish and the other Gentile. The Jewish churches continued to grow by leaps and bounds at times, when believers were added to their memberships. At the same time Gentile churches were coming into being, wherever Paul preached the gospel.

So between Acts 15:29 and Acts 21:17-26 the spiritual map of the world of that time had changed significantly.

James and Paul, and their respective groups of believers had to be taught by the Holy Spirit that neither religious background nor nationality could ever be allowed to become a dividing factor in the life of the churches. Jewish and Gentile believers had to learn that they were one (body) in Christ Jesus.

Arriving in Jerusalem the travellers rested overnight, and so the next morning was their first opportunity to meet the leaders of the Jerusalem church and the other apostles and the elders. It is not hard to imagine the scene: it is one of genuine cordiality.

> [17]*When we arrived at Jerusalem, the brothers received us warmly.* [18]*The next day Paul and the rest of us went to see*

James, and all the elders were present. [19]*Paul greeted them and reported in detail what God had done among the Gentiles through his ministry.* [20]*When they heard this, they praised God.* Acts 21:17-20

It would have been appropriate if Luke had mentioned at this point that Paul was carrying a generous offering from the Gentile churches. We imagine that it would have given Paul particular pleasure to present the gift to James. In Acts 24:17 Paul tells Felix the governor that one of his reasons for coming back to Jerusalem was: *'I came to Jerusalem to bring my people gifts for the poor and to present offerings'*.

The persecution and protection factors experienced by Paul

If we detect a slight tension in the air it is because many of those present were concerned about what the reaction of Judaism will be now that Paul has returned to Jerusalem. This is what vv. 20-26 are about.

Luke shows that the Jews vigorously opposed Paul everywhere; but he is also able to demonstrate that Christians were frequently protected by Roman officials.

The peril that Paul faced from the Jews:

The early Church was often protected by Roman Officials. We shall find this to be case on various occasions between here and the end of Acts 28.

Judaism, on the other hand, had moved from an awkward tolerance (Acts 4:23) to all-out war. Recall the martyrdom of Stephen (Acts 7:1-8:50); the attempts on Paul's life when he was converted (Acts 9:23), in Pisidian Antioch (Acts 13:49ff), in Iconium (Acts 14:5ff), at Lystra where Paul was stoned and left for dead (Acts 14:19-20), and the attack on him in Corinth (Acts 18:12ff). This a list of Jewish assaults. Attacks such the one led by Demetrius the silversmith in Ephesus (Acts 19:23ff) belong to another list.

Who could say what the current attitude of Judaism would be now that Paul was back in Jerusalem? On the basis of their past behaviour the outlook seemed black.

The precautions recommended by the Jerusalem Church (and/ or its leaders)

Perhaps the praise time (v. 20) was tactfully limited because Paul and his friends had to be briefed about changes in the church and city during their absence. It is a matter of sanctified common sense that Christians don't rush into persecution needlessly: they are discreet and behave wisely.

I warn you that what follows may try your Christian tolerance!

We can hardly believe our ears when we hear James giving Paul a glowing report of God's work among the Jews that surely caused Paul to swallow hard. Imagine James, the senior man in age and experience, counselling Paul that he is to be seen to behave as a devout Jew while he is in Jerusalem.

> *"You see, brother, how many thousands of Jews have believed, and all of them are zealous for the law."* Acts 21:20

Notice that final emphasis. Is that what the Gospel is meant to do for Jews?

James informed Paul that a campaign of slander had been waged against him

> [21]*They have been informed that you teach all the Jews who live among the Gentiles to turn away from Moses, telling them not to circumcise their children or live according to our customs.* Acts 21:21

Then it was James who seems to ask Paul for help: [22] 'What shall we do?'

Yes, Paul taught these things but it depends on who is doing the reporting (James) and the message the report is meant to convey.

Believing Jews would retail this news with their understanding of Paul's ministry in mind; unbelieving Jews would retail it with a totally different emphasis (as we shall see). Those in bondage to the Law of Moses would certainly emphasise it.

James informed Paul that his presence in the city was already known.

> [22] *They will certainly hear that you have come,* [23] *so do what we tell you.*

James informed Paul of arrangements that the Jerusalem Church had made.

He is suggesting that for as long as Paul is in the city he must behave like an orthodox Jew! He must behave in such a way as to scotch the rumours that were being circulated about him! He must go out of his way to be seen to be a devout Jew! James seems to think: keep the peace while this man is here, when we get him out of here everything will return to the status quo. Am I correct?

I hate myself for writing such a sentence about a man whom I have always admired, especially as he was the last member of Jesus' extended family to come to faith in him as God and Saviour. I always thought of him with respect.

It seems to me that the Jerusalem church was still slow to accept Gentiles. If that is so, then it is a fateful suggestion that James is making to Paul. If I am wrong about this, can someone tell me what the remainder of this chapter means? I think James' next instruction clinches the matter:

> [23]***So do what we tell you****. There are four men with us who have made a vow.* [24]*Take these men, join in their purification rites and pay their expenses, so that they can have their heads shaved. Then everybody will know there is no truth in these reports about you, but that you yourself are living in obedience to the law.*

> [25]*As for the Gentile believers, we have written to them our decision that they should abstain from food sacrificed to idols, from blood, from the meat of strangled animals and from sexual immorality."*
>
> [26]*The next day Paul took the men and purified himself along with them. Then he went to the temple to give notice of the date when the days of purification would end and the offering would be made for each of them.* Acts 21:23-26

Instead of living under the New Covenant (Hebrews 8:7-9:10), James and others like him were still living in bondage to the Law of Moses. How tragic! What James was saying was in effect: 'We are saved by grace, *but we are kept saved by the Law.'*

It seems that James' leadership had not liberated this Jewish Church, but rather confirmed its conformity to the Law of Moses. James was trying to influence religious politics in what he was saying to Paul. I'm sure that the whole idea was distasteful to Paul, yet he submitted to it. O Lord, why do such difficulties arise in Your work?

To be fair to Paul, he had a policy that he sometimes invoked in difficult situations. He followed it in an effort to win rather than turn away his enquirer or acquaintance: i.e. prospective believers. He may have been regulating his behaviour here by this policy.

> [19]*Though I am free and belong to no man, I make myself a slave to everyone, to win as many as possible.*
>
> [20]*To the Jews I became like a Jew, to win the Jews. To those under the law I became like one under the law (though I myself am not under the law), so as to win those under the law.* [21]*To those not having the law I became like one not having the law (though I am not free from God's law but am under Christ's law), so as to win those not having the law.* [22]*To the weak I became weak, to win the weak. I have become all things to all men so that by all possible means I might save some.* [23]*I do all this for the sake of the gospel that I may share in its blessings.* 1 Corinthians 9:19-23

We can try to understand Paul's reasoning; but whether we understand him or not, we need to remember that it is to his own Master that he rises or falls, and not to us

> [4] *Who are you to judge someone else's servant? To his own master he stands or falls. And he will stand, for the Lord is able to make him stand.* Romans 14:4.

The final comment on this section is simply this: how we wish that the mother church in Jerusalem, having believed in Christ alone for salvation, was enjoying the liberty of the Spirit and the fulness of the gospel in its whole Christian experience. It does not appear to have been doing so. I'm sorry, friends, but I cannot agree with James on this occasion.

THANK YOU, HEAVENLY FATHER:

For Your infinite patience with us as we engage in Your service;

For guarding and blessing us in our going out and our coming in throughout our years of service to our Lord and Saviour Jesus Christ;

For the pastoral heart and mind of Paul: when caring for and pastoring Your people, and when evangelising the lost; O Lord who is sufficient for these things?

For Your over-ruling providence when good men differ about how Your work should be carried out;

For the liberating effect of the gospel in the life of a sinner; and for the liberating work of the Holy Spirit in the life of a believer; O that we all were to come to maturity in Jesus Christ;

For the privilege of laying all relationships before you in prayer; asking that we will be willing for Your will to be done in and through us;

IN JESUS' NAME, AMEN

Acts 21: 27 - 36

PAUL'S ARREST & TRIALS

56. Acts 21: 27 - 36

PAUL ARRESTED

It was inevitable that in the course of a week during which Paul went back and forth to the temple in Jerusalem that his enemies would spot him. That is exactly what happened.

> [27]*When the seven days were nearly over, some Jews from the province of Asia saw Paul at the temple. They stirred up the whole crowd and seized him.* Acts 21:27

They are described as Jews from the province of Asia. They could well have been from Ephesus itself, because several verses later Trophimus from Ephesus had also been seen in the city.

The sighting of these two men was enough to ignite very serious riots in the city. All it took (as if they were waiting for the signal) was a shout,

> [28]*"Men of Israel, help us! This is the man who teaches all men everywhere against our people and our law and this place. And besides, he has brought Greeks into the temple area and defiled this holy place."* Acts 21: 28

People poured on to the streets in their hundreds.

> [30]*The whole city was aroused, and the people came running from all directions. Seizing Paul, they dragged him from the temple, and immediately the gates were shut.* Acts 21: 30

Beware of democratic religion! Few in the crowd could have told you why they were there. Never let the influence of a crowd (however it is made up) manipulate your personal beliefs and relationship with God. Crowds can be wrong, as at the cross of Jesus, and here in Jerusalem where they are already attempting to murder Paul (v. 30).

In previous studies I found delight in showing that while the Jews had declared all-out war on Paul, the officials of Roman Government and the representatives of Roman law frequently protected him. Such is the case here. But for the intervention of the Roman Commander Paul would have died on the spot.

The commander lost no time in rounding up some officers and soldiers and ran down to the crowd.

> [32]*When the rioters saw the commander and his soldiers, they stopped beating Paul.* [33]*The commander came up and arrested him and ordered him to be bound with two chains. Then he asked who he was and what he had done.* Acts 21:32-33

Paul's assassins knew that what they were doing was unlawful.

You cannot depend on evidence obtained from a crowd – as the Roman commander found out. In modern legal practice one witness is not enough, there must be at least two. Their identities must be made known to the court and they must have reached the age of majority. Of course special provisions apply to the accused or to the witnesses if they are not of age. A court of law needs the solid and unanimous evidence of two reliable witnesses in order to proceed with a case.

> [33]*The commander came up and arrested him and ordered him to be bound with two chains. Then he asked who he was and what he had done.* [34]*Some in the crowd shouted one thing and some another, and since the commander could not get at the truth because of the uproar, he ordered that Paul be taken into the barracks.* Acts 21:33-34

So you see, the commander gave Paul the protection of the Law without hesitation. Paul is still in one piece. The soldiers had to carry him shoulder high to get entrance to the prison such was the pressure of the mob which had begun to chant, 'Away with him.'

Please forgive me for reminding you: but do you remember the words that Paul used when in Caesarea (21:13)? *'I am ready not only to be bound, but also to die in Jerusalem for the name of the Lord Jesus.'*

I have often wondered about our dear brothers and sisters in Christ in countries where they are denied the most basic civil and religious rights: where fathers, mothers and children are murdered indiscriminately. Had they at some point earlier in their lives covenanted with their Lord that they would 'lay down their lives' if He willed it? I think that is what they do by way of preparation for martyrdom. You don't postpone your decision to die for Christ until you are looking down the barrel of a gun.

You need to do it before that. Somewhat after the Romans 12:1-2 fashion. Once you have placed yourself on the altar of sacrifice, you cannot then climb down again at some future date.

Paul has long since passed to his eternal reward. We thank God for him, and continue to pray for the suffering church of today.

THANK YOU, HEAVENLY FATHER:

For the many saints and martyrs who, down the centuries, did not count their lives dear to themselves as to shrink from death for Jesus' sake;

For those occasions where it is costly to mention our Saviour's name: give us courage that we may speak the gospel boldly as we ought to speak;

For the privilege of praying for our persecutors, who, like Saul of Tarsus at one time, are blind to the person of Jesus and the message of the gospel; may they may soon become believers in Jesus;

For the fact that You alone Lord, know the hour of our death; may we meet You gladly.

IN JESUS' NAME, AMEN

THE FIRST TRIAL

57. Acts 21:37 - 22:21

PAUL SPEAKS TO THE CROWD

[37]As the soldiers were about to take Paul into the barracks, he asked the commander, "May I say something to you?" "Do you speak Greek?" he replied.

[38]"Aren't you the Egyptian who started a revolt and led four thousand terrorists out into the desert some time ago?"

[39]Paul answered, "I am a Jew, from Tarsus in Cilicia, a citizen of no ordinary city. Please let me speak to the people."

[40]Having received the commander's permission, Paul stood on the steps and motioned to the crowd. When they were all silent, he said to them in Aramaic: Acts 21:37-40

Whatever we think about Paul, we have to admire his persistence and singleness of purpose.

Knowing the man to some extent, as we do, we know that he meant what he said. Here, when the Roman commander permitted him to speak we see him being mightily sustained by the Holy Spirit with physical and spiritual strength. In a few seconds all this will be put to the test. He decided to speak to them in Aramaic, – the lingua franca of Palestine and parts of Syria.

The effect on the crowd was that it became very quiet. Paul began his speech respectfully, addressing the crowd as 'brothers and fathers' (v. 1.)

He told them in plain words of the change that had occurred in his life since leaving Phariseeism. This information confirmed what they knew about him generally, but here they were hearing about it firsthand from Paul himself (v. 2).

He told them his name, the city of his birth and where he was educated. He had the honour of being taught by Gamaliel, a grand old man of Judaism: so that by that time (as he put it) 'he was thoroughly trained in the law of our fathers and was just as jealous for God as any of you are today' (v. 3).

Then he told them of his campaign against Christians or 'followers of this Way.' The reference was to followers of Christ, one of whose names was 'The Way (John 14:6).' He had earned himself a reputation for 'arresting both men and women and throwing them into prison.' The truthfulness of the information he had spoken to them could be confirmed by the High Priest and Jewish Council (v. 5). When he came to Damascus, the Jewish leaders there also added their authority to what Paul was doing. The prisoners were taken to Jerusalem to be punished.

That was his final action against the Christian Church and believers in Jesus because as he rode into Damascus a bright light from heaven blinded him. He fell to the ground and heard a voice saying, 'Saul! Saul! Why do you persecute me? 'Who are you, Lord?' he asked (v. 6).

"I am Jesus of Nazareth, whom you are persecuting, he replied. My friends who were with me saw the light, but could not understand the voice of the person who was speaking to me.'

'What shall I do, Lord?' I asked. 'Get up,' the Lord said, 'and go into Damascus.'

> *There you will be told all that you have been assigned to do.' [11]My companions led me by the hand into Damascus, because the brilliance of the light had blinded me.* Acts 21:10-11

A man named Ananias came to see me. He was a devout observer of the law and highly respected by all the Jews living there. He stood beside me and said, 'Brother Saul, receive your sight!' And at that very moment I was able to see him' (v. 12).

Then he said, The God of our fathers has chosen you to know his will and to see the Righteous One and to hear words from his mouth. You will his witness to all men of what you have seen and heard. And now, what are you waiting for? Get up, be baptized and wash your sins away, calling on his name.'

"When I returned to Jerusalem and was praying at the temple, I fell into a trance [18] *and saw the Lord speaking. 'Quick!' he said to me. 'Leave Jerusalem immediately, because they will not accept your testimony about me'* Acts 21:14-18

In that moment, all those years ago in Damascus, face to face with the Risen Lord Jesus Christ, Saul of Tarsus made a complete confession of the sins he had committed against Christians (v. 19). He knew himself to be guilty of serious sins, and that even as he spoke to them here in Jerusalem, the hand of every Jew was against him, not for killing Christians, but for 'preaching and teaching all men everywhere against our people and our law and this place' (21:28).

Paul concluded his speech as follows:

[19] *" 'Lord,' I replied, 'these men know that I went from one synagogue to another to imprison and beat those who believe in you.* [20]*And when the blood of your martyr Stephen was shed, I stood there giving my approval and guarding the clothes of those who were killing him.'*

[21] *"Then the Lord said to me, 'Go; I will send you far away to the Gentiles.'* " Acts 22:19-21.

There is not the slightest doubt in our minds that Paul spoke and witnessed as he did by the help of the Holy Spirit.

THANK YOU, HEAVENLY FATHER,

For the knowledge that the issues of our daily lives are in Your mighty hand;

For Your presence with us in the daily conflict between darkness and light, between truth and falsehood, between the powers of heaven and the powers of hell, in the battle for the minds and souls of people who do not know Jesus;

For Your deliverance from many dangers, seen and unseen, that You grant us daily;

For the fact that neither death nor life, neither angels nor demons, neither the present nor the future, nor any powers, neither height nor depth, nor anything else in all creation, will be able to separate us from the love of God that is in Christ Jesus our Lord.

IN JESUS' NAME, AMEN

58. Acts 22:22-29

PAUL THE ROMAN CITIZEN

We thank God that the anger of the crowd was restrained by His hand. It was certainly simmering all the while that Paul was speaking. Could we say, as a matter of fact, that there was an almost respectful silence so that everyone could hear? But what will happen when the crowd's anger boils over?

> [22]*The crowd listened to Paul until he said this. Then they raised their voices and shouted, "Rid the earth of him! He's not fit to live!"* [23]*As they were shouting and throwing off their cloaks and flinging dust into the air,* [24]*the commander ordered Paul to be taken into the barracks. He directed that he be flogged and questioned in order to find out why the people were shouting at him like this.* Acts 22:22-24

The commander sounds like an experienced man with regard to crowd control and prisoner control. From what Paul had said to the crowd the commander had learned a lot about the prisoner, but if there was anything that Paul had been holding back then the commander had ways of making him talk.

At the same time we have to say that the commander 'kept his cool' (as our young people say). When Paul was being stretched out on a rack to be flogged he spoke to a centurion standing nearby,

> [25] *"Is it legal for you to flog a Roman citizen who hasn't even been found guilty?"* Acts 22:25

The centurion was alert and saw that he could rescue his commander from making a serious mistake in his administration of Roman law.

> [26]*When the centurion heard this, he went to the commander and reported it. "What are you going to do?" he asked. "This man is a Roman citizen."* Acts 22:26

The commander was greatly alarmed and went to Paul and asked: [27]*'Tell me, are you a Roman citizen?'*

[28]Then the commander said, *'I had to pay a big price for my citizenship.'* Presumably he had purchased his citizenship on the basis of having served in the Roman army and probably also by means of an expensive bribe.

'But I was born a citizen,' Paul replied.

Those who were about to question him withdrew immediately. The commander himself was alarmed when he realised that he had put Paul, a Roman citizen, in chains. Thank God for the rule of law, particularly if the law is recognised and obeyed by the citizenry and properly administered by the judiciary and the police service.

The providence of God, that ability of His by which He works all things together for good, was busy that day in Jerusalem in the lives of everyone involved in this event.

THANK YOU, HEAVENLY FATHER:

For the rule of law in the countries where we live; it protects the law-keepers and punishes the law-breakers; where this is not the case we pray that lawlessness will cease as Your Holy Spirit raises up a standard of righteousness;

For the dedication of our servicemen and women, in the Army, Navy, Air Force, and the Merchant Navy, the Police, the Ambulance and Fire and Rescue Services, and all others who serve the country for the greater good of all our citizens;

For all who serve our country in any of the above roles, that while they are on duty their families may also experience Your divine protection;

IN JESUS' NAME, AMEN

THE SECOND TRIAL

59. Acts 22:30 - 23:11

BEFORE THE SANHEDRIN

The Commander is fascinated by this prisoner. It was he who took the initiative because there was so much more he wanted to know about Paul, particularly why he was being accused by the Jews. Therefore he released Paul temporarily, but protected him from the anger of the crowd by immediately ordering the members of the Jewish Council to convene a meeting and deal with him in accordance with their powers. Then he brought Paul and had him stand before them.

> [1]*Paul looked straight at the Sanhedrin and said, "My brothers, I have fulfilled my duty to God in all good conscience to this day."* [2]*At this the high priest Ananias ordered those standing near Paul to strike him on the mouth.* Acts 23:1-2

This trial by the Sanhedrin got off to a bad start. Ananias the priest could not abide Paul trying to convince anybody that he had a good conscience toward God. How could anyone who was campaigning against Judaism be a good Jew? Ananias ordered those standing near Paul to strike him on the mouth. Paul wasn't going to make things easy for Ananias – he could at least give him a red face by pointing out:

> [3]*"God will strike you, you whitewashed wall! You sit there to judge me according to the law, yet you yourself violate the law by commanding that I be struck."*
>
> [4]*Those who were standing near Paul said, "You dare to insult God's high priest?"* [5]*Paul replied, "Brothers, I did not realise that he was the high priest; for it is written: 'Do not speak evil about the ruler of your people."* Acts 23:4-5

So Paul collected his thoughts and continued his defence.

[6]Then Paul, knowing that some of them were Sadducees and the others Pharisees, called out in the Sanhedrin, "My brothers, I am a Pharisee, the son of a Pharisee. I stand on trial because of my hope in the resurrection of the dead." Acts 23:6

He knew that as soon as he mentioned the resurrection of the dead the Pharisees and Sadducees would immediately begin arguing with one another.

[7]When he said this, a dispute broke out between the Pharisees and the Sadducees, and the assembly was divided. [8](The Sadducees say that there is no resurrection, and that there are neither angels nor spirits, but the Pharisees acknowledge them all.) Acts 23:7-8

The situation became uproarious and some of the Pharisees seized the opportunity to speak in Paul's favour.

[9]There was a great uproar, and some of the teachers of the law who were Pharisees stood up and argued vigorously. "We find nothing wrong with this man," they said. "What if a spirit or an angel has spoken to him?" Acts 23:9

The Commander, we need to remind ourselves, had no authority whatever to participate in the affairs of the Sanhedrin; however, the good man believed it was still his duty to maintain crowd control. Not only was he resourceful, he was long-headed and took precautions to prevent any attack on Paul's life:

[10]The dispute became so violent that the commander was afraid Paul would be torn to pieces by them. He ordered the troops to go down and take him away from them by force and bring him into the barracks. Acts 23:10

So the trial by the Sanhedrin had been kept brief and was quickly closed, and from the viewpoint of the Council has achieved precisely nothing!

Here we see that the convictions that Paul had talked about in Acts 21:13ff, (when he was in Caesarea), had depth to them. During the night the Lord comforted Paul:

> [11]*The following night the Lord stood near Paul and said, "Take courage! As you have testified about me in Jerusalem, so you must also testify in Rome."* Acts 23:11

If Paul was sitting in prison that night saying to himself, 'I made a real hash of that opportunity', the opposite was the case. Paul had earned his Lord's approval.

THANK YOU HEAVENLY FATHER:

For the fact that when our life-work is ended and we stand before our Lord Jesus Christ, his evaluation of our service will be the most important; You will understand, and say 'Well done!'

For the fact that when our many attempts to serve you effectively seemed ineffective, still You were honoured by our service in Jesus' Name;

For help in Your service that sometimes came from unexpected sources, even from unbelievers;

For Your promise of 'strength for the day' – and for the fact that it has never failed;

IN JESUS' NAME, AMEN

60. Acts 23:12-22

THE PLOT TO KILL PAUL

[12]The next morning the Jews formed a conspiracy and bound themselves with an oath not to eat or drink until they had killed Paul. [13]More than forty men were involved in this plot. [14]They went to the chief priests and elders and said, "We have taken a solemn oath not to eat anything until we have killed Paul.

[15]Now then, you and the Sanhedrin petition the commander to bring him before you on the pretext of wanting more accurate information about his case. We are ready to kill him before he gets here." Acts 23:12-15

We are aware that the Jews tolerated the Roman occupation of Palestine for most of the time. But they were not a bit shy about using the law to advance their causes, whether legal or illegal. They did not have the authority to execute anyone. That power was in the hands of the Romans. So we assume that it was their intention when Paul was being brought out by the Commander the next morning they would have enough men and enough force to ambush Paul and kill him – and then escape the law themselves. So they had to set the trap.

Little jugs have big ears! A youth overheard the plot being laid. We don't know what age this nephew of Paul's was, perhaps a young teenager, but he had his wits about him. First he told Paul what he had learned and on his uncle's bidding went to the barracks, gained admission to the Commander and told him about the plot to kill Paul.

Paul asked a centurion who was nearby to take the boy to the commander: 'He has something to tell him,' he said. So the boy stood in front of the commander within a few minutes. The centurion introduced the lad.

> *[18]The centurion said, "Paul, the prisoner, sent for me and asked me to bring this young man to you because he has something to tell you." [19]The commander took the young man by the hand, drew him aside and asked, "What is it you want to tell me?"*
>
> *[20]He said: "The Jews have agreed to ask you to bring Paul before the Sanhedrin tomorrow on the pretext of wanting more accurate information about him. [21]Don't give in to them, because more than forty of them are waiting in ambush for him. They have taken an oath not to eat or drink until they have killed him. They are ready now, waiting for your consent to their request."*
>
> *[22]The commander dismissed the young man and cautioned him, "Don't tell anyone that you have reported this to me."* Acts 23:18-20

THANK YOU, HEAVENLY FATHER;

For the fact that heaven's court never adjourns, it is always in session; Job found that to be true (Job 1 & 2) and Paul found this to be true. Therefore the Jews' plan to kill Paul was quashed by heaven.

For another truth of Scripture (close in meaning to the one above) 'Vengeance is mine, I will repay,' says the Lord;

For the fact that the eyes of the Lord are on the righteous and his ears are open to their cry;

For the promise You have made to your people. 'Never will I leave you; never will I forsake you.' So we say with confidence, 'The Lord is my helper; I will not be afraid. What can man do to me?'

IN JESUS' NAME, AMEN

61. Acts 23: 23 - 35

PAUL TRANSFERRED TO CAESAREA

[23]Then he (the Commander) called two of his centurions and ordered them, "Get ready a detachment of two hundred soldiers, seventy horsemen and two hundred spearmen to go to Caesarea at nine tonight. [24]Provide mounts for Paul so that he may be taken safely to Governor Felix." Acts 23:23-24

In a previous study I asked if Paul ever travelled on mules or donkeys (Study 49). At that point I couldn't recall whether he did or not. Well, in case anyone has been losing sleep wondering, here is evidence that he could at least sit on a horse! In Acts 23:24 his friend, the Roman Commander ordered two centurions to provide mounts for Paul.

I wonder did Paul ever stop to think how much he owed this Roman for taking care of his personal safety. He could not have paid the man in currency. That was uncalled for, and perhaps would have been regarded as something of a bribe. But did Paul ever thank the man? If he forgot Paul for everything else, he would remember him for saying thanks.

For the Roman it was a case of 'never having lost a prisoner yet' – for Paul it was the gift from God's hand of another day in which to serve Jesus. That is how it is with all of us. Another day, another gift from God.

Claudius Lysias, the Roman commander wrote a letter as follows:.

'For the attention of His Excellency, Governor Felix' Greetings.

[27]This man was seized by the Jews and they were about to kill him, but I came with my troops and rescued him, for I had learned that he is a Roman citizen.

> [28]*I wanted to know why they were accusing him, so I brought him to their Sanhedrin.* [29]*I found that the accusation had to do with questions about their law, but there was no charge against him that deserved death or imprisonment.*
>
> [30]*When I was informed of a plot to be carried out against the man, I sent him to you at once. I also ordered his accusers to present to you their case against him.* Acts 23:27-30

After having secured the prisoner so well, and having written to Felix to say he was on his way to be tried by him, the commander was taking no risks. Paul was accompanied by two hundred soldiers, seventy horsemen, and two hundred spearmen to leave for Caesarea by nine o'clock that night (vv.23-24). The first stage of the journey took them to Antipatris, midway between Caesarea and Jerusalem, in fact on the northern border of Judea. The next day the cavalry went on with Paul and the horsemen returned to the barracks.

The rest of this instalment is easily told:

> [33]*When the cavalry arrived in Caesarea, they delivered the letter to the governor and handed Paul over to him.* [34]*The governor read the letter and asked what province he was from.*
>
> *Learning that he was from Cilicia,* [35]*he said, "I will hear your case when your accusers get here." Then he ordered that Paul be kept under guard in Herod's palace.* Acts 23:33-35

THANK YOU, HEAVENLY FATHER;

For the fact that *'the king's heart is in the hand of the Lord; he directs it like a watercourse wherever he pleases'* (Proverbs 21:1);

For *'even the darkness will not be dark to You; the night will shine like the day, the darkness is as light to You'* (Psalm 139:10-12);

For Your goodness and mercy that have followed me all the days of my life and I will dwell in the house of the Lord forever (Psalm 23);

IN JESUS' NAME, AMEN

THE THIRD TRIAL

62. Acts 24:1-27

THE TRIAL BEFORE FELIX

> [1]*Five days later the high priest Ananias went down to Caesarea with some of the elders and a lawyer named Tertullus, and they brought their charges against Paul before the governor.* Acts 24:1

Order is being observed.

Not a word connected with the case is spoken until the prisoner is brought into court.

> [2]*When Paul was called in, Tertullus presented his case before Felix: "We have enjoyed a long period of peace under you, and your foresight has brought about reforms in this nation.* [3]*Everywhere and in every way, most excellent Felix, we acknowledge this with profound gratitude.* [4]*But in order not to weary you further, I would request that you be kind enough to hear us briefly.* Acts 24:2

Those were just a few saccharine words to sweeten up Felix (if his mood required them that morning). It was an attempt to capture the judge's goodwill.

Tertullus gets to the point.

> [5]*"We have found this man to be a troublemaker, stirring up riots among the Jews all over the world. He is a ringleader of the Nazarene sect* [6]*and even tried to desecrate the temple; so we seized him and wanted to judge him according to our law. But the commander, Lysias, came and with the use of much force snatched him from our hands and ordered his accusers to come before you.* [8]*By examining him yourself you will be able to learn the truth about all these charges we are bringing against him."* Acts 24:5-8

[Some MSS omit verses 6-8.]

Terrullus affirmed that the Jewish crowd joined in these accusations asserting that these things were true (v. 9),

Felix motioned that Paul could speak.

> [10]*When the governor motioned for him to speak, Paul replied: "I know that for a number of years you have been a judge over this nation; so I gladly make my defence.* [11]*You can easily verify that no more than twelve days ago I went up to Jerusalem to worship.*
>
> [12]*My accusers did not find me arguing with anyone at the temple, or stirring up a crowd in the synagogues or anywhere else in the city.* [13]*And they cannot prove to you the charges they are now making against me.* Acts 24:10-13

Paul decided to answer the false charges against him. He challenged anyone to contradict his defence, because he was speaking the truth.

> [14]*However, I admit that I worship the God of our fathers as a follower of the Way, which they call a sect. I believe everything that agrees with the Law and that is written in the Prophets,* [15]*and I have the same hope in God as these men, that there will be a resurrection of both the righteous and the wicked.* [16]*So I strive always to keep my conscience clear before God and man.* Acts 24:14-16

Paul is maintaining that he is not a deviant, but is loyal to the ancestral faith. Nor is he a sectarian or a heretic for he stood squarely in mainstream Judaism. As a follower of 'the Way' (a name for the followers of Jesus) he was in direct continuity with the Old Testament, because the scriptures witnessed to Jesus Christ as the one in whom God's promises had been fulfilled.

Another accusation against him was that he profaned the temple. Paul answered:

> [17]*"After an absence of several years, I came to Jerusalem to bring my people gifts for the poor and to present offerings.* [18]*I was ceremonially clean when they found me in the temple courts*

doing this. There was no crowd with me, nor was I involved in any disturbance.

[19]But there are some Jews from the province of Asia, who ought to be here before you and bring charges if they have anything against me. [20]Or these who are here should state what crime they found in me when I stood before the Sanhedrin— [21]unless it was this one thing I shouted as I stood in their presence: 'It is concerning the resurrection of the dead that I am on trial before you today.' " Acts 24:17-21

In other words the court had convened and some witnesses had not been called; witnesses who ought to have been heard (vv. 19-21).

The Court Adjourned by Felix.

[22]Then Felix, who was well acquainted with the Way, adjourned the proceedings. "When Lysias the commander comes," he said, "I will decide your case." Acts 24:22

The thing that was getting under the skin of these Roman officials was that the Jews did not have a legal complaint to make against Paul – their complaints and charges were about Jewish law and Jewish worship and had nothing to do with Roman law. Nor were the officials going to get themselves a bad name by denying the prisoner any legal rights or by treating him inhumanely. So we begin to see the exceptional features of Roman law.

So when Felix made provision for Paul's welfare he made excellent arrangements.

[23]He ordered the centurion to keep Paul under guard but to give him some freedom and permit his friends to take care of his needs. Acts 24:23

Paul meets Drusilla, the wife of Felix.

[24] Several days later Felix came with his wife Drusilla, who was a Jewess. He sent for Paul and listened to him as ***he spoke about faith in Christ Jesus.*** Acts 24:24

There we have Paul's theme: otherwise the signature tune of evangelicalism.

> [25]*As Paul discoursed on righteousness, self-control and the judgment to come, Felix was afraid and said, "That's enough for now! You may leave. When I find it convenient, I will send for you."* Acts 24:25

The King James Version of the Bible has a priceless rendering of this verse:

> [25] *And as he reasoned of righteousness, temperance, and judgment to come,* ***Felix trembled****, and answered, 'Go thy way for this time; when I have a convenient season, I will call for thee.'*

A grand old man of Irish Baptists, the late Pastor Louis Edward Deens (who spent the greater part of his ministry in Dublin), was a wonderful preacher and a genius at homiletics. He preached a famous sermon on this two-word text in Acts 24:25 KJV many times. For him, the emphases of the text were as follows. (1) Felix Trembled; (2) Only Felix Trembled; & (3) Felix Only Trembled. Many a preacher would give his eye-teeth to be able to express a text in such succinct terms.

Felix found an escape route from Paul's penetrating preaching:

> [25]*As Paul discoursed on righteousness, self-control and the judgment to come, Felix was afraid and said, "That's enough for now! You may leave. When I find it convenient, I will send for you."* Acts 24:25

It was unbridled lust and total lack of self-control that had brought Felix and Druscilla together in the first place.

> [26]*At the same time he was hoping that Paul would offer him a bribe, so he sent for him frequently and talked with him.* Acts 24:26

Sadly there is no evidence that Felix ever came to know Jesus and find something more than gold.

Felix wasn't a man of his word:

> [27]*When two years had passed, Felix was succeeded by Porcius Festus, but because Felix wanted to grant a favour to the Jews, he left Paul in prison.* Acts 24:27

THANK YOU, HEAVENLY FATHER:

For Paul's witness to Felix and Priscilla, despite which both of them opted for the whole world and lost their own souls;

For many good people whose callings and careers mean that they live in high places; we thank You for the Christian witnesses who are in their employment and whose testimonies they respect;

For every humble believer in Jesus who thanks You *'that one day in a quiet place, they met the Master face to face';*

For the gospel story of Your love for a world of sinners, for whom You gave Your one and only Son, that whoever believes in him, shall not perish but have eternal life.

IN JESUS' NAME, AMEN

THE FOURTH TRIAL

63. Acts 25:1-12

THE TRIAL BEFORE FESTUS

> 1*Three days after arriving in the province, Festus went up from Caesarea to Jerusalem, 2where the chief priests and Jewish leaders appeared before him and presented the charges against Paul. Acts 25:1-2*

How brazen and unprincipled can men be? Notice the party was led by the chief priests and Jewish leaders who had come to present charges. But look at what this group asked the properly appointed and installed Roman Governor to do:

> [3]*They urgently requested Festus, as a favour to them, to have Paul transferred to Jerusalem, for they were preparing an ambush to kill him along the way.* Acts 25:3

They wanted rid of Paul, by whose hand or by whatever means it was possible to have him killed.

Festus never batted an eyelid (as we say) but was firm and unbending in his reply:

> [4]*Festus answered, "Paul is being held at Caesarea, and I myself am going there soon.* [5]*Let some of your leaders come with me and press charges against the man there, if he has done anything wrong."* Acts 25:4-5

Festus wasn't going to be pushed around. Nor was he in the slightest hurry:

> [6]*After spending eight or ten days with them, he went down to Caesarea, and the next day he convened the court and ordered that Paul be brought before him.* [7]*When Paul appeared, the Jews who had come down from Jerusalem stood around him, bringing many serious charges, which they could not prove.* Acts 25:6-7

Paul was permitted to make his defence

> [8]*Then Paul made his defence: "I have done nothing wrong against the law of the Jews or against the temple or against Caesar."* Acts 25:8

Festus is an old dog, and you can't teach an old dog new tricks

> [9]*Festus, wishing to do the Jews a favour, said to Paul, "Are you willing to go up to Jerusalem and stand trial before me there on these charges?"* Acts 25:9

Do you see what Festus has done? The Jews were absolutely blazing with anger that they had to make the journey from Jerusalem to Caesarea – and not the other way round. In their view Paul and company ought to be doing the travelling – that was why they badgered Paul in v. 7. If looks could kill – then they would have needed a mortician and a Rabbi to conduct his funeral service.

Paul was no 'dozer' either (as we say) and I think he was enjoying the discomfort of the Jews. Paul's reply is priceless.

> [10]*Paul answered: "I am now standing before Caesar's court, where I ought to be tried. I have not done any wrong to the Jews, as you yourself know very well.*
>
> [11]*If, however, I am guilty of doing anything deserving death, I do not refuse to die. But if the charges brought against me by these Jews are not true, no-one has the right to hand me over to them."*
>
> *"I appeal to Caesar!"* Acts 25:10-11

Paul has extricated himself from the hands of the Jews in a few words!

After a brief aside to confer with his council, Festus affirmed:

> [12]*After Festus had conferred with his council, he declared: "You have appealed to Caesar. To Caesar you will go!"* Acts 25:12

THANK YOU, HEAVENLY FATHER:

For a Christian's love of the truth: the Jews who were charging Paul with crimes against their faith, were the most unscrupulous of men, scheming to kill Paul. They cared nothing for truth;

For Paul's awareness of what was going on; and his adamant testimony that he had done nothing wrong either in Jewish or Roman Law;

For the working of Divine Providence in such situations; so that wrong is exposed and right is exalted;

For Your will that Paul should travel to Rome and bear testimony there for the glory of his Saviour and Lord;

IN JESUS' NAME, AMEN

THE FIFTH TRIAL

64. Acts 25:13 - 26:32

PAUL BEFORE AGRIPPA.

[13]A few days later King Agrippa and Bernice arrived at Caesarea to pay their respects to Festus. [14]Since they were spending many days there, Festus discussed Paul's case with the king. He said: "There is a man here whom Felix left as a prisoner. [15]When I went to Jerusalem, the chief priests and elders of the Jews brought charges against him and asked that he be condemned.

[16]"I told them that it is not the Roman custom to hand over any man before he has faced his accusers and has had an opportunity to defend himself against their charges. [17]When they came here with me, I did not delay the case, but convened the court the next day and ordered the man to be brought in.

[18]When his accusers got up to speak, they did not charge him with any of the crimes I had expected. [19]Instead, they had some points of dispute with him about their own religion and about a dead man named Jesus whom Paul claimed was alive. [20]I was at a loss how to investigate such matters; so I asked if he would be willing to go to Jerusalem and stand trial there on these charges. [21]When Paul made his appeal to be held over for the Emperor's decision, I ordered him to be held until I could send him to Caesar."

[22]Then Agrippa said to Festus, "I would like to hear this man myself." He replied, "Tomorrow you will hear him." Acts 25:13-22

Felix was in no hurry to deal with the prisoner and close his case. Two years passed during which time Paul languished in prison. One day Felix was entertaining King Agrippa and his queen Bernice at Caesarea and thought to himself, 'It might be a good way to pass an hour or two. Let them meet Paul.'

So with a few remarks about how he kept the Jews (Paul's accusers) in line, Felix and Herod set a time when they will have Paul before them the next day (v. 22).

Paul before Agrippa

Can't we see them all, the men bursting their uniforms and looking resplendent in their formal dress? Bernice and the ladies were likewise attired for this formal gathering.

> [23]*The next day Agrippa and Bernice came with great pomp and entered the audience room with the high ranking officers and the leading men of the city. At the command of Festus, Paul was brought in.* Acts 25:23

Festus opened the proceedings:

> [24]*Festus said: "King Agrippa and all who are present with us, you see this man!*
>
> *The whole Jewish community has petitioned me about him in Jerusalem and here in Caesarea, shouting that he ought not to live any longer.* [25]*I found he had done nothing deserving of death, but because he made his appeal to the Emperor I decided to send him to Rome.* [26]*But I have nothing definite to write to His Majesty about him.*
>
> *Therefore I have brought him before all of you, and especially before you, King Agrippa, so that as a result of this investigation I may have something to write.* [27]*For I think it is unreasonable to send on a prisoner without specifying the charges against him."* Acts 25:24-27

The case is now underway.

> [1]*Then Agrippa said to Paul, "You have permission to speak for yourself." So Paul motioned with his hand and began his defence:* [2]*"King Agrippa, I consider myself fortunate to stand before you today as I make my defence against all the accusations of the Jews,* [3]*and especially so because you are well acquainted*

with all the Jewish customs and controversies. Therefore, I beg you to listen to me patiently. Acts 24:1-3

Paul addressed King Agrippa with respect.

He made it clear that he was defending himself against the accusations of the Jews. He believed that the King was very experienced in dealing with Jewish customs and controversies.

> [4]*"The Jews all know the way I have lived ever since I was a child, from the beginning of my life in my own country, and also in Jerusalem.* [5]*They have known me for a long time and can testify, if they are willing, that according to the strictest sect of our religion, I lived as a Pharisee.*
>
> [6]*And now it is because of my hope in what God has promised our fathers that I am on trial today.* [7]*This is the promise our twelve tribes are hoping to see fulfilled as they earnestly serve God day and night. O King, it is because of this hope that the Jews are accusing me.* [8]*Why should any of you consider it incredible that God raises the dead?* Acts 26:4-8

Paul is not arguing against the administration of Jewish Law, he has no complaint. The Jews are taking up the time of a Roman Court with their religious disputes. But Paul has to explain his position vis-à-vis the message of the prophets about the Messiah Jesus, and the significance of his life, death and resurrection. But he did not always think like this.

> [9]*"I too was convinced that I ought to do all that was possible to oppose the name of Jesus of Nazareth.* [10]*And that is just what I did in Jerusalem. On the authority of the chief priests I put many of the saints in prison, and when they were put to death, I cast my vote against them.* [11]*Many a time I went from one synagogue to another to have them punished, and I tried to force them to blaspheme. In my obsession against them, I even went to foreign cities to persecute them.* Acts 26:9-11

Now it is the turn of Agrippa to hear Paul's testimony:

> *[12]"On one of these journeys I was going to Damascus with the authority and commission of the chief priests. [13]About noon, O King, as I was on the road, I saw a light from heaven, brighter than the sun, blazing around me and my companions. [14]We all fell to the ground, and I heard a voice saying to me in Aramaic, 'Saul, Saul, why do you persecute me? It is hard for you to kick against the goads.'*
>
> *[15]"Then I asked, 'Who are you, Lord?' 'I am Jesus, whom you are persecuting,' the Lord replied. [16] 'Now get up and stand on your feet. I have appeared to you to appoint you as a servant and as a witness of what you have seen of me and what I will show you. [17]I will rescue you from your own people and from the Gentiles. I am sending you to them [18]to open their eyes and turn them from darkness to light, and from the power of Satan to God, so that they may receive forgiveness of sins and a place among those who are sanctified by faith in me.'* Acts 26:12-18

You may be thinking that with an able speaker with the ability of Paul, these proceedings are going to shorten the afternoon. Just watch Festus. He is embarrassed in the presence of King Agrippa.

> *[19]"So then, King Agrippa, I was not disobedient to the vision from heaven. [20]First to those in Damascus, then to those in Jerusalem and in all Judea, and to the Gentiles also, I preached that they should repent and turn to God and prove their repentance by their deeds. [21]That is why the Jews seized me in the temple courts and tried to kill me. [22]But I have had God's help to this very day, and so I stand here and testify to small and great alike. I am saying nothing beyond what the prophets and Moses said would happen— [23]that the Christ would suffer and, as the first to rise from the dead, would proclaim light to his own people and to the Gentiles."* Acts 26:19-23

[24]At this point Festus interrupted Paul's defence.

> *"You are out of your mind, Paul!" he shouted. "Your great learning is driving you insane." [25]"I am not insane, most*

excellent Festus," Paul replied. "What I am saying is true and reasonable". Acts 26:24-25

Asking Paul to stop was like trying to stop the tide coming in.

[26]The king is familiar with these things, and I can speak freely to him. I am convinced that none of this has escaped his notice, because it was not done in a corner. [27]King Agrippa, do you believe the prophets? I know you do." Acts 26:26-27

Paul had addressed the King directly and got himself a very quick 'put-down'

[28]Then Agrippa said to Paul, "Do you think that in such a short time you can persuade me to be a Christian?" [29]Paul replied, "Short time or long—I pray God that not only you but all who are listening to me today may become what I am, except for these chains." Acts 26:28-29

So the case closed without a verdict

There was no verdict; the court had not been convened as such that afternoon, merely for the entertainment of the King and Queen. Agrippa gave his opinion to Festus privately as the two men left the room. They found themselves in agreement.

[30]The king rose, and with him the governor and Bernice and those sitting with them. [31]They left the room, and while talking with one another, they said, "This man is not doing anything that deserves death or imprisonment." [32]Agrippa said to Festus, "This man could have been set free if he had not appealed to Caesar." Acts 26:30-32

And so this unproductive episode closes. The enormous machinery of law and order that the Roman Empire relied on for its smooth functioning, was unstoppable.

Paul was bound for Rome. He had demanded to go there to avoid being killed at the whim of the Jews, or as the victim of one of their murderous plots. He had not broken any law of Rome, not had he found guilty of any crime. It was unnecessary for him to appeal to Caesar because of the nature of his case. Politically speaking, only the Emperor could save Paul now.

THANK YOU, HEAVENLY FATHER:

For the legal rights of citizenship, protected by civil law and recognised diligently when the occasion demands; enabling all citizens to behave so as to protect these rights for all;

For the protection of Paul's life and travel when so many of his Jewish enemies were actively plotting to kill him by all means, legal or otherwise;

For Paul's demeanour when on trial, respectful to the officers of the court, courageous in his defence when wrongly accused, not ashamed to speak of his Saviour when given the opportunity to speak;

For all Your people who are prison because they were wrongfully accused and arrested for faith crimes. Oh God, give them your strength and your joy inexpressible and full of glory. Be with parents and children, husbands and wives who are so cruelly separated;

IN JESUS' NAME, AMEN

Acts 27:1 – 28:1

ROME AT LAST

65. Acts 27: 1-12

PAUL SAILS FOR ROME

> [1]*When it was decided that we would sail for Italy, Paul and some other prisoners were handed over to a centurion named Julius, who belonged to the Imperial Regiment.* Acts 27:1

Paul's itinerary takes him to sea for the very long journey to Rome, and at a very awkward time of the year for seafarers. Ships' captains would soon be coming off the sea for the winter months because storms on the Mediterranaen Sea were renowned for their ferocity.

The ship that was ready to depart was a coastal vessel that did a kind of 'milk run' for the ports she could access.

> [2] *We boarded a ship from Adramyttium about to sail for ports along the coast of the province of Asia, and we put out to sea. Aristarchus, a Macedonian from Thessalonica, was with us.* Acts 27:2

Perhaps they knew of Aristarchus' plan to travel with them: it doesn't sound like too much of a surprise. However, he would be welcome company. He had travelled with Paul in Greece. And at a future date Paul would refer to him as 'my fellow-prisoner'.

It's interesting that Luke was able to travel with Paul. Again the fellowship factor would be high. A very pleasant experience awaited them at their next port of call.

> [3]*The next day we landed at Sidon; and Julius, in kindness to Paul, allowed him to go to his friends so they might provide for his needs.* Acts 27:3

From Sidon on the Syrian shore they sailed west across the sea to pass on the lee side of Crete. Strong winds buffeted them all the way

(v. 4). Despite the difficulty, they made it to southern Turkey and the coast of Silicia and Pamphylia, landing at Myra in Lycia (v. 5).

A Change of Ship

> *[6]There the centurion found an Alexandrian ship sailing for Italy and put us on board. [7]We made slow headway for many days and had difficulty arriving off Cnidus. When the wind did not allow us to hold our course, we sailed to the lee of Crete, opposite Salmone. [8]We moved along the coast with difficulty and came to a place called Fair Havens, near the town of Lasea.* Acts 27:6-8

They were travelling late in the year, hence the serious storm

> *[9]Much time had been lost, and sailing had already become dangerous because by now it was after the Fast (After Pentecost). So Paul warned them, [10]"Men, I can see that our voyage is going to be disastrous and bring great loss to ship and cargo, and to our own lives also."*

> *[11]But the centurion, instead of listening to what Paul said, followed the advice of the pilot and of the owner of the ship. [12]Since the harbour was unsuitable to winter in, the majority decided that we should sail on, hoping to reach Phoenix and winter there. This was a harbour in Crete, facing both south-west and north-west.* Acts 27:9-12

What would you have thought if the captain of a ship on which you were sailing was being advised by one of the passengers, whose advice he seemed to ignore (vv. 9 -11)?

Paul was advising that they should not proceed. What qualifications did he have to advise the captain? He was a servant of God, but that might not have meant anything to the captain. Would you have thought anything the less of him for ignoring Paul's advice?

What if you were also aware that the pilot of the ship, who also owned the ship, ignored the advice of Paul, and settled the matter by having the passengers vote on it (v. 12)? Naturally the vote turned out that they proceed on the journey hoping to reach Phoenix, and spend the winter there.

The second ship we should note was much larger, was carrying 276 passengers and a cargo of grain. It would have been unwieldy in heavy seas wallowing between the waves rather than rising on them to dip again to meet and ride up the following wave.

We will leave them there for a while, pondering the choice they had made. They would have to winter somewhere.

THANK YOU HEAVENLY FATHER:

For the fact that we influence others who do not see things as we do by prayer and example, rather than by argument or a superior, know-it-all attitude;

For those in peril on the sea, especially the Fishing Fleets, the Merchant Navy and Ferry Masters, who import so much of our food and essential materials, in peace time as in wartime;

For those whose work at sea takes them away from home for long periods of separation from wives and children; O God, answer their prayers for their families;

For the privilege of committing our way to the Lord, whenever, however and wherever we travel, and for every safe journey we make;

IN JESUS' NAME, AMEN

66. Acts 27:13 - 26

THE STORM (EUROCLYDON)

Read v. 13 and share the relief of the passengers.

> [13]*When a gentle south wind began to blow, they thought they had obtained what they wanted; so they weighed anchor and sailed along the shore of Crete.* Acts 27:13

Anyone who wasn't observing the clouds might not have been worried. Weren't they the brave souls who had decided to sail on when they were south of Crete?

They weren't so brave perhaps, when *'a tempestuous wind, known as Euroclydon'* rose against them (KJV v. 14)

> [14]*Before very long, a wind of hurricane force, called the "north-easter", swept down from the island.* [15]*The ship was caught by the storm and could not head into the wind; so we gave way to it and were driven along.* [16]*As we passed to the lee of a small island called Cauda, we were hardly able to make the lifeboat secure.*
>
> [17]*When the men had hoisted it aboard, they passed ropes under the ship itself to hold it together. Fearing that they would run aground on the sand-bars of Syrtis, they lowered the sea anchor and let the ship be driven along.* [18]*We took such a violent battering from the storm that the next day they began to throw the cargo overboard.* [19]*On the third day, they threw the ship's tackle overboard with their own hands.*
>
> [20]*When neither sun nor stars appeared for many days and the storm continued raging, we finally gave up all hope of being saved.* Acts 27:14-20

That is a picture of lostness (v. 20). They hadn't a clue where they were, because the heavenly bodies could not be seen in the darkness of the storm. They were without navigation.

Would any of them listen to Paul now?

> [21]*After the men had gone a long time without food, Paul stood up before them and said: "Men, you should have taken my advice not to sail from Crete; then you would have spared yourselves this damage and loss.* [22]*But now I urge you to keep up your courage, because not one of you will be lost; only the ship will be destroyed.*
>
> [23]*Last night an angel of the God whose I am and whom I serve stood beside me* [24]*and said, 'Do not be afraid, Paul. You must stand trial before Caesar; and God has graciously given you the lives of all who sail with you.*
>
> [25]*So keep up your courage, men, for I have faith in God that it will happen just as he told me.* [26]*Nevertheless, we must run aground on some island."* Acts 27:21-25

THANK YOU, HEAVENLY FATHER:

For the numerous narratives in the Old and New Testaments in which the sea has a prominent part: all the way from Genesis when God called the gathered waters 'seas' to the day in which the sea gives up the dead which are in it (Rev. 20:13);

For the illustrative use of the sea in the scriptures: a picture of restlessness (the wicked are like the troubled sea); a place of forgetfulness (where God has cast our sins), and a picture of calm in obedience to the voice of Jesus the Lord of Creation;

For all who are travelling today by land, by sea and by air, taking the Gospel of Jesus Christ to the nations of the world;

IN JESUS' NAME, AMEN

67. Acts 27:27-44

THE SHIPWRECK

> [27]**On the fourteenth night** *we were still being driven across the Adriatic Sea, when about midnight the sailors sensed they were approaching land.* [28]*They took soundings and found that the water was one hundred and twenty feet deep. A short time later they took soundings again and found it was ninety feet deep.* [29]*Fearing that we would be dashed against the rocks, they dropped four anchors from the stern and prayed for daylight.* Acts 27:27-29

I have often thought that people who have spent days and night at sea, with or without a boat, and lived to tell the tale must be remarkable people not only with strong character but strong determination. Such stories abounded in wartime when, for instance, German U-Boats sank ships in the Allied Convoys that were crossing the Atlantic bringing essential supplies to Europe.

In this case, I think things are bad when sailors begin to pray (v. 29). There cannot be a lonelier place on earth than to be alone at sea, without help, and in the unlikely event of any coming along.

The sailors took other measures to save the ship and its human cargo:

> [30]*In an attempt to escape from the ship, the sailors let the lifeboat down into the sea, pretending they were going to lower some anchors from the bow.* [31]*Then Paul said to the centurion and the soldiers, "Unless these men stay with the ship, you cannot be saved."* [32]*So the soldiers cut the ropes that held the lifeboat and let it fall away.* Acts 27:30-32

They were going to save themselves first by trying to escape on the lifeboat. Paul spotted what they were doing and told them that the safety of all on board depended on their remaining on board.

[33]Just before dawn Paul urged them all to eat. "For the last fourteen days," he said, "you have been in constant suspense and have gone without food—you haven't eaten anything. [34]Now I urge you to take some food. You need it to survive. Not one of you will lose a single hair from his head." [35]After he said this, he took some bread and gave thanks to God in front of them all. Then he broke it and began to eat. [36]They were all encouraged and ate some food themselves.

[37]Altogether there were 276 of us on board. [38]When they had eaten as much as they wanted, they lightened the ship by throwing the grain into the sea. Acts 27:33-38

Thank God for daylight

It changes everything. For one thing it scatters the fears of the night.

[39]When daylight came, they did not recognise the land, but they saw a bay with a sandy beach, where they decided to run the ship aground if they could. [40]Cutting loose the anchors, they left them in the sea and at the same time untied the ropes that held the rudders. Then they hoisted the foresail to the wind and made for the beach. [41]But the ship struck a sand-bar and ran aground. The bow stuck fast and would not move, and the stern was broken to pieces by the pounding of the surf. Acts 27:39-41

We try to imagine that voyage of fourteen nights and days, most of the journey spent tacking into the wind and being driven every way by the ferocity of the storm. I think many stories would be told by firesides when they would all reach home eventually.

After such brave attempts to save life, the Roman soldiers were planning to kill their prisoners to prevent any of them from swimming away and escaping.

Here is another time when a friendly Centurion saves Paul's life.

[43] But ***the centurion wanted to spare Paul's life*** *and kept them from carrying out their plan. He ordered those who could swim to jump overboard first and get to land. [44]The rest were to get*

there on planks or on pieces of the ship. In this way everyone reached land in safety. Acts 27:43-44

THANK YOU HEAVENLY FATHER:

For the spirit of prayer that descended on the survivors of the (now famous) shipwreck; we thank You that the sea and its moods can give people a sense of God;

For the convenient food supply on board the ship, albeit that the bulk of it had to be thrown overboard; it sustained life and was sufficient to meet the need.

For the fact that *'You plant Your footsteps in the sea, and ride upon the storm.'*

IN JESUS' NAME, AMEN

68. Acts 28:1-10
ASHORE ON MALTA

> [1]*Once safely on shore, we found out that the island was called Malta.* [2]*The islanders showed us unusual kindness. They built a fire and welcomed us all because it was raining and cold.*
> Acts 28:1-2

Wonders never cease

What a grand thing that reception was that the Maltese people gave to the survivors of the shipwreck. Evidently they met them coming ashore. Someone had built a fire and welcomed them because it was raining and cold (v. 2). Paul was showing his gratitude to them by getting involved in the arrangements they were making.

> [3]*Paul gathered a pile of brushwood and, as he put it on the fire, a viper, driven out by the heat, fastened itself on his hand.* [4]*When the islanders saw the snake hanging from his hand, they said to each other, "This man must be a murderer; for though he escaped from the sea, Justice has not allowed him to live."*
>
> [5]*But Paul shook the snake off into the fire and suffered no ill effects.* [6]*The people expected him to swell up or suddenly fall dead, but after waiting a long time and seeing nothing unusual happen to him, they changed their minds and said he was a god.*
> Acts 28:1- 6

On the hundreds, perhaps thousands of little islands dotted on the Mediterranean Sea there was a lot of superstition. This explains why the islanders thought that Paul was a god. I imagine he soon scotched that rumour. Had he been a mere man, in their estimation he surely would have been bitten and died.

Here is a different and very welcome kind of miracle. I wonder did they ask questions about the living God after this wonderful event.

[7]There was an estate nearby that belonged to Publius, the chief official of the island. He welcomed us to his home and for three days entertained us hospitably.

[8]His father was sick in bed, suffering from fever and dysentery. Paul went in to see him and, after prayer, placed his hands on him and healed him.

[9]When this had happened, the rest of the sick on the island came and were cured.

[10]They honoured us in many ways and when we were ready to sail, they furnished us with the supplies we needed. Acts 28:7-10

God never stops working

None of the people from the ship had heard of Publius, chief official of the island, nor did they know he had a father who was very sick with the effects of fever and dysentery. Paul placed his hands on the old man and he was healed.

When this had happened, the rest of the sick people on the island came and were cured.

We thank God for the wonderful deliverance he gave the passengers of that ship, and that the people could see and examine the miracles of healing that had been performed.

A kindness repaid

The travellers made preparations and made ready to sail, but not before the Maltese people honoured them in many ways. Furthermore, when they were ready to sail, they furnished the travellers with the supplies they needed.

THANK YOU, HEAVENLY FATHER:

For the numerous ways and varied circumstances by which You make Your way into the hearts of sinners;

For the safe landing and friendly reception that Paul and the other travellers were privileged to enjoy, and for lasting friendships formed that day;

For the very natural way that You gained entrance to the home of Publius and his sick and elderly father, so that no one felt embarrassed;

For every home around the Mediterranean basin, into which You came because Paul and others of your servants were received and welcomed there first;

IN JESUS' NAME, AMEN

69. Acts 28: 11 - 16

ARRIVAL AT ROME

The journey from Malta was made in an Alexandrian ship – which sounds a bit like a Spanish galleon of later centuries. It carried the figurehead of the twin gods of Castor and Pollux. In Greek mythology Castor was a horseman, and Pollux a prize boxer. Sometimes they were referred to as 'Gemini' or 'the Twins'. These two had the reputation of being favourable to sailors, which is why this ship was named in their honour.

The next day a favourable south wind came up and they made good speed to Puteoli, a well-known seaport located in the Bay of Naples. Paul and Luke and their party found Christian brethren there and had hospitality shown to them for seven days before continuing for Rome.

On arrival at the outskirts of Rome they were met by some believers, who having heard of their coming, had travelled out to the Forum of Appius and the Three Taverns to meet them, a distance of about thirty miles.

> [15]*The brothers there had heard that we were coming, and they travelled as far as the Forum of Appius and the Three Taverns to meet us. At the sight of these men Paul thanked God and was encouraged.* Acts 28:15

Their sea journey had ended. The rest of the journey would be on foot.

> [16]*When we got to Rome, Paul was allowed to live by himself, with a soldier to guard him.* Acts 28:16

THANK YOU HEAVENLY FATHER:

For preserving the lives of Your servants and for using them to Your glory during their long journey to Rome;

For fulfilling Your word to Your servant Paul, that he would testify for You in Rome also;

For the spirit of fellowship created by the Holy Spirit between believers wherever they meet on earth;

IN JESUS' NAME, AMEN

70. Acts 28: 17 to 31

PAUL PREACHES AT ROME

We really feel thankful about the wording of the final sentence in v. 16.

> [16]*When we got to Rome, Paul was allowed to live by himself, with a soldier to guard him.* Acts 28:16

Never mind the presence of the Roman soldier, I imagine the cell, or room, or house (whatever it was) must have been next door to heaven as Paul was able to read and pray and write and think. The recovery of health and strength after his journey was also very important.

V. 17 reveals that he was thinking big thoughts! Within three days he had organised a meeting and invited all the local Jews to come along.

> [17]*"Three days later he called together the leaders of the Jews. When they had assembled, Paul said to them: "My brothers, although I have done nothing against our people or against the customs of our ancestors, I was arrested in Jerusalem and handed over to the Romans."*
>
> [18]*"They examined me and wanted to release me, because I was not guilty of any crime deserving death."*
>
> [19] *"But when the Jews objected, I was compelled to appeal to Caesar—not that I had any charge to bring against my own people."* Acts 28:17-19

So if any of his friends were unclear about why Paul had come to Rome, they knew now. Did you notice Paul's three special emphases? These are the reasons why he is in Rome.

[15.] "***The Romans*** *examined me and wanted to release me, because I was not guilty of any crime deserving death.*"

[19] "*But when* ***the Jews*** *objected, I was compelled to appeal to Caesar—not that I had any charge to bring against my own people.*"

[20] "*For this reason* ***I have asked to see you and talk with you.*** *It is because of the hope of Israel that I am bound with this chain.*"

I think it is evident that the Jews in Rome, although living at the heart of the Empire, were far removed from the heart of Christianity in Jerusalem and Judea. Some of the things Paul was talking about seemed to be remote to them.

For a moment go back to vv. 21-22

[21]*They replied, "We have not received any letters from Judea concerning you, and none of the brothers who have come from there has reported or said anything bad about you.*

[22]*But we want to hear what your views are, for we know that people everywhere are talking against this sect."* Acts 28:21-22

The Roman Jews were not only remote from Paul, but remote from what was happening in Judaism.

Now please move on to vv. 23–25.

[23]*They arranged to meet Paul on a certain day, and came in even larger numbers to the place where he was staying. From morning till evening he explained and declared to them the kingdom of God and tried to convince them about Jesus from the Law of Moses and from the Prophets.*

[24]***Some were convinced by what he said, but others would not believe.***

[25]*They disagreed among themselves and began to leave after Paul had made this final statement: "The Holy Spirit spoke*

the truth to your forefathers when he said through Isaiah the prophet:

Here follows Isaiah 6:9-10

> [26] *'Go to this people and say, "You will be ever hearing but never understanding; you will be ever seeing but never perceiving.* [27] *For this people's heart has become calloused; they hardly hear with their ears, and they have closed their eyes. Otherwise they might see with their eyes, hear with their ears, understand with their hearts and turn, and I would heal them.'*[28] *"Therefore I want you to know that God's salvation has been sent to the Gentiles, and they will listen!"* Acts 28:23-28

The truth of the matter was that the Jews in Rome were ignorant of what it meant to be a believer in Jesus; or 'a completed Jew' as some Messianic groups are pleased to call themselves to-day. To others, believers like Paul and his friends were only members of a sect.

Why Acts 28 ends abruptly we cannot be sure.

There may be some clues in the following observations.

-> Paul had not come to trial. He was free to meet with people.

-> Rome's attitude to Christianity ('this new sect') was one of tolerance.

-> There was evangelism to be done among both Jews and Gentiles.

The ending is most appropriate, and we thank God for it.

> [30] ***For two whole years Paul stayed there in his own rented house and welcomed all who came to see him.***

> [31] ***Boldly and without hindrance he preached the kingdom of God and taught about the Lord Jesus Christ.***

I imagine that Luke got pleasure from that ending also.

THANK YOU, HEAVENLY FATHER;

For the innumerable conversations about Jesus that took place in Paul's rented house; and the many who became believers in Jesus there;

For Your wise and wonderful providence that guided and guarded Paul's footsteps all his life through, until he saw Jesus face to face in heaven;

For the many times our hearts turned to You following our Bible reading, just to tell You how much we love You;

IN JESUS' NAME, AMEN

Pastor Rea Grant's two books belong together.
You will be glad that you have both of them to use
for your personal Bible reading and as useful commentaries
on Luke's two books.
Purchase these books
through your local Christian Bookshop
or by Mail Order from Amazon.com
from anywhere in the world.

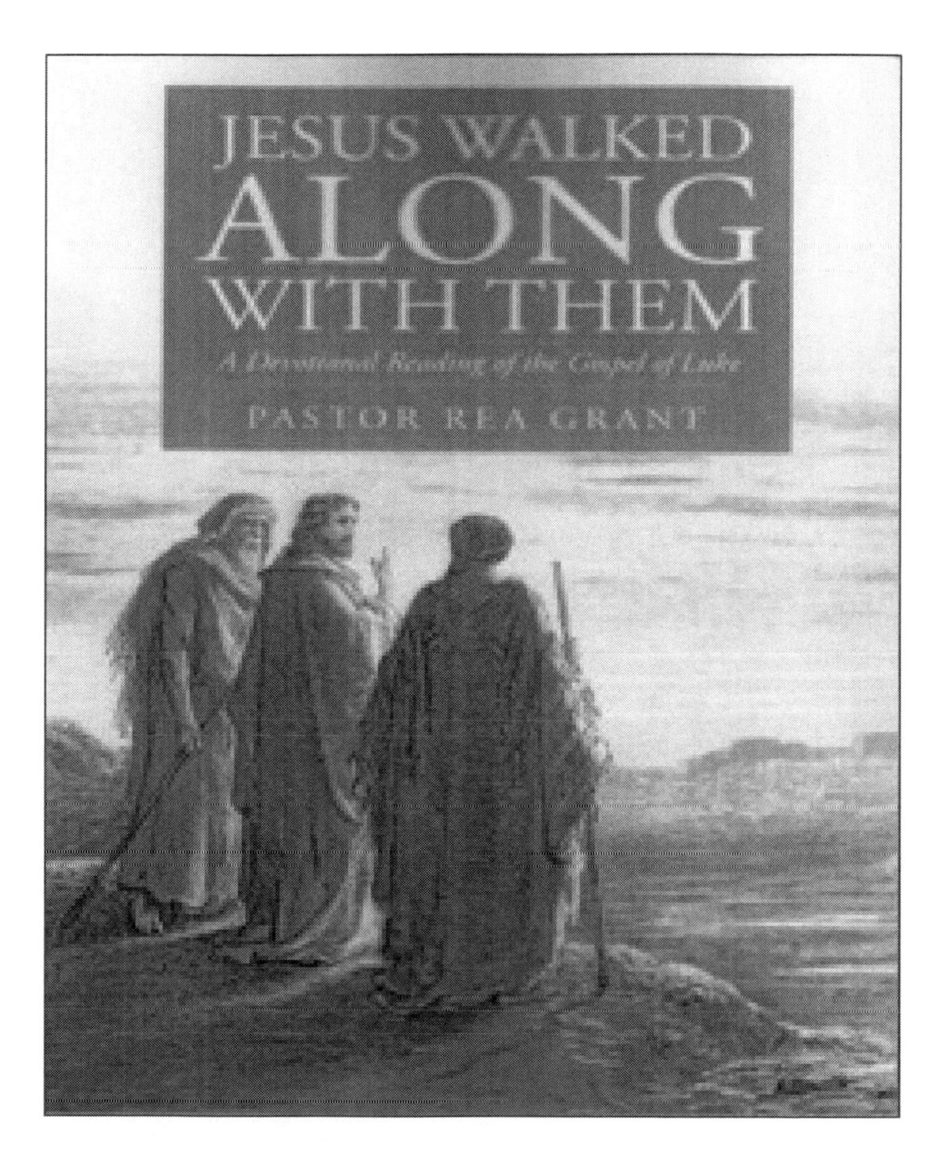
JESUS WALKED
ALONG
WITH THEM
A Devotional Reading of the Gospel of Luke
PASTOR REA GRANT